The Culture Concept

Critical American Studies Series

GEORGE LIPSITZ

UNIVERSITY OF CALIFORNIA—SAN DIEGO

SERIES EDITOR

The Culture Concept

Writing and Difference in the
Age of Realism

MICHAEL A. ELLIOTT

Critical American Studies

University of Minnesota Press
Minneapolis • London

An alternate version of chapter 4 was published as "Ethnography, Reform, and the Problem of the Real: James Mooney's *Ghost-Dance Religion*," *American Quarterly* 50, no. 2; reprinted by permission of The Johns Hopkins University Press.

Published by the University of Minnesota Press
111 Third Avenue South, Suite 290
Minneapolis, MN 55401-2520
http://www.upress.umn.edu

Library of Congress Cataloging-in-Publication Data

Elliott, Michael A.
   The culture concept : writing and difference in the Age of Realism /
Michael A. Elliott.
      p. cm.—(Critical American studies series)
Includes bibliographical references and index.
   ISBN 0-8166-3971-X (alk. paper)—ISBN 0-8166-3972-8
(pbk. : alk. paper)
      1. American literature—African American authors—History
and criticism. 2. Literature and anthropology—United States.
3. Boas, Franz, 1858–1942—Influence. 4. Difference (Psychology) in literature.
5. African Americans in literature. 6. Ethnology in literature.
7. Indians in literature. 8. Realism in literature. 9. Culture in literature.
   I. Title. II. Series.
   PS153.N5 E38 2002
   810.9'896073—dc21

                                    2002003115

Contents

Acknowledgments

This book focuses on institutions and networks of people who made certain forms of writing possible in the late nineteenth and early twentieth centuries. In a similar fashion, this book has only been possible because of the institutional and individual aid I have received. I began this project as a dissertation, and my advisors in that process aided me in ways far beyond what any graduate student could reasonably expect. In fact, each continued to offer substantial assistance well after the dissertation was safely deposited. Robert A. Ferguson was the model director: meticulous in his careful attention, aggressive in his commentary, and sympathetic to the ultimate goals of the project. Priscilla Wald challenged me at every turn to pursue the most difficult questions of the project and played a crucial role in my reformulation of the dissertation into a genuine book. And Arnold Krupat proved to be much more than an "outside reader"; his good-natured skepticism, impressive knowledge of my subjects, and scholarly generosity have been critical to me. I want to thank each of these three for their time, attention, and intellectual camaraderie. I cannot overstate the depth of my gratitude to them.

The Department of English and Comparative Literature at Columbia University was an exciting place to be an Americanist during the years I studied there. I would like to acknowledge the members of the Americanist dissertation group who labored over the ideas that finally came to fruition in this book, particularly Lilian Carswell, Sarah Chinn, Caleb Crain, Andrew Epstein, Jonathan Gill, Audrey Goodman, John Matteson, and Joshua Miller.

I completed the manuscript of the book during a year-long fellowship at the Charles Warren Center for Studies in American History at Harvard University. I am grateful to Lizabeth Cohen, Werner Sollors, and Laurel Thatcher Ulrich for making that year possible, as well as to the center's administrator, Susan Hunt, for her practical and good-humored help. In addition, the other fellows at the center contributed to my writing, often in intangible ways. I would also like to thank Hildegard Hoeller and Augusta Rohrbach for their deeply helpful responses to my Warren Center presentation of material related to chapter 1.

I am grateful to the American Philosophical Society (APS) for awarding me a summer fellowship, sponsored by the Mellon Foundation, to work with the papers of Franz Boas. The superb librarians at the APS were often able to anticipate my research needs faster than I could articulate them.

My colleagues, Americanists and non-Americanists alike, in the Department of English at Emory University have made the writing of this book easier through the countless ways they have shown their support for me and my research. Their advice and offers of assistance have been especially useful in the final stages of the project, and I would like to publicly thank Mark Bauerlein, Frances Smith Foster, Christopher Lane, Cristine Levenduski, and Richard Rambuss for opening their doors to me. I am grateful to the university for providing me with summer research grants and with a subvention from the Quadrangle Fund to pay photograph permission fees.

The fourth chapter of this book originally appeared in article form in *American Quarterly*, and I received insightful commentary on that article draft from Curtis M. Hinsley and Michael Hittman, as well as thoughtful advice from the journal's editor, Lucy Maddox. I worked out several key arguments to chapter 5 in a talk at the University of Illinois at Urbana-Champaign, and I would like to thank Julia A. Walker, William J. Maxwell, and Suvir Kaul for facilitating that visit. Among the many others whom I must thank for commentary on portions of this book are Lee D. Baker, Stanley Corkin, Andrew Delbanco, Lauren Muller, William J. Peace, and Siobhan Senier. Dana Nelson, Joel Pfister, and Alan Trachtenberg provided rigorous and highly useful readings of the final manuscript, and Richard Morrison has been responsive, shrewd, and sympathetic in his office of editor at the University of Minnesota Press.

Barry O'Connell has been a friend and mentor for more than ten years, and this book would not be a reality if it had not been for his encouragement and teaching. More recently, Claudia Stokes has become a formidable intellectual interlocutor—one whom I rely on almost daily. Her intense labor on a draft of this book has made the final version much better than it might otherwise have been. I would also like to thank my parents, Arthur and Barbara, and my brothers, Sean and Peter, for their kindness and unstinting affection during my years of academic study.

Finally, no one has endured more for this book than Jennifer Mathews, who simply cannot be thanked sufficiently in a scholarly monograph. I will say only that the extent of her influence cannot really be measured at this point, nor is it likely to be ever adequately appreciated.

INTRODUCTION

American Word Culture

In 1989, the German medical historian Barbara Duden commented on the usage of the word "culture" to designate a distinct way of life. "We often forget how recent it is that learned discourse started using the term 'culture,'" she stated. "When I was in my early twenties and studying at the University of Vienna, I recall that the only way to refer to this notion was to say 'Kultur im Sinene des amerikanischen Wortes *culture*'—*Kultur* as in the meaning of the American word 'culture.'"[1] Her remarks raise the questions that have motivated my interest in the history of the concept of culture. What does it mean for this anthropological definition of culture to be identified as the intellectual product of the United States, for "culture" to be an "American" word? How has the American context affected the role the culture concept has played in "learned discourse"? And what other American words may have facilitated the emergence of this key term of our critical vocabulary?

For Duden, the "American word 'culture'" means thinking of culture as socially constructed networks of meaning that divide one human group from another. This definition of culture, with its rejection of social evolution and its implicit endorsement of a kind of relativism, was delineated by a branch of American anthropology headed by Franz Boas, himself a

German immigrant who arrived in the United States in the 1880s. Boas and the others investigating cultural difference in the late nineteenth century believed their study of culture required a professional methodology of observation and transcription, and therefore their enterprise relied upon an ambitious program of textual production that influenced, and was influenced by, similar documentary projects being conducted outside of anthropology, including literary ones. In this way, the efforts that eventually led to the dissemination of this "American word 'culture'" played a critical role in shaping the broader American culture of words.

A premise of this book is that this process took shape long before Boas's definition of culture actually entered widespread "learned discourse" in the 1920s and 1930s, that the influence of the culture concept upon the textual documentation of group-based difference reaches back at least as far as the last two decades of the nineteenth century, the period when Boas began formulating his ideas about culture. From the 1880s to the turn of the twentieth century, the interest in what anthropologist E. B. Tylor had tagged in 1871 the "wide ethnographic sense" of culture generated a profusion of social scientific and literary texts based on the observation of difference. These texts not only demonstrate the impact of the debates about culture in which Tylor, Boas, and other anthropologists participated, but the ways in which they register those debates can also help us to comprehend better the contours of the Boasian culture concept that would later play such a pivotal role in twentieth-century thought.

By unraveling the shifting definitions of culture at work in American writing during this period, my purpose is therefore twofold: to understand a chapter of the history of writing about difference in the United States, and to use this body of writing to inquire into the history of this "American word."

This focus precludes me from either charting all of the meanings associated with the word "culture" or giving a complete genealogy of its intellectual roots. Such histories of the term commonly emphasize its double set of roots in Europe. On the one hand, the definition of culture as group identity is directly related to what French thinkers of the late eighteenth century began to call *civilisation:* the achievement of human advancement manifest in certain customs and standards of living. *Civilisation* is relational and hierarchical; it makes one group (Western Europe) distinct by comparing it to less advanced ones mired in so-called barbarism or savagery, and it belongs to all members of that group. Equally important, *civilisation* is the endpoint of a process of cultivation that takes place over the course of generations and centuries. German *Kultur*, on the other hand, is static and bound to a particular time and place. As developed by the romantic nationalist Johann Gottfried von Herder, *Kultur* came to be identified with the spiritual identity of a nation, embodied by its peasant *Volk. Kultur* figured as the connective tissue of the organically whole nation and gave to it a unique character. Individuals therefore had an obligation to cultivate their relationship to the national *Kultur* in order to achieve a sense of rootedness and harmony with their society.[2]

Both *civilisation* and *Kultur* shaped conceptions of group-based difference in the late-nineteenth- and early-twentieth-century United States. At the risk of oversimplifying complex intellectual histories, we might say that French *civilisation* found its home in the evolutionary anthropology that arose in the wake of social Darwinism. Like the original explicators of *civilisation*, cultural evolutionists looked to difference as a means of measuring and revealing the mechanics of *progress*. Boas and his students, on the other hand, responded by developing a concept of culture that owed much to the German tradition of *Kultur*.[3] The Boasians stressed that a culture was not a universal history but a configuration of manners, mores, and beliefs peculiar to a people; for that reason, this model is often referred to as "cultural particularism." Each culture, in this sense, possesses integrity, and one more accurately speaks of *cultures* in the plural rather than of a singular culture that confers different degrees of status upon broad divisions of humanity, as in the French model. In turn, Boasian cultural particularism fostered twentieth-century cultural relativism, a belief that, in the words of Boas's student Alfred L. Kroeber, "any cultural phenomenon must be understood and evaluated in terms of the culture of which it forms part."[4]

In the late nineteenth century, the study of culture revolved around professional practices that valorized the firsthand observation and textual representation of group-based difference. These methods produced writing that attempted to capture the elusive essence of cultural difference on the page, a kind of writing that I refer to as *culturalist* throughout this book. In treating scientific ethnography as an enterprise of writing, I am hardly presuming anything new. As I hope the notes to this book make clear, I am indebted to a generation of critical anthropologists who have interrogated their own disciplinary practices by using literary theories to read texts produced in the name of social science. Their scholarship, in turn, has helped me to make sense of the affinities between the ethnographic works produced by anthropologists and the works published in a variety of forms by literary authors during the same age. In particular, I focus on how the theories and institutions of American literary realism, which flourished during the last two decades of the nineteenth century, fostered the production of culturalist texts that shared many of the goals of social scientific ethnography. Like social science, literary realism valued the careful and accurate depiction of those phenomena—language, dress, rituals—that gave groups a distinguishing identity. Editors and critics who considered themselves "realists," moreover, generally believed that such works could have a salutary effect on the relationships between their readers and those represented.

As an account of textual practices that influenced and were influenced by the emergence of the culture concept later popularized by American anthropology, this book does not argue for a unilinear history of causation. It does not demonstrate that American literary realism produced the Boasian culture concept, or that the proliferation of ethnography single-handedly determined the fate of letters in the late-nineteenth-century United States. Instead, it claims that ethnography and literary realism developed similar strategies of publication that responded to problems related to the textual representation of group-based difference. While it is possible to make an argument for the mutual influence of these two kinds of writing, this book is more concerned with how these affinities can be used to illuminate the mechanics and logic of the documentation of culture. The very fact of such a similarity had—and indeed continues to have—a dramatic effect on the history of writing about difference in the United States, and on the articulation of culture as a model for understanding that difference.

In the late nineteenth century, the production of such ethnographic texts, whether recognized as literature, social science, or some combination of the two, could strike decidedly against the grain of the time. As Matthew Jacobson has convincingly shown in his recent history of how the United States simultaneously confronted domestic and foreign otherness, an over-arching belief in American "civilization" as the pinnacle of evolution dominated the period comprised of the last two decades of the nineteenth century and the first two decades of the twentieth. A dramatic rise in the number of foreign immigrants arriving from abroad, as well as the expansion of American interests overseas, Jacobson writes, "took place at a time when a passion for 'progress' defined both the national character as it was popularly conceived and the nature of the world's peoples as they appeared through the ethnocentric lens of an 'Anglo-Saxon' cultural mission."[5] This triumphalism went hand in hand, in other words, with a chauvinism that at best generated sentimental projects aimed at domesticating foreignness through Americanization, and at worst fostered the virulence of white supremacy. The textual documentation of culture, to be sure, could be complicit with this ideology of progress, but it also reveals an alternative, cross-disciplinary history of writing by those made uneasy by their contemporaries' unquestioned faith in progress; it reveals a history of writing that attempted to engage with foreignness by searching for a new set of concepts and terms.

If the vocabulary of ethnographic culture proved a means of confronting difference, it also offered an answer to the contradictory threat of homogenization. Charles Dudley Warner's 1889 novel *A Little Journey in the World* begins with a knowing nod toward this growing fear. "It is a suggestive thought," the book states, "that at a given hour all over the United States innumerable clubs might be considering the Want of Diversity in American Life."[6] At a time when many believed the leveling forces of modernity would eliminate local and regional distinctions, texts were seen as preserving such distinctions to be consumed by cosmopolitan readers as well as studied by social scientists. The ultimate purpose of the salvage imperative that united local color writing, folkloric writing, and scientific ethnography was not to reverse or forestall the processes of cultural unification. Indeed, this writing representing group-based distinction found a ready audience in those who considered a bland national sameness all but inevitable. As Hamlin Garland contended in his 1894 literary polemic *Crumbling Idols*, "It is the differences which interest us; the similarities do not please, do not forever stimulate and feed us as the differences."[7]

The writing of culture responded to the perception of antithetical dangers—diversity and homogeneity—but it emerged during a period when other approaches to social identity, those based on older theories of biological differentiation and on newer ones of evolution, were responding to the fears of those same threats in more dramatic ways. Anyone with a cursory knowledge of the late-nineteenth- and early-twentieth-century history of the United States will be familiar with actions taken or attempted against those considered foreign to the Anglo-Saxon heritage: the institutionalization of Jim Crow laws and the spread of anti-black violence, including lynching; the drive to dismantle the tribal societies of American Indians through territorial dispossession; the varied attempts (some successful, others not) to restrict immigration of both non-whites and persons from southern and eastern Europe. The turn toward ethnographic culture by a small group of scientists and authors hardly constituted an adequate political reaction to such developments, yet it did afford an arena for those who desired a new way of speaking, thinking, and writing about group-based difference. Boas, for instance, repeatedly used anthropology to argue that racial discrimination had no scientific basis, and many writers and editors associated with literary realism believed that they were promoting a literary democracy accessible to members of all racial and ethnic groups. When the leading proponent of American literary realism, William Dean Howells, commented in the course of reviewing the stories of Charles W. Chesnutt that in the "department of literature ... there is, happily, no color line," he indicated the strength of his conviction that the realm of literary publication could succeed where the larger society had so obviously failed.[8] His hope was not to erase the portrayal of difference in literature, but to ensure that literature offered an access to representation more egalitarian than that afforded by other political and social arenas.

Both Howells and Boas also function as synecdoches for the professionalization of their respective fields. In the case of Howells, his version of American literary realism staked out a territory for the professional author for whom writing was the primary means of self-support. Critics of American literary realism have long recognized how its works frequently express anxiety over maintaining a space of professional authorship distinct from the popular press yet still financially remunerative. Boas, meanwhile, participated in and facilitated the creation of professional institutions in academic anthropology—professional societies, journals, degree programs—that took the discipline out of the hands of the self-taught and put it into those of persons trained in research universities. In each case, the methodology of professional, distanced observation enacted a position of objectivity as a means of establishing discursive authority. While the textualization of this distance occurred in dramatically different forms, ethnographic writing and the literature of American realism shared a stated bias against sentimental forms; in each field, sentimentalism was understood to produce inaccurate representation, distortion that led to erroneous interpretations of group-based differences and that sapped the power of American society to overcome barriers related to race, ethnicity, and region.

This turn against sentimentalism mattered not only because of its role in the formation of ethnographic writing as a professional practice, but also because of the ties so convincingly explicated by Laura Wexler between the sentimental mode and the project of domesticating difference in the late nineteenth century. Wexler shows how, even as the practice of sentimental literary strategies declined during this period, a sentimental ideology persisted that enabled white Americans to ignore the violence of imposing U.S. imperial power on people of color at home and abroad.[9] Culturalist writing produced by professional observers of difference could be pressed

into service by this reform program of Americanization; however, by emphasizing their break with the logic of sympathy and sentiment, literary
realists and anthropologists could distance themselves from that agenda—
and I hope to show how their ethnographic texts could articulate an often
complicated set of responses to it.

My pairing of Howells and Boas here may come as a surprise to those
readers familiar with other recent efforts to link American literary production with the anthropological concept of culture. Marc Manganaro,
Walter Benn Michaels, and Susan Hegeman have all insisted upon the importance of cultural anthropology to the literary *modernism* of the United
States in the first half of the twentieth century.[10] Such works draw upon the
chronological coincidence of high modernism in the 1920s and 1930s with
the best-known works of Boasian anthropology, such as Margaret Mead's
Coming of Age in Samoa (1928) and Ruth Benedict's *Patterns of Culture*
(1934), as well as on the well-documented instances in which modernists
such as D. H. Lawrence and T. S. Eliot drew upon the anthropological
representations of difference as sources of inspiration. This scholarship
elaborates the position of Raymond Williams, who in 1973 described in *The
Country and City* how the longing of estranged authors and critics for the
wholeness and harmony of rural culture produced both literary modernism and the profession of literary criticism.[11]

My reason for insisting upon American literary realism as a necessary
context for investigating the importance of the culture concept to writing goes beyond a simple desire to unearth a prologue to this same story
about culture and modernism. By shifting attention to the period in which
the culture concept had not yet gained institutional authority or even been
fully articulated, I want to show it to be a more complex, more provisional and historically contingent idea than has recently been understood.
Recuperating the culture concept in this way, as the product of a history
of contestation with nineteenth-century paradigms of evolution and racial
biology, may help us to understand better its appeal throughout the twentieth century, as well as its limitations. Moreover, attending to the formation of the culture concept constitutes the strategy I will employ in
reading a variety of texts—some belonging to scientific ethnography, some
to literary realism, and some to both genres—crucial to the history of
writing about difference in the United States.

One of the many qualities that separate this book from the histories of
anthropology so necessary to my work is a methodology that will strike
many as patently ahistorical. Instead of offering a chronological account of
how the definition of culture changed over time, I take the Boasian culture

concept articulated in the early twentieth century and use it to explicate literary and scientific texts composed during the previous decades. In other words, I am not making claims for the direct impact of Boasian culture upon this or that work. I can (and do) make claims about the constellation of ideas and texts that employ the logic and lexicon of the culture concept, even if they do not yet have the benefit of Boas's vocabulary. Proceeding in this manner allows me to address the disciplinary crucible in which Boas formed the ideas that his students would later make better known, as well as to show how shifting definitions of culture in late-nineteenth-century America would have unforeseen and seemingly contradictory consequences.

One of those consequences was a convergence of scientific and literary representations of group-based difference. Scientific ethnography—the written description of a single people or practice by an anthropologist—flourished in the last two decades of the nineteenth century as an increasingly professional practice, thanks in large part to the founding in 1879 of the Bureau of American Ethnology by the U.S. government. The artistic movement now known as American literary realism enjoyed its greatest prominence during these same decades. While "realism" could hardly be said to be a unified or coherent enterprise, it was, as I shall demonstrate in chapters 2 and 3, characterized by an interest in the precise portrayal of group-based difference, as evidenced by the large number of collections of local-color fiction and dialect tales published and praised by realist editors and critics. Scientific ethnography and literary realism shared an interest in the documentation of difference, and, while the disciplinary practices that divide the fields must be taken seriously, their overlap affected the shifting definitions of culture that governed the textual representation of otherness.

The configuration of this convergence produced a "cultural realism," a rubric I shall use to cover a wide variety of texts drawing from ethnography and literature. Over the course of the book, I hope to show the significance of the variety of forms that cultural realism could take; for the moment, I offer the following passage from Howells's *A Hazard of New Fortunes* (1890) as an illustration of its prevalence. Howells's protagonist, magazine editor Basil March, has been roaming New York with an eye for the "continual entertainment" that the city and its population afford him—and will also furnish his readers when he begins to write literary sketches of the city for his new magazine. Looking for the home of a friend living in the impoverished and vibrant East Side, March encounters a man selling printed sheets of ballads. The passage is a long one, but merits attention for what it can and cannot explain about the ballads:

They were mostly tragical or doleful; some of them dealt with the wrongs of the working man; others appealed to a gay experience of the high seas; but vastly the greater part to memories and associations of an Irish origin; some still uttered the poetry of plantation life in the artless accents of the end man. Where they trusted themselves, with syntax that yielded promptly to any exigency of rhythmic art, to the ordinary American speech, it was to strike directly for the affectations, to celebrate the domestic ties, and above all, to embalm the memories of angel and martyr mothers whose dissipated sons deplored their sufferings too late. March thought this not at all a bad thing in them; he smiled in patronage of their simple pathos; he paid the tribute of a laugh when the poet turned, as he sometimes did, from his conception of angel and martyr motherhood and portrayed the mother in her more familiar phases of virtue and duty, with the retributive shingle or slipper in her hand. He bought a pocketful of this literature, popular in a sense which the most successful book can never be.[12]

Why exactly *does* March buy a "pocketful of this literature"? Howells suggests that March does not respond to these ballads in the way that their authors intended. He smiles at their pathos; he laughs when they turn serious; and he hardly seems to be affected by the embalmed "memories of angel and martyr mothers." March, therefore, cannot be interested in this "popular" literature simply as literature; indeed, these sentimental ballads seem to embody the emotional excess that March (and his creator, Howells) deplored in literary expression. Their attraction instead emanates from their "artless accents" and from their "origin" in a rural, foreign way of life, tellingly centered on a "plantation." March buys the ballads because they are cultural artifacts—because they derive from a way of life he believes distinct from his own. He judges them by a standard different from that he would use to judge the latest opera or novel, a standard that might indeed win the lyrics publication in a magazine like the one he edits. To be "popular" as these ballads are (and as Howells's novels were not) is to be an authentic product of a culture outside the urban center that March and the ballad seller inhabit.

The ballads that March purchases sit at the convergence of literary realism and ethnography, for they are examples of precisely the vernacular expression prized by both disciplines at the time of Howells's writing. March might have as easily read such ballads in the journal of the recently founded American Folk-Lore Society, an illustrated collection assembled in book form for a general audience, or even in the five-volume scholarly edition of *The English and Scottish Popular Ballads*, published between 1882 and 1898 and edited by Francis James Child, the first chair of English at Harvard University. What Howells registers in his depiction of March's purchase is that the proliferation of such texts relied upon the degree to which their readers could draw upon these diverse scholarly and artistic frameworks to assign them value. March does not want the ballads merely because they convey ethnographic information about, for example, the agricultural practices of the Irish or their dialect of English; instead, he takes pleasure in the pieces, even if his pleasure—the smile at the pathos, for instance—does not comport directly with the pleasure accorded the ballads by their original audience. Nonetheless, the assessment of the accuracy of the texts as representations of actual songs sung by the actual Irish "working man," an evaluative standard directly imported from social science, is necessary for March's pleasure. The ballads express the "poetry of plantation life" (just as did printed versions of African American stories and songs) because they are produced in presumably "artless accents" by people who never imagined that they would be heard, much less read, outside that setting. What gives March pleasure, finally, is the possibility of confronting an otherness through a written text, a possibility framed by an understanding of group-based difference that I will call "cultural."

If March's interest in the transcriptions of ballads encapsulates the complexity and prevalence of the late-nineteenth-century textualization of culture, it also dramatizes the difficulties that this process could create. Most obviously, March purchases these artifacts of cultural difference as inexpensive commodities in a kind of wholesale bulk that precludes discriminating among them. Given that much of the plot of the novel revolves around the financial fortunes of March's magazine and its producers—writers, illustrators, editors—the sheer cheapness of this "pocketful" stands in striking contrast to the value that March and his colleague put upon their own services. The ballads are economic goods, but poorly remunerative ones for the seller, let alone for their creators. Just as the editors of highbrow magazines such as the *Atlantic, Century,* and *Harper's* could pick and choose which products of ethnographic culture they would print, March has the luxury of buying however many or few ballads he desires. The ballads may speak of the "wrongs" suffered by the "working man," but March does not seem to recognize the discrepancy in power between himself and their purveyors.

Even more important to my argument, Howells does not make clear the ultimate effect of March's reading of the ballads. The very fact that the ballads appear before March's eyes as written texts enforces a distance between him and the people from whom they were collected. In spite of the fact that such documents purport to be a direct representation of an oral performance, their existence as written texts gives March freedom as an observer—to skim or to read with care, for example—that he would not have enjoyed had he heard them as performed songs. This distance gives someone like March the opportunity to regard such texts as more than repositories of factual ethnographic information. Engaging texts in this way creates the possibility that readers can ascribe to them artistic properties, and experience an aesthetic pleasure. One reason, for example, that March feels free to take a pleasure different from that of the original audience is that he is not actually in the presence of that audience, a separation that enables him to give free play to the education and taste that have shaped his interest in cultural difference. The quality of attention that March gives the ballads results from both his faith in their accuracy and his critical orientation as a producer and editor of literary realism. What this passage illustrates is how the textualization of culture in the late nineteenth century aestheticized difference through the techniques and idiom of ethnography.

The realist age taught its readers to value authentic cultural difference as both a scientific and an aesthetic object, and it fostered the production of texts that could serve these functions simultaneously. March enjoys the ballads because they portray a rural culture, distant and different from his own, authentic but not threatening in its difference. The original creators of the ballads become an afterthought, as March treats their songs like museum objects preserved for his appreciation, artifacts that help him solidify his position as a realist capable of recognizing authenticity. However, the attention that March devotes to the ballads reminds us that the proliferation of interest in culturalist texts created opportunities for literary artists who could represent on the page certain kinds of experience. Moreover, A Hazard of New Fortunes itself shows that texts dwelling at this convergence of literature and ethnography could even make possible the interrogation of the terms by which culture was being textualized. Howells makes March's condescension as a connoisseur and purveyor of culture recognizable to the reader. March's pleasure in hearing songs about the "wrongs of the working man" in Ireland stands in vivid contrast to his obliviousness of the wrongs suffered by the working classes that surround him in New York, an irony sharpened, at the conclusion of the novel, by the violence of a streetcar strike.

In this way, March dramatizes the same shift that Walter Benn Michaels has described in a recent article calling upon criticism to move beyond questions of difference and identity. According to Michaels, attention to difference, including the debate over whether identities are inherited or socially constructed, has supplanted the primacy of ideology in critical discourse. Cultural difference, in other words, has replaced political disagreement.[13] Michaels's conclusion seems compelling in light of Howells's novel, in which March's interest in the ballads is more pronounced than his interest in class struggle. Yet I am not wholly convinced that the division between political engagement and attention to cultural difference was as easy to delineate in the late nineteenth century as Michaels suggests it is in our own time. For several figures I will discuss, the documentation of culture offered a necessary means of addressing, rather than avoiding, questions of power and ideology. In particular, at their most canny and sophisticated, culturalist texts could reveal how certain stances toward cultural difference deliberately or incidentally ignored the kind of political questions to which Michaels wants us to return. My response to Michaels's provocative analysis is that our critical task should not be simply to leave behind those who have valued group-based difference, but rather to revisit the texts produced in the name of "culture" without being governed by the same obsession with authenticity crucial to their initial reception. Doing so, I hope, will prevent us from prizing difference for its own sake and help us to decipher how the writing of culture could communicate meanings of aesthetic and social significance not legible in any other medium.

My contention that the ethnographic notion of culture had some positive effects, including the creation of opportunities to critique the limitations of that same concept, means that I am offering a more optimistic account of culture as an idea than are most others writing about the concept, whether in literary criticism or anthropology, at the turn of the twenty-first century. Throughout *The Culture Concept*, I restate and build upon many recent criticisms leveled against "culture": that it is a nostalgic longing for rural harmony, that it ignores political and economic power, that it simplifies and valorizes group-based differences in ways that do not reflect how people actually live their lives. These claims are all valid, and this study owes a debt to those who have made them (such as Johann Fabian, Christopher Herbert, and Adam Kuper), a debt that is not adequately reflected by my endnotes. This book is not an attempt to respond to their collective critique by arguing "for" culture—as though one could argue simply for or against an idea so pervasive in current intellectual life. Instead, what I try to offer is a sense of what the anthropological culture concept might have offered at the turn of the twentieth century and how the same forces that produced this concept also produced crucial chapters in the history of the literary prose representing racial and ethnic difference. This very literature, meanwhile, enables me to explore the origins and ultimate effects of the limitations named by recent critics of the culture concept.

To show how I can make this claim, I borrow two questions posed by Scott Michaelsen in a study that, like my own, considers the anthropology of Native American peoples as a way of addressing larger questions of group-based identity and difference. Michaelsen asks, "Can 'culture,' born in evolutionism, ever truly be redeveloped and deployed in a nonhierarchical, nonjudgmental manner? And can 'culture,' as the replacement concept for 'race,' evade the problems of racial theorizing by emphasizing history over nature?"[14] For Michaelsen, the answer to both questions is "no." He argues that culture always values ethnic identity in a way that prizes essentialism and redeploys the chauvinism at the heart of both nineteenth-century evolutionism and racialism. In many ways, the readings that I conduct in the following chapters support Michaelsen's thesis, but I also wish to consider seriously the fact that, at the turn of the twentieth century, a group of American writers and social scientists believed that the answer to both questions was, in fact, "yes"—that culture could indeed offer a way of speaking about group difference in manner both "nonhierarchical and nonjudgmental." That the literary and ethnographic texts I examine struggle with the problems that Michaelsen identifies makes it all the more imperative to describe what was at stake: a new way of depicting identity on the page that simultaneously fostered and resulted from the emergence of what has come to be known as the culture concept.

I consider an account of such projects necessary because, even though cultural particularism played a central role in *twentieth*-century thought, its contours were shaped by the *nineteenth*-century struggles that Michaelsen highlights. In particular, I insist that the evolutionary, racialist paradigm that dominated late-nineteenth-century thought forms an indispensable context for understanding how Boas eventually articulated his definition of culture. What I argue is that the shift from cultural evolution (which understood culture as a uniform, global process) to Boasian culture (which understood culture as an aggregation of the practices and beliefs specific to a particular group) involved a radical change in the *narrative* organization of knowledge about group-based alterity. Narratives do more than place events into chronological sequence; they arrange those events according to patterns of causation in a way that enables the author and the reader to create order out of the chaos of everyday life. The ethnographers and literary realists attempting to document culture produced texts that demonstrated a widespread concern with this role of narrativization. While the responses to the problems of narrative structure varied widely in their form and content, the texts that I consider in this study bear the marks of struggles over the dual, interlocking questions of what to convey and how to convey it. The framed stories of Charles Chesnutt's conjure tales (chapter 3), the circular emplotment of James Mooney's ethnography of the Ghost Dance (chapter 4), and the chronologically narrow memoir of Francis La Flesche's experiences in a mission boarding school (chapter 5) all illustrate how problems of narrative structure were intimately bound to the representation of cultural difference in the realist age.

In my discussion of the intersection of literary realism and scientific ethnography in the late-nineteenth-century United States, I do not hope to provide a complete account of either American literary realism (for this, see Nancy Glazener, Amy Kaplan, Kenneth W. Warren, and Michael Davitt Bell) or of American anthropology during this period (see Regna Darnell, Curtis M. Hinsley, and George W. Stocking Jr.).[15] Nor do I provide a complete reckoning of the politics of difference—the racial oppression of African Americans, the dispossession of American Indians, the debates over immigration—that are so important to this historical moment. Matters of policy, though, often form the frame of my textual analysis, particularly in the chapters dealing with Native American texts, and I gesture toward the political implications of the textual strategies described. Indeed, one cannot avoid politics if one wishes to address the authors and scientists that I do, for these were writers who believed their work of lasting benefit to the victims of nineteenth-century racism. While my study may question the efficacy of their tactics, it does not doubt their sincerity. Their logic, vocabulary, and even methodology have often seemed to me similar to that which informed late-twentieth-century (and now early-twenty-first-century) debates of the same matters: culture, race, difference, representation. Indeed, the premises of literary realism—that responsible literature should accurately reflect the social world, and in doing so could change it—are nearly identical to the motives behind the curriculum reform and multiculturalism of the past twenty-five years. Literary realists like Howells believed that the literature of the United States should reflect the diversity of the people living within its borders, and that this attention to difference would somehow make it possible for the diverse groups to coexist. Ethnographers, similarly, held that the precise documentation and measurement of difference could reveal shared principles of human behavior and therefore bring about a more enlightened and just social order.

At its core, the version of culture at issue simultaneously connotes division and solidarity; cultural difference divides us, it says, but all groups are alike in that they have culture. If this sounds like a bumper sticker from the heyday of multiculturalism—Unity in Diversity!—that is not accidental. My entrance into higher education as an undergraduate in the late 1980s coincided with the peak of optimism concerning the power and importance of the concept of culture to facilitate tolerance in American life. The effects of this widespread adoption of "culture" as a force for progressive change, particularly in education, could be seen everywhere during this era: in the prevalence of the term "multiculturalism" (as well as its antonym, "dead white male") in the popular media, in the debates over college curricula at universities throughout the nation, and even in the publication of texts such as the *Heath Anthology of American Literature*, which first appeared in 1990 as an alternative to the less culturally inclusive *Norton*. (The *Norton* has since, in fact, made significant adjustments, including the addition of several of the Ghost Dance songs I discuss in chapter 3.) However, another phenomenon may be more illustrative, one that was perhaps not new but that seemed to me representative of a newly shared concern about culture. I recall as an undergraduate wandering the stacks of textbooks arranged by course and discipline at the college bookstore and being struck by the sheer number of literary works, especially novels, being assigned in disciplines *outside* of English and other literature departments. Many of these courses, to be sure, were offered by interdisciplinary programs—women's studies, black studies, American studies—but others were in decidedly non-literary fields such as history, anthropology, religion, and political science. These books were being read, therefore, for the information that they conveyed rather than primarily for their properties as creations of literary imagination. All of these works were written by persons representing groups outside the dominant culture, and the majority, from what I remember, were by women: Leslie Marmon Silko, Toni Morrison, Maxine Hong Kingston, Alice Walker.

Of course, I did not enroll in all of these courses, and I would not want to misrepresent the complex reasons that led professors from these disciplines to assign these writers. But I see in such curricular decisions a premise, which I believe was first put forward during the period this book addresses—namely, that literature has a unique ability to document the experience of cultural alterity (as well as of gendered difference) in a truthful and instructive matter. Such a belief, I am suggesting, owes a good deal to the definition of culture that I describe here and to its history in the age of realism. That the culture concept and the representation of culture created their own vexing questions was something of which my college professors were undoubtedly aware as well, for they certainly communicated that sense to me. The year I entered college was also, after all, the year that James Clifford's *The Predicament of Culture* first appeared, a book that simultaneously identified "culture" as a disciplinary fiction and demonstrated its centrality to contemporary thought. "Culture," Clifford writes there, "is a deeply compromised idea I cannot yet do without."[16] If nothing else, I hope that the chapters that follow convey the depth of my agreement with Clifford on this point.

The Culture Concept begins with a chapter-long explication and interpretation of the culture concept put forward, both explicitly and implicitly, in the work of anthropologist Franz Boas. Rather than contend with the full, vast corpus of Boas's writing, I focus on works from the first half of his career, from his first fieldwork in North America through the first decade of the twentieth century. While the ideas that Boas elucidated during this period would not gain widespread currency until the 1920s and 1930s, this chapter demonstrates how his conception of cultural pluralism was framed as a direct response to the evolutionary and racialist assumptions of late-nineteenth-century thought. I describe how Boas attempted to shift the emphasis of his discipline away from a preoccupation with arranging peoples into narratives of development and toward the accumulation of cultural data produced by a single temporal moment. The Boasian culture concept could therefore function as an antidote to the chauvinism of social Darwinism; however, it also suffered from a crucial limitation, the inability to account for cultural change. Chapter 1 concludes by turning to Boas's only known work of fiction, a short story written later in his career, to contend that it offers a meditation on this problem.

Chapters 2 through 5 engage texts that antedate the peak of Boasian anthropology, but that coincide with Boas's own development as a scientist and intellectual in the last two decades of the nineteenth century. Each of these chapters employs the Boasian model of culture as a lens through which to read the struggles over representation, authenticity, and the narrative organization of knowledge that these texts share. Chapter 2 begins this process by showing how the critical feuds over the nature and necessity of "realism" utilized a vocabulary similar to the one employed by anthropologists to debate the meaning of culture. Like ethnography, literary realism came to value the first-hand observation of group-based difference and to develop conventions by which that difference would be textualized. The emphasis upon the documentation of difference recreated something similar to the ethnographic description of culture, and it furthermore established the possibility that readers could regard markers of cultural difference as aesthetic objects.

Chapter 3 extends this argument by describing how the culturalism of literary realism, particularly the conventions of dialect literature, shaped the careers of two African American writers, Paul Laurence Dunbar and Charles W. Chesnutt. Dunbar and Chesnutt illustrate how culture could create opportunities for writers of African American heritage to address the "highbrow" audience predisposed to realism, but they also show that the confusion surrounding culture dramatically restricted how that audience would receive such authors. The culturalist orientation toward static, synchronic description made it difficult for both Dunbar and Chesnutt to use the culturalist forms of realism in a way that escaped the plantation nostalgia dominating literary depictions of African Americans in the late nineteenth century.

Accurate representation and the identification of "real" authenticity were equally crucial to writing about American Indians in the late-nineteenth-century United States, as ethnographers dedicated themselves to detailed cultural description that moved closer to the Boasian model of cultural particularism. Chapter 4 uses the example of James Mooney's monograph *The Ghost-Dance Religion and the Sioux Outbreak of 1890* (1896) to show how this effort to document cultural phenomena led ethnographers to consider the dilemma of narrative form. Working under John Wesley Powell, who endorsed social evolution and its stagist, developmental model of human history, Mooney crafted a style of ethnography that responded to the realist imperative of social relevance, yet simultaneously resisted the narrative structure of evolutionary history. His *Ghost-Dance Religion* wrestles with the difficulty of conveying a sense of the power and complexity of this tribal phenomenon at a time when neither the government nor those interested in "Indian reform" were prepared to recognize its political significance.

In chapters 2 through 4, I make claims about the manner in which literary realism and scientific ethnography from the late nineteenth century exhibit similar discursive strategies in the pursuit of the documentation of culture. In chapter 5, "Culture and the Making of Native American Literature," I argue more directly that these two genres of writing converged to produce written texts that recorded vernacular expression, functioned as repositories of cultural information, and obtained recognition as bearers of aesthetic value. This disciplinary intersection frames my discussion of a variety of texts representing the experience of Native Americans published in the years just before and just after the turn of the twentieth century. More specifically, this chapter demonstrates how three American Indian writers—Charles A. Eastman, Zitkala-Ša, and Francis La Flesche—situated their prose at the convergence of realism and ethnography around the emerging concept of culture, and how they used this convergence to interrogate the meaning and application of the concept. I turn to the work of La Flesche, an Omaha man who became an ethnographer for the Bureau of American Ethnology, as an extended example of how the study of culture could be embraced by an American Indian intellectual of this period and yet raise troubling contradictions about the nature of group identity.

The final chapter offers a chronological coda. Writers like Dunbar, Mooney, and La Flesche worked to document culture in the years before the Boasian culture concept became widely understood. Zora Neale Hurston, on the other hand, was an ethnographer and novelist trained in the method and theory of Boas's school. By way of assessing the legacy of Boasian culture to twentieth-century American literature, and as a means of arguing that the inception of culture in the age of realism continued to wield influence even into the modernist age, I therefore take up Hurston's ethnography and fiction. My purpose is not to give a full account of her intellectual development or written work. Instead, I examine Hurston's writing as an example of how the principles of cultural realism have been deployed within works that inquire into the potential and the limits of the culture concept itself. In fact, I argue that this line of investigation in Hurston's work has contributed to its enthusiastic reception during the past twenty-five years. The rediscovery and canonization of Hurston represent a final demonstration of how the culture concept continues to matter to the world of American letters. The subtle history of the culturalist writing that precedes Hurston's, in turn, affords us an opportunity to understand the nuances of a crucial experience of readers of our own time, the reading of literature to confront matters of group-based difference. To ignore the nuances of this experience, either in previous periods or in our own, risks not only repeating earlier errors but neglecting a complex chapter in the history of the American cultures of words.

1

Culture, Race, and Narrative: Reading Franz Boas

I begin in May 1887, with two periodicals that index the disciplinary debates at the center of this study. That month, the "letters" section of *Science* included a contribution from its twenty-nine-year-old geography editor, a recent immigrant to the United States from Germany named Franz Boas (1858–1942).[1] The letter, published with the title "The Occurrence of Similar Inventions in Areas Wide Apart," criticized the display of ethnological artifacts in the U.S. National Museum in Washington. Under the aegis of Otis T. Mason, a more established and better recognized figure than Boas, these collections had been divided according to typological inventions, so that each display case arranged artifacts from across the globe into an evolutionary sequence that demonstrated the development of more sophisticated, complex tools from simpler, "primitive" ones.[2]

In his letter, Boas argued that this method of presentation was misleading: Mason had presumed that the tools and other artifacts represented a single, global pattern of history, but similar inventions of disparate peoples may have come about for different reasons. "Unlike causes," Boas contended, "produce like effects." The only way, therefore, that one could convey the significance of a tool or a basket or an item of clothing would be to display it in the context from which it was gathered. "By regarding a single implement outside of its surroundings, outside of other inventions of the people to whom it belongs, and outside of other phenomena affecting that people and its productions, we cannot understand its *meaning*" (emphasis added). Proper display of ethnological artifacts required the careful presentation of "a complete collection of a single tribe."[3]

The same month that Boas launched his battle against the American anthropological establishment, William Dean Howells (1837–1920) published, in *Harper's Monthly*, one of his series of broadsides in his campaign for literary realism. Unlike Boas, who was still relatively unknown and without institutional resources, Howells in 1887 was near the height of his professional career. Fifty years of age, Howells had served as editor of the *Atlantic Monthly*, published many of the novels for which he is best known today, and begun to write the "Editor's Study" columns for *Harper's* that made him the most visible literary critic in the United States. The "Editor's Study" articles—many later collected into the volume *Criticism and Fiction* (1891)—represent Howells's most sustained attempt to describe the realist aesthetic he so earnestly championed.

Howells's "Editor's Study" of May 1887 is typical of these efforts. After discussing recently published books, Howells moves to a litany of claims on behalf of a realist fiction characterized by accuracy, moderation, and utility:

> Let fiction cease to lie about life; let it portray men and women as they are, actuated by the motives and the passions in the measure we all know; let it leave off painting dolls and working them by springs and wires; ... let it not put on fine literary airs; let it speak the dialect, the language, that most Americans know—the language of unaffected people everywhere— and we believe that even its masterpieces will find a response in all readers.[4]

Howells was convinced that realism could usher in an era in which literature would be more honest, more democratic, and better received by the American public. In turn, he hoped such a literature could help shape the society that read it.

The disputes in which Boas and Howells were engaged, one about anthropological science, the other about literary art, overlapped in conceptual vocabulary and logic. At the most basic level, both Boas and Howells were making arguments about representation and accuracy in 1887. Boas claimed that certain arrangements of museum artifacts could lead patrons to false conclusions; Howells contended that certain literary portrayals gave their readers a distorted understanding of the world. Less obviously, each of these polemics contained arguments about the way meaning is imparted through narrative. For Howells, fictional narratives that exaggerated emotions, instead of presenting them "in the measure we all know," failed to serve readers. For Boas, Mason's method of display conveyed to viewers a narrative of a unified, global evolution of humanity that ignored the real complexities of human history. A "collection of string instruments, flutes, or drums of 'savage' tribes and the modern orchestra," Boas wrote, is of no use in telling its audience about the development or meaning of music within the context of any group's lived experience.[5] Anthropology therefore needed to change the way that it told its stories.

I will return to Howells and to literary realism in the next chapter, but the connections between Howells's arguments and Boas's are central to my discussion of Boas and the single idea, the "culture concept," for which he is best known. Boas's efforts to elucidate and describe his version of culture contained an occupation with the very matters that concerned Howells: the nature of representation, the way in which meaning is created, and the methods by which disciplines convey their knowledge of the world. Not only was literary realism affected by this notion of culture, but the inverse was true as well; the culture concept so crucial to twentieth-century thought was formed in the age of realist apprehension about the shape and role of narrative.

This chapter is devoted to Boas's articulation of what culture is and how it operates, because his work crystallizes the possibilities and the dilemmas of the documentation of culture that figure in the chapters that follow. In the early twentieth century, Boas offered a clarity and logical consistency in his writing about culture rarely present in the works that I consider from the last two decades of the nineteenth century. In part, Boas had the benefit of hindsight, and the full-fledged Boasian anthropology of the twentieth century can be understood as a continuation of the intersecting efforts of scientific ethnography and American literary realism to document culture and, in so doing, to define its nature. However, Boas does not necessarily solve the problems of the late nineteenth century, the period when he was developing his ideas and methods. Instead, Boas's work brings into relief the difficulties facing those who would document culture; it helps explain why so many of his contemporaries were engaged in precisely that project; and it sheds light on the strategies they used. Finally, Boas's model of culture helps to explain why the effort of American literary realism, in Howells's words, to "portray men and women as they are" shared the idiom of ethnography—and what the consequences of this discursive overlap have been for the history of literature in the United States.

Franz Boas and the Culture Concept: A Brief Introduction

The version of culture put forward by Franz Boas would not reach a widespread audience until the second and third decades of the twentieth century, when popular works by his students first appeared, such as Margaret Mead's *Coming of Age in Samoa* (1928) and Ruth Benedict's *Patterns of Culture* (1934), and when Boas and his students would be called upon as scientific experts to denounce the racialist theories of the German Third Reich.[6] (Boas was even featured on the cover of *Time* in 1936.)[7] By then, Boas had shifted American anthropology from a museum-based enterprise to one centered in the university; under his influence, the doctoral degree earned through fieldwork became a requirement of the profession. Boas trained his own students at Columbia University, where he began teaching in 1896 and was appointed to a full professorship in 1899, and by the 1920s many of those same students were installed in anthropology departments throughout the country.[8] Until his death in 1942—he is reported to have died falling into the arms of Claude Lévi-Strauss while speaking at the Columbia Faculty Club—Boas stood at the center of a continually growing network of professional academic anthropologists in the United States.[9]

At the time of Boas's debate with Otis Mason in 1887, that shift toward the professionalization of the social sciences, in particular anthropology, was underway. The United States Congress had agreed to create one of the most visible institutions of the discipline, the Bureau of American Ethnology, in 1879; during the late 1880s, Harvard University and the University of Pennsylvania appointed the first professors of anthropology in the country; and two of the journals central to the field, *American Anthropologist* and the *Journal of American Folk-Lore*, appeared for the first time in 1888, the products of new scientific organizations.[10] While anthropology was still the home of scientists without any formal training or, like Boas himself, with training in other disciplines, in the final decades of the nineteenth century anthropologists joined the ranks of other professional social scientists whose standards of training and methodology secured their authority.[11] As they became recognized as arbiters of scientific knowledge, anthropologists would speak more frequently to non-scientific audiences as experts on questions relating to foreign peoples both at home and abroad: the indigenous populations living within the United States, the increasing ranks of immigrants, and those brought under U.S. jurisdiction through the nation's imperial ventures.

The dispute between Mason and Boas over the proper arrangement of museum artifacts participated in this process of professional formation, for it concerned the methods by which anthropologists would display the results of their research for a lay audience. Equally important, Boas's arguments demonstrate how his ideas about culture were firmly rooted in the intellectual questions of the nineteenth century. While Boas never uses the word in his 1887 *Science* letter, *culture* clearly constitutes the grounds upon which he would like to reform museum display. As I have noted, he argues that phenomena—here, artifacts such as tools—only have meaning within the context of the specific conditions that surround them. "We have to study each ethnological specimen in its history and in its medium," Boas writes.[12] That "medium," he would later call "culture."

More than fifteen years earlier, in his two-volume *Primitive Culture* (1871) the English anthropologist E. B. Tylor had published a definition of culture still frequently cited as the first such attempt by an anthropologist:

> Culture or Civilization, taken in its wide ethnographic sense, is that complex whole which includes knowledge, belief, art, morals, law, custom, and any other capabilities and habits acquired by man as a member of society.[13]

Tylor's definition borrowed from the competing traditions described in the introduction—the German idea of *Kultur* and the French notion of *civilisation*—to label culture an aggregate of global, observable phenomena, including morals and beliefs. Tylor's "wide ethnographic sense" of culture contrasts with the definition advanced by Matthew Arnold only a few years previously in *Culture and Anarchy* (1869). For Arnold, culture is an individual pursuit, the realization of "harmonious perfection" and an "inward condition of mind and spirit" that occurs through engagement with profound works of art.[14] For Tylor, culture is outward, behavioral, and tangible; it is the whole way of life of a group, and every group engagement.[15] Both Arnold and Tylor consider culture a kind of achievement that can be measured in a hierarchical manner, but for Arnold the achievement is individual, for Tylor, the product of a group. Unlike Arnold, Tylor believes that such a thing as "primitive culture" exists, but he does not consider it to be on the same plane as the "civilization" of industrial Europe.[16] Writing in the midst of the evolutionary fervor that followed the publication of Darwin's *Origin of Species* (1859), Tylor is interested in culture as a historical process by which some peoples become cultured and others do not.

While Boas shared Tylor's sense of culture "in the wide ethnographic sense" as something to be observed and integrated into a "complex whole," he stressed that each of these wholes is peculiar to a particular group. The question of museum display illustrates how this Boasian definition of culture changed the orientation and evidentiary requirements of anthropology.

Instead of needing a sampling of, say, farming implements from around the world to sketch out the development of the modern plow, Boas proposed that one must collect all the information that one can from each cultural context to be accurate in what one says about such tools. It is only a short step from this contention to Boas's requirement that his students see the objects of their study firsthand through fieldwork rather than relying upon the accounts and collections of others in the manner of "armchair anthropologists" like Tylor.

Boas also tried to change the kinds of conclusions that anthropologists could reach from their observations of cultural evidence. In contesting Mason's arrangement of museum artifacts, Boas was, in a narrow way, making a concerted effort to displace the definition of culture tied to an evolutionary paradigm. Cultural evolution, elucidated in works like Tylor's *Primitive Culture* and Lewis Henry Morgan's *Ancient Society* (1877), defined culture as something that occurs in progressive stages—stages labeled by Morgan as "savagery," "barbarism," and "civilization."[17] Under such a model, the task of anthropology was to document this process of cultural development and then to identify the necessary features of each stage and the ways such phenomena were transformed. Otis Mason's exhibits, therefore, presented viewers illustrations of the evolution of a loom or a violin from its "primitive" origins, regardless of to which continents or centuries the makers of such objects belonged. (See Figure 1.)

Boas wanted to eliminate this evolutionary model from anthropology. He argued in *Science* that it was impossible to establish the chain of historical causality that would verify the accuracy of such arrangements. In bringing artifacts together in this manner, Mason and others were presuming that such objects were created by the same forces regardless of the social or geographical environment of the peoples who created them. Because "unlike causes produce like effects," Boas wrote, one could never be sure that similar objects had the same purpose or meaning among dissimilar peoples.[18] Boas refocused the efforts of American anthropology away from the recreation of an entire history or invention (or institution such as marriage or law); instead, anthropology would strive to recreate the complete context of a single moment in time—a cultural moment. Therefore, when he had the opportunity to preside over exhibition at the American Museum of Natural History in New York, he used mannequins to present a "life-group," so that the audience could see tribal objects in a more complete cultural context.[19] (See Figure 2.)

Even in Boas's 1887 debate with Mason, in which the culture concept remains incipient and ill-defined, the Boasian model leads directly to an argument about the kind of narrative structures that anthropology should use to organize its knowledge and to communicate with the public. Boas would have his discipline limit itself to a more recent, knowable past rather than seek an understanding of the global progression of humanity through cultural stages. Boas realized that the progressive narrative of cultural evolution was a means of arranging groups along a chronological hierarchy; according to that model, "primitive peoples," even if living in the present age, represented an earlier and inferior time. In contrast, Boas hoped that anthropology would demonstrate something vastly different to its public. As he noted in another *Science* letter concerning museum display, "It is my opinion that the main object of ethnological collections should be that civilization is not something absolute, but that it is relative, and that *our ideas and conceptions are true only so far as our civilization goes*" (emphasis added).[20] In other words, Boas believed that one should not, as did evolutionists like Tylor, speak of culture as a singular process that unites diverse peoples in a progressive hierarchy. Rather, one should, as Boas himself did later, speak of cultures in the plural.[21]

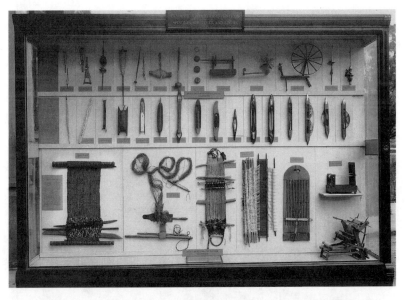

Figure 1. A display case from the U.S. National Museum (circa 1890), prepared under the supervision of Otis T. Mason. The plaque over the case reads, "Synoptic History of Inventions: Spindles, Shuttles, and Looms." Employing artifacts gathered from around the globe, this exhibit portrays the evolution of weaving instruments from the "savage" to the "civilized." Reproduced by permission of the Smithsonian Institution Archives. Negative 21389, *Synoptic History of Inventions*, Smithsonian Institution Archives, Record Unit 95, Photograph Collection, 1850s–.

I show in later chapters how the competition between these two notions of culture affected not only anthropology but other forms of writing. Because "cultural relativism"—a phrase that Boas did not actually use—became a critical buzzword of the late twentieth century, it is worth pausing to consider what he is and is not claiming for this conception of cultural difference. His point is not to preclude one culture from making a moral judgment about another's practice, although he may indirectly discourage such judgments.[22] Instead, he is making an argument about interpretation and meaning; he "repeatedly insists that two culture elements are not the same if they *mean* different things to different people."[23] Boas's idea of culture, like that of the cultural evolutionists, vests everyday objects and practices with significance; it rests upon the tangible, not upon Arnold's inward state of "harmonious perfection." Unlike the evolutionists, Boas presents the problem of interpretation as a complex, challenging process that forces anthropologists and museum patrons alike to realize that all patterns of thought, including their own, are contingent upon the dense contextual web called culture.

Figure 2. This "life group" exhibit (circa 1902) at the American Museum of Natural History was curated by Franz Boas. The exhibit uses mannequins to display artifacts as used in their original context. Reproduced by permission of the American Museum of Natural History. Negative 338764 from the American Museum of Natural History Library; copy by J. Beckett.

For Boas, museums were not the best places for this difficult process of interpretation, and physical artifacts were not always the most valuable objects for cultural interpretation.[24] One of the many trends that he influenced over the course of his career was the shift of American anthropology toward the production and study of *written texts*.[25] While Boas remained interested in the cultural information that the visual could convey, an interest that later resulted in his *Primitive Art* (1928), during the years that he emerged as an influential figure within the discipline, he stressed the need to secure publication outlets for texts adhering to the rigorous standards he advocated. He and his students were therefore heavily involved in the editing and publication of journals such as *American Anthropologist*, which became a national journal in 1898, and the *Journal of American Folk-Lore*.[26] These serials would help constitute anthropology as a professional discipline, by providing a means of communication among trained social scientists, and they would reinforce the emphasis upon textual production fostered by Boas. Of the four fields around which he organized the discipline—linguistics, cultural anthropology, physical anthropology, and archaeology—the two with which Boas was most often associated, linguistics and cultural anthropology, were text-based disciplines. Linguistics had always required accurate recordings of indigenous languages, and Boas inherited from the German philological tradition a belief that the textual reproduction of stories, songs, and histories constituted data necessary to the accurate interpretation of culture. "Not only would linguistically rigorous corpora of native-language texts constitute the materials to sustain current research," Charles L. Briggs and Richard Bauman have observed of Boasian anthropology, "but they would be the chief legacy that anthropologists might provide to future scholars."[27]

Through its series of *Annual Reports* and *Bulletins,* the Bureau of American Ethnology also fostered this emphasis upon the writing and publication of cultural material—what I refer to as "ethnography." Like the dialect literature and local color writing discussed in the two following chapters, scientific ethnography proceeded from the premise that, through the appropriate methodology, crucial group-based differences could be rendered upon the page. In the late-nineteenth and early-twentieth centuries, this project, today often referred to as "salvage ethnography," took on particular urgency because of the commonly held belief that the carriers of traditional Indian languages and forms of knowledge would soon disappear. In an 1878 report that helped persuade Congress to create the Bureau, its future director, John Wesley Powell, explained why the study of Native peoples "should be pushed with utmost vigor," and in doing so described the kind of information the Bureau would seek to record: "The field of research is speedily narrowing because of the rapid change in the Indian population now in progress; all habits, customs, and opinions are fading away; even languages are disappearing; and in a few years it will be impossible to study our North American Indians in their primitive conditions, except from recorded history."[28] Boas, too, regularly invoked the salvage imperative. For instance, when requesting funds for his aptly named project on the "Vanishing Tribes of North America," he argued that future generations "will owe a debt of gratitude to him who enables us to preserve this knowledge, which, without a great effort on the part of our own generation, will be lost forever."[29]

The imperative for preservation articulated here by Powell and Boas was central to the textualization of group difference in the late-nineteenth and early-twentieth centuries, and in fact formed the basis of all ethnographic writing, whether in literature or in social science. On the one hand, the salvage mode ties ethnographic texts to the antimodernist response to feared homogenization that T. Jackson Lears describes in *No Place of Grace*.[30] Like the Arts and Crafts movement or the revival of interest in the Middle Ages, salvage ethnography preserved markers of difference threatened by industrialization and mass communication. On the other hand, during a period of intensifying discrimination against African Americans and deepening anti-immigrant nativism, the textualization of group-based difference created a forum for confronting the racial and ethnic diversity of the United States outside of the blatant chauvinism of white supremacy. Ethnographic texts could afford readers the chance to encounter voices rarely present in political debate.

In the case of anthropology, the presumed necessity of salvaging culture also contributed to the way the ethnographic texts of Boas and others continued the object-based tradition of American anthropology. Like the museum collections of objects, such texts "constituted a body of material that would endure through time and provide the basis for future analysis and interpretation."[31] This sense that texts had the status of scientific specimens rather than artistic creations seems particularly true of Boas's own ethnography. Volumes such as *Chinook Texts* (1894), *Kathlamet Texts* (1901), and *Tsimshian Texts* (1902) transcribe and translate verbal artifacts, but without explanation or interpretation. "The following pages contain nothing but the texts and translations," Boas writes at the conclusion of his two-page introduction to *Chinook Texts*.[32] Boas sometimes offered interpretations of such texts in subsequent monographs; more often he did not. In one well-known work, *The Ethnology of the Kwakiutl* (1921), he prints page after page of Kwakiutl (or Kwakwaka'wakw) recipes for the preparation of salmon and blueberries with little commentary about the significance of such material. As Briggs and Bauman have recently pointed out, "Boas's failure to provide even minimal *explications de texte* . . . can be understood as part of his efforts to construct the texts as self-contained artifacts and scholarly objects."[33] He was building, in other words, a textual museum that would survive those whose words he recorded.

One can also understand Boas's publishing practices as a testament to his belief in the complexity of all cultures. For while he pushed for the discovery of scientific truths about culture, he also insisted that one could not arrive at such conclusions until one had accumulated all the necessary evidence, something that his famed "five-foot" shelf of Kwakiutl ethnographies suggests would require a lifetime of effort. This skepticism about the possibility of arriving at verifiable truths has led Arnold Krupat to label Boasian anthropology as a science in the "ironic mode." As an ironic science, Boasian anthropology encourages its practitioners to seek meaningful conclusions while simultaneously articulating impossibly high standards for arriving at such meaning.[34] Even Boas's 1887 comments about museum display sound hopelessly rigorous; could a museum ever actually exhibit the "complete collection of a single tribe" that Boas deemed necessary to provide adequate context?

The never-ending relentless drive to accumulate and publish cultural material in the late-nineteenth and early-twentieth centuries created a new emphasis on textual representation and analysis and forged new relationships between anthropology—particularly the field concerned with such writing, ethnography—and other discursive movements of the period. The sheer quantity of the original texts, coupled with the paucity of analysis and interpretation, forced Boasian anthropologists to read them in a different way than did their predecessors or British contemporaries. Rather than searching, as James George Frazer did in the *Golden Bough* (1890; 1911–15), for patterns and similarities *among* cultures, the Boasians looked for characteristics intrinsic and internal to the texts of a particular culture. While the Boasian anthropologists still considered themselves scientists deriving empirical truths, the type of interpretation they used was something like the mode of reading experienced by the audiences of Joel Chandler Harris's *Uncle Remus* or Paul Laurence Dunbar's dialect poetry, to name two examples discussed in chapter 3. In each case, the reader of the vernacular work was asked to come to terms with a linguistic specimen framed by an authoritative voice, a voice that testified to the authenticity of the text as a representation of group difference but did not provide a definitive interpretation of the meaning of the text. Through this textual arrangement, works of scientific ethnography provided for an aesthetic component to the reading of cultural documents, and conversely the literary reading of such realist texts seemed, to many, scientific in nature.

Philosophers and other students of aesthetics typically describe the necessary condition for aesthetic judgment—that is, a judgment about a work's beauty or artistic qualities that produce pleasure, rather than an evaluation of its scientific significance—as a distance allowing disinterested contemplation.[35] Placing a mask or a vase under a glass case in a museum instantiates such a distance between the observer and the artifact; similarly, the recording and publication of oral expression by a scientific authority can place the reader at the necessary remove from the text to engage in disinterested contemplation. This intersection of ethnography and literary realism around the project of cultural documentation enables readers to engage cultural difference as both a scientific and aesthetic phenomenon. Howells hints at the possibilities as well as the problems of the aestheticization of culture in an offhand remark he makes about the return of Basil and Isabel March to New York, in *The Hazard of New Fortunes* (1890): "The main difference was that they saw it more now as a life, and then they had only regarded it as a spectacle."[36] The rise of ethnographic notions of culture made it possible for people like the Marches to view other ways of life as constituting more than a "spectacle," even if the pleasure they took in viewing it upon the page or in the museum still retained an air of condescension.

The aesthetic possibilities of cultural documentation—a project described in *The Hazard of New Fortunes*—at the end of the nineteenth century were deepened by the agenda articulated by Boas for his discipline. The evolutionary paradigm that held sway throughout this period promised that the rules determining human existence were within reach. Many in the middle and professional classes believed, as Lears observes, that science "was a kind of Easter-egg hunt; once the eggs were gathered the game would be over: the laws governing the universe would be fully known."[37] The evidentiary requirements of cultural analysis, as set forward by Boas, deliberately frustrated such a search. Under the rigors of Boasian anthropology, it became easier to reach judgments that seemed more aesthetic in nature about the symbolic significance of a particular cultural artifact or document, but more difficult to make determinations about its place in a scientifically verifiable system of development. How and why Boas tried to thwart his contemporaries from reaching such conclusions stems from the historical moment in which he elucidated the culture concept, a moment in which Boas was preoccupied with the dominance of the biological determinism of race.

From Race to Culture

While Boas may have inserted himself into the public debates of his time by denouncing racist theories of identity, in the pages of publications such as *The Nation* and *The New Republic,* his more sustained energies were directed at the disciplines of social science, particularly anthropology, for which he attempted to differentiate between notions today still omnipresent in the American academy: race and culture.[38] Boas pursued this goal as he simultaneously attempted to redefine the concept of culture itself, to replace the interpretation of culture as something that exists in progressive stages with a definition of culture as something existing in complex entities that cannot be arranged according to either chronology or hierarchy. Central to this two-pronged argument—that race was separate from culture and that cultures should be studied as discrete wholes— was Boas's preoccupation with diminishing the role of *narrative,* with its emphasis upon chronology, in interpreting the human condition. Evolutionists of all stripes were attempting to describe the narrative patterns that produced the events of global human history; Boas responded by trying to divorce the study of culture from this narrative organization.

The challenge of charting the shifting definitions of "race" and "culture" at the turn of the twentieth century has been complicated by the frequency with which these terms are even today used as nearly interchangeable. One of the most widely read discussions of this confusion, Walter Benn Michaels's *Our America: Nativism, Modernism, and Pluralism,* contends that, through American modernism, the idea of culture became a mask beneath which the primacy of racial identity continued to be propagated in the United States. For Michaels, the discussion of cultural identities, both in the period he describes and in our own, has been nearly always a poorly disguised discussion of racial ones.[39] In the period prior to modernism, the relationship between race and culture could be even more complex. At the end of the nineteenth century, Boas posited socially determined culture as a deliberate alternative to biologically determined race as a means of explaining group-based differences. While this version of culture never fully supplanted the concept of race (as Michaels shows), it did affect the ways thinkers across discursive disciplines described group-based differences through narrative forms. In other words, the introduction of the culture concept affected not only *what* stories Americans might tell about their social divisions, but also *how* they might tell those stories.

Before the early twentieth century, the vocabulary of social identity provided no reliable lexicon for dividing those characteristics that people inherited from their ancestors from those they did not. Though it existed in a variety of forms, hereditarianism played a role in all conceptions of group difference.[40] Since their arrival in the Americas, Europeans have persisted in attempting to enumerate and define the differences between themselves and descendants of peoples of other continents, and this long history of efforts demonstrates how intertwined the cultural and racial versions of identity are. For example, in one of the best-known statements on difference in the history of American letters, "Query XIV" of *Notes on the State of Virginia*, Thomas Jefferson describes the distinctions between blacks and whites as being "physical and moral"—terms that seem at first to approximate a division between biological race and social culture. The "physical" and the "moral," however, are not discrete categories for Jefferson. His discussion of "the negro" progresses easily from skin color ("the foundation of a greater or less share of beauty in the two races") to hair and body odor to the ways in which blacks approach love, sleep, and grief.[41] My point is not to condemn Jefferson for his racialist presumption that social inequities are founded in the biological differentiation of racial inheritance (nor for his more obvious racism in writing that blacks smell worse than whites, or that blacks need less sleep because they make time for some social activity after being forced to "hard labour" all day). Rather, I bring up Jefferson to remind us that, for him, these phenomena are intimately connected; each empirical observation contributes equally to what for Jefferson is a coherent portrait of blacks "as inferior to the whites in the endowments both of body and mind."[42]

The connection between the "physical" and the "moral," between "body" and "mind," formed the cornerstone of the so-called racial science of antebellum America. Led by Samuel Morton, the American school of ethnology investigated the measurement of skulls to prove differing intellectual capacities of the races. The race scientists of this era provided an empirical prop for chattel slavery and for the continued oppression of American Indians by contending that their findings supported the theory of polygenesis—the belief that races of humanity did not share a common origin.[43] Polygenesis offered a powerful argument for those white Americans searching to justify the prevailing social order through the language of the natural world. The world-renowned Swiss naturalist Louis Agassiz, who began teaching at Harvard in 1847, wrote in the introduction to one widely read polygenesist work that "the differences existing between distinct races are often greater than those distinguishing species of animals one with the other."[44]

Polygenesis and this brand of race science fell victim to two broad developments, one political, the other scientific. The outcome of the Civil War, together with the passage of constitutional amendments guaranteeing blacks certain rights, robbed such research of its relevance as an apologia to slavery, though the beliefs it propagated resurfaced repeatedly throughout the post-Reconstruction debates over the status of African Americans in the United States. During the same period, the reorientation of scientific thought in the wake of Charles Darwin's *Origin of Species* influenced the discussion of race in an immediate way. Darwinism suggested that races shared a common origin, but that their differentiation took place in the ancient past—in effect, a compromise between monogenesis and polygenesis. Darwinism did not provide an immediately accessible framework for disentangling inherited qualities from acquired ones. In fact, regardless of the original intentions of Darwin himself, Darwinism's emphasis upon biological development furnished a vocabulary for racialists of the late nineteenth century who argued that the connection between biological difference and social inferiority was undeniable.[45] Equally important, the new vocabulary of evolution shifted scientific attention to the question of development, to how races might and might not change. Discovering the laws of development might help clarify the past, but the real import would be to help shape and predict the future of humanity. In the late nineteenth century, evolution could therefore be invoked both by white supremacists arguing that the "struggle for existence" necessitated intraracial solidarity and by progressive thinkers claiming that evolution necessitated reforms leading to a more humane society.[46]

During this same period, the evolutionary anthropology of E. B. Tylor and Lewis Henry Morgan paid little attention to actual biological origins for social differences. Instead, cultural evolutionism drew upon an organic analogy that portrayed the development of a people as occurring in a manner similar to the evolution of a species of plant or animal. Cultures "grew" more complex and specialized over time, just as species changed from simple organisms to more advanced ones with highly differentiated parts; both followed Herbert Spencer's maxim of progress from homogeneity to heterogeneity. In describing culture in this way, works like Tylor's *Primitive Culture* and Morgan's *Ancient Society* managed to skirt the question of biological determinism altogether. Racial inheritance was not described as a crucial factor in cultural evolution, but evolutionary anthropologists habitually divided cultural groups along the same lines that scientists such as Agassiz used to separate racial stocks. This arrangement according to the degree to which peoples had "progressed" toward the goal of civilization reproduced the hierarchy of earlier racial science.

In the shadow that evolutionism cast in the concluding decades of the nineteenth century, biologically inherited race and socially constructed culture became linked concepts, a double lens through which intellectuals could view populations of the United States. W. E. B. Du Bois's "The Conservation of Races" (1897) exemplifies this tie: "But while race differences have followed mainly physical race lines, yet no mere physical distinctions would really define or explain the deeper differences—the cohesiveness and continuity of these groups. The deeper differences are spiritual, psychical, differences—undoubtedly based on the physical, but infinitely transcending them."[47] In attempting to describe these "deeper differences," Du Bois is reaching for the social force that we have come to call culture. Yet his second sentence falls back upon biological race, the "physical," as the underlying basis of this force. For Du Bois, endorsing the notion of inherited behavior is still a necessary strategy.[48]

Du Bois later refuted this logic; he wrote in his 1940 autobiography *Dusk of Dawn* that the "real essence" of African American kinship "is its *social* heritage of slavery" (emphasis added).[49] Lee D. Baker has shown how Du Bois adopted a Boasian, culturalist position in the early twentieth century, a period when, Du Bois and Boas, both educated in German universities, cultivated a professional relationship important to each. Boas's scientific credentials made his critiques of biologically based theories of racial difference a useful authority for Du Bois and his colleagues. At Du Bois's invitation, meanwhile, Boas participated in the African American struggle for political equality—for instance, by lecturing at Atlanta University, speaking at the first meeting of the National Association for the Advancement of Colored People (NAACP), and writing for the NAACP's *The Crisis*—and in so doing gained a new audience for his brand of anthropology.[50]

Boas's primary tool against the racial determinism espoused by white supremacists was a relentless empiricism. Rather than simply dismiss the racialist premise that a hierarchical social order was grounded in biological differences among races, he sought to use the techniques of physical anthropology to prove that social inequities were not rooted in natural divisions of humanity. By using the same methodology often employed by racial scientists to argue the inferiority of non-white peoples, Boas caused himself to seem, to some, limited by devotion to scientific rigor.[51] However,

Boas believed such efforts could use the authority of objective scientific procedure to dispel deep-seated beliefs about the nature of biologically inherited race. Boas's most elaborate and best-known effort of this kind was his study of the offspring of immigrants to the United States, conducted from 1908 to 1910 under the auspices of the U.S. Immigration Commission. Created as a result of nativist efforts to restrict immigration, the commission was firmly set against the record numbers of immigrants arriving from eastern and southern Europe.[52] In the end, it produced forty-two volumes of reports, and, as John Higham writes, "cast its mountainous social and economic data in the form of an invidious contrast between the northwestern and southeastern Europeans in the United States at that time."[53]

Boas's contribution to the commission did little to support this argument. Instead of fueling nativist fears, he used anthropometric data to assure Americans that they need not worry that immigrants from southern and eastern Europe would change the literal face of the nation. The 573-page report to Congress, published as *Changes in Bodily Form of Descendants of Immigrants* (1911), demonstrated that, after living in the United States, children of immigrants physically more resembled one another (and other native-born Americans) than their European progenitors.[54] Supported by page after page of empirical measurements, Boas argued that the environment of the United States had affected the physical features of American-born children, even though he could not explain precisely why.[55] Boas's study is an effort to undermine the idea of biological heredity as a major determinant of group-based behavior by showing that the supposedly stable marker of racial inheritance, bodily form, is not a reliable marker of heredity. The popular press interpreted such findings as a victory of the American environment over the racial divisions of the so-called Old World, and as an answer to worries that the new immigration would alter the "face" of the United States. As the *New York Globe*, one of the many newspapers and magazines reporting Boas's findings, put it: "[T]he caricatures of Uncle Sam in a hundred years from now will present the same essential features as now—the same lankiness, the same protuberance of nose."[56]

Like his later efforts to denounce Aryanism, Boas's stance on immigration and his work with Du Bois remind us that he understood that abstract ideas such as race and culture could have immediate and dramatic consequences. By striving to make the separation of the physical from the cultural a central premise of anthropology, he sought to have the discipline, in turn, move the public closer to his position of racial equipotentiality. Fostering egalitarianism, however, required more than severing the relationship between race and culture; it required redefining the cultural in a manner different than that of evolutionary anthropologists. For the Boasians, cultural difference marked the boundaries between alternative systems of understanding the world, systems so incongruent that they could not be arranged in any temporal, developmental scheme.

The articulation of a pluralistic model of culture therefore compelled Boas and his students to contest the role of chronology in cultural evolution. "The Aims of Anthropology," an 1895 address to the American Association for the Advancement of Science (AAAS) by its president, Daniel G. Brinton, succinctly demonstrates how central were questions of time to the complicated relationships among race, culture, and evolution that the Boasians hoped to alter.[57] In his talk, Brinton (1837–1899), a Civil War surgeon who became one of the first professors of anthropology in the United States, announced what he called the "corner stone of true anthropology," a "discovery little less than marvelous":

> This discovery is that of the physical unity of man, the parallelism of his development everywhere and in all time; ... the nigh absolute uniformity of his thoughts and actions, his aims and methods, when in the same degree of development, no matter where he is or in what epoch living.[58]

Brinton neatly encapsulates here the premise of evolutionary anthropology: the "absolute uniformity" of humanity's development through different stages or degrees. The ultimate goal of the discipline, according to this formulation, was to understand the process of this development so that those at its most advanced stage, "civilization," could progress even farther (71).

This search for the "universal in humanity" (65) proceeds from what Johannes Fabian has labeled the "denial of coevalness," the assumption that peoples living in the same moment of history actually represent different chronological stages of development.[59] In this framework, anthropology could examine, for example, the Indians of North America as representatives of the prehistory of European "civilization." Brinton argues that the "careful study of what are called 'ethnographic parallels'—that is, similarities or identities of laws, games, customs, myths, arts, etc., in primitive tribes located far asunder on the earth's surface" would both conclusively prove the unity of cultural development and highlight its most important features (65). When Otis Mason had displayed specimens from throughout the Earth in a single sequence, he had followed precisely the same logic. Chronological sequence was the first step toward deriving the laws that drove human development.

Chronology marks one group-based difference that Brinton describes in this talk; peoples may differ because of the place they occupy in this history of progress. In this sense, Native American groups were "older" than the Euro-Americans who were their neighbors. Brinton, however, also explicitly addresses another difference: biologically rooted race. Despite his avowed belief in the "physical unity" of humanity, Brinton returns to biological differences at the end of his address in order to "deny that all races are equally endowed" (68). He continues, "The black, the brown, and the red races differ anatomically so much from the white, especially in their splanchnic organs, that even with equal cerebral capacity they never could rival its results by equal efforts." Though all human groups shared a common path of development, the racial inferiority of some groups would prevent them, according to Brinton, from progressing as far down that path as others.[60]

Brinton's evolutionary account of the nature of group-based differences arranges its knowledge in a highly narrativized form. This model empha- sizes the forging of connections among chronologically disparate events through patterns of causation. In other words, Brinton understands cul- ture as a narrative, which is more than a sequence of events; narrative, in the sense that I am using it here, purports to recount such a sequence according to some principle of order. It is not history in the sense of an empirical representation of the past, but history with a telos and a discernible logic.[61] Cultural evolution used people living in both the past and the present to chart an evolutionary genealogy that described how people acted (their culture) at different moments in human history—and it simultaneously suggested that groups moved at different rates through this narrative ladder because of biological make-up (their race). Brinton's narrative delineated a clear hierarchy that he, despite his belief in the unity of humanity, would not disrupt. Brinton's earlier *Races and Peoples: Lec- tures on the Science of Ethnography* (1890) illustrated the practical applica- tion of such a model; there, he urged white women to avoid "the embrace of a colored man" in order to "preserve the purity of the type, and with it the claims of the race to be the highest. They have no holier duty, no more sacred mission, than that of transmitting in its integrity the heritage of ethnic endowment gained by the race throughout generations of strug- gle."[62] Brinton's injunction reveals the extent to which his conception of human difference is narrativized, centered on the way in which "heritage" links people over time. The "sacred mission" is the transmission of cultural achievement through the propagation of "racial purity." Culture in this evolutionary model has both a temporal component—a clear trajectory of progress over time—and a biological one.

One year after Brinton gave "The Aims of Anthropology" as his AAAS presidential address, Boas, at the organization's annual meeting, delivered a paper that reads like a direct rebuttal to Brinton.[63] "The Limitations of Comparative Anthropology" (1896) in many ways extends the argument that Boas had voiced in the late 1880s on the topic of museum display.[64] The flaw in the model of cultural evolution, he argued, was its presumption "that if an ethnological phenomenon has developed independently in a number of places its development has been the same everywhere; or, expressed in a different form, that the same ethnological phenomena are always due to the same causes" (273). Masks, for example, frequently appear in cultures throughout humankind, but they are not always created for the same reason; some commemorate a deceased person, some protect the wearer against spirits, and some form a crucial element of theater (274). One cannot presume that masks universally accompany other elements of culture or that masks are necessary to the development of some other phenomenon. Instead, the anthropologist can attempt a "detailed study of customs in their relation to the total culture of the tribe practicing them," a method that Boas contends will determine "with considerable accuracy" the meaning and history of such phenomena (276).

Boas's culture-specific method produces a profoundly new relationship between anthropology and narrative time. The evolutionary anthropology of Tylor, Morgan, and Brinton establishes chronological discrepancies among cultural groups, even those who actually lived during the same literal moment, and it does so by positing a narrative that describes how these groups developed from the earliest moments of human history. For Boas, on the other hand, questions about deep time could not be addressed by anthropology because the only past that is verifiable is the recent past of a single culture. In fact, the Boasian culture concept goes so far as to scuttle the question of time altogether, to reorient anthropology from *diachronic* (and universal) history to *synchronic* (and culturally specific) description and analysis.[65]

This theoretical shift affected ethnography—the documentation of cultural difference and the publication of vernacular texts—in ways illustrated by the ethnographic work of Boas himself. The following paragraph comes from the introduction of *Chinook Texts*, a work published in 1894 as a Bulletin of the Bureau of American Ethnology. Here, Boas describes his efforts to collect accurate and authentic texts in the Chinook dialect of the Salishan language in 1890 and 1891:

I went to search for this remnant of the Clatsop and Chinook peoples and found them located at Bay Center, Pacific county, Washington. They proved to be the last survivors of the Chinook, who at one time occupied the greater part of Shoalwater bay and the northern bank of Columbia river as far as Greys Harbor. The tribe has adopted the Chehalis language in the same way in which the Clatsop have adopted the Nehelim. The only individuals who spoke Chinook were Charles Cultee and Catherine. While I was unable to obtain anything from the latter, Cultee (or more properly Qᵢɛltē') proved to be a veritable storehouse of information. His mother's mother was a Katlamat, and his mother's father a Quilā'pax; his father's mother was a Clatsop, and his father's father a Tinneh of the interior. His wife is a Chehalis, and at present he speaks Chehalis almost exclusively, this being also the language of his children. He has lived for a long time in Katlamat, on the southern bank of [the] Columbia river, his mother's town, and for this reason speaks the Katlamat dialect as well as the Chinook dialect. He uses the former dialect in conversing with Samson, a Katlamat Indian, who is also located at Bay Center. Until a few years ago he spoke Chinook with one of his relatives, while he uses it now only rarely when conversing with Catherine, who lives a few miles from Bay Center. Possibly this Chinook is to a certain extent mixed with Katlamat expressions, but from a close study of the material I conclude that it is on the whole pure and trustworthy.[66]

Boas frames the hundreds of pages of texts and translations that follow this introduction with what is essentially a salvage story. In locating Cultee, the "veritable storehouse of information," Boas claims to have preserved the Chinook dialect and its tales before the extinction of its speakers. (In fact, Cultee also served as the single source for Boas's *Kathlamet Texts*.) From the background and circumstances of Cultee we can infer why Chinook has been reduced to the lone pair of speakers that Boas names. Presumably due to disease, violence, and territorial dispossession—Boas does not explicitly say—the "once powerful tribes" (Boas's words) of the lower Columbia river have been reduced to small populations that have become more unified over time, a consolidation most likely facilitated by an increasing rate of intermarriage and the adoption of a common dialect.

The contrast between the dynamic history of cultural transformation and exchange that Boas alludes to in these prefatory remarks and the texts that follow dramatizes the extent of Boas's rejection of diachronic narrative. For while the passage reprinted above raises a variety of questions about the effects of dramatic alterations in tribal life, the texts themselves stand alone as an authoritative, "pure and trustworthy," ahistorical depiction of the Chinook language and culture. Of the thirty-three texts collected in the volume, thirty-one are placed under the headings of either

"Myths" or "Beliefs, Customs, and Tales." The remaining two, which conclude the book, are labeled "Historical Tales"; one tells a brief story of an intertribal battle, and the other speaks of "The First Ship Seen by the Clatsop." The placement of the latter as the concluding text in the volume adds to the sense that Cultee's stories and depictions of tribal life represent some unspecified moment prior to the arrival of Europeans (let alone of intertribal borrowing) when the speakers of Chinook occupied the larger geographical territory Boas describes. What Boas saves, therefore, is not only a language, but a whole way of living and imagining the world that no longer exists except as encoded in these texts.

In other instances, Boas is known to have taken steps to ensure that the ethnographic texts he published represented a tribal culture free from outside influence—removing, for example, English phrases that Indian informants inserted into their own speech.[67] Boas's quest for the culturally "pure" is important, but equally relevant is the bifurcated relationship to temporality of a work like *Chinook Texts*. While Boas's introduction provides a narrative of Cultee's life and Boas's documentation of culture, the main body of the work describes Chinook culture without any explicit narrative structure whatsoever. Of course, each text features Cultee as a narrator, yet the division and arrangement of the texts asserts their status as descriptive acts that produce a taxonomy of tribal life. By removing all traces of the histories evoked in the introduction, including both the general history of European-Native relations and the specific history of the ethnographic encounter between himself and Cultee, Boas leaves us with texts that portray culture as a synchronic, static entity.

To borrow the rubric of Georg Lukács's well-known essay "Narrate or Describe?" Boasian ethnography adopted description as its philosophy of composition. "Description," Lukács contends, "debases characters to the level of inanimate objects" by forcing readers to become "merely observers" of that which the text describes.[68] The experience of reading ethnographic texts produced by Boas, as well as the dialect tales and collections of local color writing that the following chapters examine, relies upon an objectifying observation analogous to what Lukács finds in descriptive fiction. Unlike Lukács, though, I do not consider this readerly observation to be wholly negative, for the distance required for such observation makes possible the aesthetic contemplation of ethnographic texts. *Chinook Texts* provides an example, in fact, of how a work valued initially as a scientific specimen has over time become redefined as an aesthetic achievement— for one of Cultee's trickster tales appears in the most recent edition of the *Norton Anthology of American Literature*.[69] While the mode of ethnographic observation that Boas's volume insists upon may divorce culture from history—description, Lukács states, "contemporizes everything"[70]—it has also allowed readers to engage these texts as complicated works of verbal art.

The temporal disjunction between Boas's introduction and Cultee's texts constitutes a variation of a pattern that occurs throughout the publication of vernacular expression in the late nineteenth century, not just in scientific ethnography but also in works associated with American literary realism. In Joel Chandler Harris's *Uncle Remus: His Songs and Sayings* (1880), for instance, the association of the narrative frame with the chronological present contrasts with the "timeless" quality of the tales of the African American raconteur. Even the arrangement of *Uncle Remus* bears something in common with *Chinook Texts*, for Harris follows Boas in putting a single historical narrative (in this case, "A Story of the War") in a separate category from the more characteristic and ahistorical "legends."[71] The stories of Uncle Remus are presumed to evoke a pleasant version of antebellum plantation life, but they do so without referencing the complex and painful history of life under slavery. Instead, the sense of antiquity in Remus's stories places them at a distance from both the young white boy to whom Remus tells them and Harris's audience who reads them, a phenomenon registered in the number of titles of books of dialect expression or local color writing that include the word "old," such as Thomas Nelson Page's *In Ole Virginia* (1887), Zitkala-Ša's *Old Indian Legends* (1900), and Paul Laurence Dunbar's *In Old Plantation Days* (1903) (to name a few books that figure in later chapters). Both scientific ethnography and literary realism engaged in what Richard H. Brodhead has identified as "the habit while purporting to grasp an alien cultural system of covertly lifting it out of history, constituting it as a self-contained form belonging to the past rather than an interactive force still adapting to the present."[72] Boas goes farther than authors of literature by trying to extricate Cultee's texts from chronology altogether—to render them as purely descriptive as possible by removing the temporal dimension inherent to narrative.

One comment Lukács makes about the limitations of description may help to explain why Boas took such drastic steps to orient the ethnographic project around the descriptive, rather than the narrative, mode. "The levelling inherent in the descriptive method," Lukács writes, "makes everything episodic." Boas aimed for precisely this "levelling." The more narrativized forms of anthropology had established a progressive, evolutionary version of culture that, as Brinton's "Aims of Anthropology" demonstrates, was linked to chauvinistic beliefs in racial hierarchy. In response, Boas offered descriptions of culture that were indeed "episodic" insofar as they were comprised of synchronic observations that could not be arranged into a satisfactory, unified chronology exhibiting the pattern of causation Lukács and others identify as characteristic of narrative. For this reason, the guiding principle of Boasian ethnography may be better described as cultural *particularism* than cultural pluralism. It insists upon interpreting cultural phenomena as the products of an individual episode of culture, as well as upon emphasizing the ways that such evidence often disproves the validity of global, cross-cultural narratives about human experience.[73]

For Boas, abandoning the search for a "grand system of the evolution of society" was a necessary step for anthropology to become a science that did more than simply furnish the data to justify the domination of so-called civilized people over primitive ones.[74] Culture would uncover local truths, like the Chinook stories told by Charles Cultee, not universal laws. As one of Boas's allies put it in 1918, "Culture cannot be forced into the straitjacket of any theory, whatever it may be, nor can it be reduced to chemical or mathematical formulas. As nature has no laws, so culture has none."[75] Removing the quest for such laws from the discipline of anthropology necessarily resulted in a shortening of its temporal depth. Broad diachronic narratives bore too much in common with the racially-based (and racially-biased) theories of evolution that went hand-in-hand with social Darwinism. Time became the wedge that Boas used to pry apart biological race and socially constructed culture.

Instead of unfolding the global history of evolution, Boas emphasized the study of local "forms of thought," a phrase that he used in the 1911 book *The Mind of Primitive Man* to refer to everything from definitions of color to concepts of illness, to fashion, to table manners. The goal of the ethnographer became to set down the quotidian phenomena of everyday life that revealed how "groups of man belonging to distinct social strata do not behave in the same manner."[76] As the title of Boas's book—the first he wrote for a general audience—suggests, the ultimate purpose of study of such group-oriented behavior was to reveal its complex psychological significance, its meaning that could only be discovered through investigation of a particular cultural context. In *The Mind of Primitive Man*, Boas argues that this manner of interpreting foreign behavior would reduce ethnic chauvinism: "The general theory of valuation of human activities, as developed by anthropological research, teaches us a higher tolerance than the one we now profess."[77]

This tolerance comes at the cost of rendering culture an unwieldy interpretive tool. Throughout *The Mind of Primitive Man*, Boas emphasizes the almost numbing complexity of culture: "There are a thousand activities and modes of thought that constitute our daily life—of which we are not conscious at all until we come into contact with other types of life, or until we are prevented from acting according to our custom—that cannot in any way be claimed to be more reasonable than others, and to which, nevertheless, we cling."[78] Understanding a culture fully not only requires documenting and decoding each of these "thousand activities," but also determining how they are integrated into a whole.[79] The sheer difficulty of comprehending a single cultural system precludes, in turn, the Boasian anthropologist from discerning how cultures *change*. The disjunction between the introduction and the main body of a work like *Chinook Texts* illustrates this limitation. While Boas may allude to the developments that have dramatically altered tribal life in the geographical region in question, developments that surely affected not only the content but the manner of Cultee's speech, the texts themselves stand as timeless artifacts seemingly unchanged from an unnamed moment prior to this history. The difficulty of reconciling the documentation of culture as a static phenomenon with the necessity of accounting for cultural change remains an issue debated within cultural anthropology to this day.[80]

Critics have pointed out that, because Boasian ethnography treats each culture as a singular, complex entity, this model emphasizes unadulterated purity, instead of recognizing the degree to which all human groups are continually shaped by a variety of forces, including exchange and contact with other groups.[81] Yet Boas's treatment of culture as a "closed system of signification"—to use the phrase of one such critic—also distinguishes Boasian cultural *particularism* from the racially inflected cultural *pluralism* advocated in the late 1910s and 1920s by figures such as Horace Kallen.[82] As Werner Sollors has argued, Kallen's anti-assimilationist pluralism embraced an American ethnic diversity (or at least a diversity of immigrants from Europe) but reaffirmed "the eternal power of descent, birth, *natio*, and race" as the ultimate determinant of identity.[83] For Kallen, each person carried an "intrinsic" ethnic identity that affected his or her behavior; "[W]hatever else he changes," he states in "Democracy versus the Melting-Pot" (1915), a man "cannot change his grandfather."[84]

By way of contrast, recall the complex genealogy that Boas gives for Charles Cultee in the introduction to *Chinook Texts:* Cultee's "mother's mother was a Katlamat, and his mother's father a Quilā'pax; his father's mother was a Clatsop, and his father's father a Tinneh of the interior."[85] Boas is not claiming that Cultee can "change his grandfather"—or his grandmother, for that matter. In fact, Cultee's descent from four different groups seems of hardly any relevance for Boas at all; it certainly plays no role in the presentation of the texts. Instead, Boas vigorously enforces a division between race and culture in a way that Kallen does not. Cultee's descent is not significant except insofar as it may shed light on the synchronic description of Chinook culture that he provides, and Boas implies (perhaps wrongly) that it does not shed any light at all. While the result may be a work that seems incongruent with the cultural mixing that most likely accompanied the marriages included in Cultee's genealogy, the work focuses its attention on what Cultee *tells* as an informant, not who Cultee *is* as a product of biology.

Unlike Kallen's cultural pluralism, the Boasian model of culture urges the primacy of social *meaning* rather than *identity*, of unraveling how phenomena signify rather than uncovering who people are. What the study of culture yields is a system for understanding how members of a group share customs, behavior, and institutions that have meanings particular to that culture. No single, hidden truth confers that significance; instead, the elements of culture derive meaning from their organization in a dense, contextual web. The sheer volume of ethnographic texts that Boas himself published demonstrates how inexhaustible he believed the project of documenting culture, and the extent to which he was invigorated by the complexity of cultural systems. By treating cultures as integrated wholes, the Boasian model produces two effects of importance to this book. First, it reinforces the distance among groups by insisting upon their ultimate differences and generating a search for the most authentic markers of these differences. "Culture," as Adam Kuper writes, "is always defined in opposition to something else."[86] Second, it invites the observer to contemplate each culture as a system of internal connections rather than as a chapter in evolutionary history. The first corollary creates a distance between an observer and the cultural artifact, similar to the distance required for aesthetic judgment; the second corollary creates an imperative for observers to employ this distance by engaging in an interpretive act about the meaning of the artifact, much as one interprets an object of art.

Boas considered himself first and last a scientist, and his dedication to scientific fact and method should not be discounted. However, the emergence of this manner of thinking about culture participated in a larger trend of thinking about culturally specific differences as having both aesthetic and scientific meanings. The textual preservation of culture, particularly the recording of vernacular verbal expression, played an especially significant role in this new way of thinking of difference because the anthropological writing of culture intersected with contemporary discursive movements originating outside of social science. The ethnographic emphasis on particularism, local setting, and forms of language made this combination of anthropological investigation and literary expression nearly inevitable.

Well after American literary realism made ethnographic forms of writing visible, and after Boas had articulated the culture concept and completed the vast majority of his work in ethnography, he created a short work that dwells precisely on this disciplinary convergence. This text, a short story entitled "An Eskimo Winter," encapsulates questions at the heart of this book. How can the anthropological model of culture be incorporated into literary narrative? Can literature help address the weaknesses of the culture concept, particularly the problem of how cultural change occurs? Inquiring into how Boas may have answered these questions through his only published work of fiction invites us, further, to consider the changes in culture that he experienced in his own life.

A Story of Culture: "An Eskimo Winter"

Boas agonized over making clear the distinction between culture and race throughout his entire professional life, but he avoided using either of these concepts to examine his own motivations as a scholar, teacher, and activist. For Boas, a secular Jew and a German immigrant, debates about assimilation, Americanization, and cultural pluralism provided crucial opportunities for science to show the larger society a path toward more rational and more just policies; they were not occasions for autobiographical reflection.[87] As the Third Reich came to power in Germany, Boas devoted himself to denouncing publicly Nazi racial theories and to aiding Jewish refugees hoping to relocate to the United States. When reading such articles by and about Boas in the late 1920s and 1930s, the public may have assumed that Boas was Jewish, but he never, as far as I can tell, explicitly referred to himself in published writing as being of Jewish ancestry.[88]

Julia E. Liss has shown that the letters Boas wrote as a university student at Heidelberg and Bonn in the late 1870s reveal a deep ambivalence toward other Jewish students and toward those whom he identified as "glorious German youth." During this time and that of his subsequent studies at the University of Kiel, anti-Semitism provoked Boas into quarrels and at least one duel, but such altercations did not create in him a greater sense of ethnic or religious loyalty.[89] After becoming established in the United States, Boas participated in the secular Ethical Culture movement, and like many other German Jews living in New York in the early twentieth century, he identified as German rather than Jewish.[90] Liss documents how "Boas's early efforts to establish himself in America had the effect of affirming a German identity which, as a Jew in Germany, had been very problematic for him."[91]

Boas's reluctance to discuss his Jewish ancestry may also have resulted from a professional decision. Given his devotion to overturning doctrines of racial hierarchy, he would not have desired to distract possible supporters of the culture concept with the issue of his own heritage. Instead, Boas hoped to portray himself as a detached, objective scientist, far removed from personal considerations. In his 1908 address on "Race Problems in America," one of the articles later incorporated into *The Mind of Primitive Man*, Boas went so far as to speak of the "people of eastern and southern Europe" who were emigrating to the United States as belonging to "types distinct from our own." While the phrase may be technically correct—Boas was a *central* European Jew—this rhetoric aligns him with his audience as removed from the ethnicity of a controversial wave of immigration.[92] On at least one occasion, Boas's failure to identify himself as a Jew yielded comic results. The *McClure's Magazine* story on Boas's immigrant study stated, "Nearly anybody can tell a Jew on sight, and yet, it is very difficult to define the typical Jewish characteristics." Either the editors of *McClure's* were ignorant of Boas's background or they were capable of pulling an extraordinary inside joke; on the page opposite this statement, they printed Boas's portrait.[93]

If Boas chuckled over this juxtaposition, he never let on. Throughout his life, he attempted to present himself as not only deracinated but also detached from any single set of cultural influences.[94] When American "patriots" raised eyebrows at his World War I pacifism, Boas countered that his principles were those of a global, not national, citizen. He went further in 1919 by publishing "Scientists as Spies," an article denouncing the employment of anthropologists as covert agents by the U.S. government and arguing that science should stand above and apart from the narrow conflicts of nation-states. This article, in turn, resulted in Boas being censured by the American Anthropological Association.[95] During this same period, he grew increasingly concerned with the problem of the *individual* in culture, for although Boasian culture explains human difference in a way that resists hierarchical narratives, it does so by focusing upon the differences between groups and upon how group identities shape individuals. The models and methods of Boasian anthropology do not account for how those who, like Boas himself, feel themselves at odds with the culture in which they live. An offhand remark in *The Mind of Primitive Man* is revealing: "While in primitive civilization the traditional material is doubted and examined by only a very few individuals, the number of thinkers who try to free themselves from the fetters of tradition increases as civilization advances" (206).[96] Even though Boasian anthropology celebrated the diversity and complexity of culture, Boas could also regard it as a set of "fetters."

Remarkably, Boas may have elected to address the difficult tension between the individual and culture through an entirely different narrative form—his only known work of fiction. In 1920, Elsie Clews Parsons decided to publish a volume of short fiction written by anthropologists about Native American cultures, and the book was published two years later under the title *American Indian Life*. Parsons had earned her doctorate in sociology, but she eventually became a full-fledged Boasian folklorist, editing *The Journal of American Folk-Lore* and publishing several accomplished volumes of her own work.[97] Unlike her colleagues, Parsons had access to substantial financial resources, and her patronage of Boasian anthropology (as well as her personal charm) may have played a part in the success she enjoyed in cajoling a group of social scientists to turn their efforts toward writing short fiction. Alfred L. Kroeber, who had been Boas's first doctoral student at Columbia, wrote the book's introduction. He told Parsons, "I shall always marvel at the way you drove them—us, I should say—one after another to delivery for the story book."[98]

Kroeber also feared that "the value of the book will average rather low as science or literature," as though the attempt to be both literary and scientific would necessarily preclude the book's success on either front.[99] What Kroeber did not acknowledge was that the book would "average" quite high as an index to this historical moment in the discipline. The list of contributors to *American Indian Life* reads like a who's who of Boasian anthropology from this period; Kroeber, A. A. Goldenweiser, Paul Radin, Frank Speck, Clark Wissler, Robert Lowie, Pliny Goddard, John R. Swanton, and Edward Sapir all wrote stories, as did Boas himself. Parsons chose to end the volume with Boas's contribution, a gesture signaling Boas's position as the central figure of this group and placing his word on matters of Native American culture as the final one.

Curiously, Boas elected not to write about the Kwakiutls, his most frequent ethnographic subject, or about any of the other Northwest cultures that had received his most recent and closest attention. Instead, his story, "An Eskimo Winter," returned Boas to his earliest field-work, the 1883–84 expedition to Baffin Island that transformed him from a geographer-physicist into an anthropologist.[100] This journey had been crucial to Boas's professional and theoretical development; here, he began to develop the ideas that he would later articulate in *The Mind of Primitive Man*.[101] His "letter-diary" from the expedition is worth quoting at length:

> I often ask myself what advantages our "good society" possesses over that of the "savages" and find, the more I see of their customs, the more I realize that we have no right to look down upon them. Where amongst our people would you find such true hospitality as here? Where are people so willing to perform *every* task asked of them? We have no right to blame them for their forms and superstitions which may seem ridiculous to us. We "highly educated people" are much worse, relatively speaking. The fear of tradition and old customs is deeply implanted in mankind, and in the same way as it regulates life here, it halts all progress for us. I believe it is a difficult struggle for every individual and every people to give up tradition and follow the path to truth.[102]

The expedition led Boas to form the guiding principles of his career as a social scientist. The task of cultural anthropology, as he described it in the years that followed, was to document the operation of these "forms and superstitions" while maintaining a proper respect for them. We are all creatures of culture, Boas maintained, products of "tradition and old

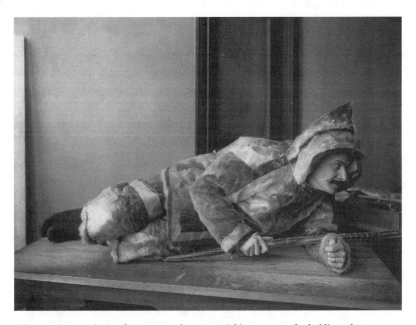

Figure 3. Boas posing to demonstrate the correct Eskimo posture for holding a harpoon—presumably to aid in the production of an accurate mannequin for museum display. Reproduced by permission of the American Museum of Natural History. Negative 3220 from the American Museum of Natural History Library; copy by R. Weber.

customs" so "deeply implanted" that it becomes nearly impossible to dis-
entangle their roots. The mission of anthropology, according to the logic
of the letter-diary, is both to foster respect for the complexity and power
of culture everywhere *and* somehow to enable select individuals to emancipate themselves from that same powerful force. [103]

Like the other stories in *American Indian Life*, "An Eskimo Winter"
directs most energy toward the first of these goals, by detailing Eskimo cultural practices, a documentary strategy leading one reviewer to compare
the volume to a textbook overloaded with "sugar coated" information—
the veneer of literary storytelling barely disguising the ethnographic data
these anthropologists consider valuable.[104] By reading Boas's story, one
learns how Eskimos (or Inuit) hunt, dine, build shelter, and heal their
sick. The story gives Boas an opportunity to mention some of his favorite
examples of cultural difference, including the taboo against eating caribou
and seal meat together and the custom of weak, elder Eskimos choosing
to commit suicide by wandering off into the wilderness so as not to be a
burden to their families. As with other contributions to the volume, "An
Eskimo Winter" privileges description over narrative and plot. Parsons
calls *American Indian Life* "a book of pictures" in her preface, and she
could not have been more accurate.[105] Because Boas's culture concept makes
it nearly impossible to describe how a particular cultural practice or event
came into being, an anthropologist will be on safe ground by telling only
how things are at a particular moment, not how things came to be.

The project of *American Indian Life* is to take advantage of the natural
affinity between the expository description of prose fiction and scientific
ethnography. Yet the format of the book also forces Boas and his fellow
anthropologists to arrange that description into the form of narratives that
will attract a lay audience. To qualify as a genuine "story," even a sequence
of descriptions must have plot and character, and Boas loosely frames
the action of "An Eskimo Winter" around two figures. Pakkak is a village
leader, a successful hunter "held in particular awe, for he was not only
strong in body and skilled in the use of the knife, lance and bow, but he
was endowed with supernatural powers" (365). No-tongue, on the other
hand, is a much less fortunate individual in the community, but manages
to persist in spite of the difficulties that confront him: "He relied upon the
good luck and the help of his friends who might be expected to assist
him, in case they should have skins to spare" (365). When No-tongue
finds himself trapped on a drifting ice floe, he sings a song ironically pro-
claiming his pleasure, the only indication in the entire book that Native
Americans might have a sense of humor:[106]

Aya, I am joyful; this is good!
Aya, there is nothing but ice around me, that is good!
Aya, I am joyful; this is good!
My country is nothing but slush, that is good!
Aya, when indeed, will this end? this is good!
I am tired of watching and waking, this is good! (368)

Like the Eskimo man from whom Boas first heard this song, the character of No-tongue must endure a week floating on the sea before being washed back to shore.[107]

The value of "An Eskimo Winter" rests upon the assumption that Pakkak and No-tongue do *not* represent extraordinary lives. As seemingly opposite characters, they teach presumably non-Eskimo readers about the variations of Eskimo culture by functioning as contrasting products of it. They are, though, also the products of their non-Eskimo creator. In the final three paragraphs of the story, Boas leaves us with a twist. No-tongue, after being harassed by Pakkak's younger, overbearing brother, makes a decision:

Now No-tongue was prompted to leave the village in which he had spent many years. For a long time he had been talking of the distant home from which he had come with his mother, when he was a very young man. At that time he wanted to see the world, and he had drifted from village to village along the whole coast line until finally he had settled down with his wife. The memory of his old home had never left him, and he longed to go back and see his relatives and the scenes of his childhood. (377–78)

For an anthropologist who had spent years persuading others of the power of culture over the individual, of the crucial role of tradition and custom, the resolution of "An Eskimo Winter" seems unlikely. In this moment, No-tongue sounds much more like Boas himself than like any Eskimo man he ever reported knowing. Like No-tongue, Boas had left the land of his birth "when he was a young man" (though without his mother!) desiring to "see the world." Boas, too, had thrown his lot in with a new culture, a new "village," but felt occasionally nostalgic for the old one. He even considered himself treated unfairly by more than one scientific "brother"; he wrote "An Eskimo Winter" about a year after his colleagues in the American Anthropological Association censured him for the "Scientists as Spies" article.

These parallels between Boas and his character may help explain why Boas raises the possibility of abandoning "tradition" that he first mentioned in his letter-diary of the 1880s. The final image of Boas's story, and in fact of the volume altogether, is the image of No-tongue and his wife leaving the regular rhythms of their own culture to depart upon a journey that will take "several years" of travel across the ice and snow—an image far more ambiguous than Boas's earlier hope that the resistance to culture could lead one to "follow the path to truth." Boas's diction even leaves the reader unclear as to how much No-tongue feels coerced (or "prompted") to leave the village, and how much he might be making a conscious decision. Regardless, in this conclusion to a largely descriptive work, Boas has introduced classic elements of narrative action—a wronged protagonist, a conflict, and a climactic exit. Equally important, even though Boas employs culture as the appropriate means of explaining the daily routine of Eskimo life, this narrative development comes from an individual in the process of doing something extraordinary. The story ends on a note of dramatic change: No-tongue rejects his village and stands practically alone, alone in search of another place where he can practice the culture that he bears. Nothing in *American Indian Life* or in Boas's earlier writing about his concept of culture prepares us for such an individual.

For Boas, narrative action and the change it produces come from a conflict between an individual and his or her culture, not from the narrative development of culture itself. "An Eskimo Winter" does not deny that culture has a coercive power; the reader feels both No-tongue's pain at leaving one village and his keen desire to return to another. Yet the end of the story leaves No-tongue in a deliberately liminal symbolic space in which he stands, momentarily, outside culture. We can either read the ending as No-tongue's triumph over the hold that the village had over him or as a victory of the culture of his birthplace that has reclaimed him; the story's uncertainty is deliberate. The vast stretches of ice and snow are places of silence for the aptly named No-tongue, but they are also places that demand an individuated courage.

Boas spent his entire scientific career studying and analyzing the nature of group identity. The narrative legacy that this story highlights, however, relies upon the tension between the celebration of culture and the difficult fate of those individuals capable of bristling at its controlling influence, between the ethnographic description of static cultural practices and the narrative change effected by those living within these practices and, at least at times, dissatisfied with them. The first half of this intellectual tradition, the celebration of culture, later developed into the more full-blown belief of cultural relativism, an idea central to twentieth-century intellectual history. The second half, Boas's seemingly contradictory concern for the individual unwilling to acculturate, has remained a seldom-considered strand of Boas's thinking.

Although Boas appears not to have been too impressed by his own literary efforts—the most complete version of his bibliography omits "An Eskimo Winter" altogether[108]—fiction served him on this occasion in two ways. First, it afforded the possibility of mimetic representation in a way similar to ethnography; it provided, in other words, a space in which culture could be written. Second, fiction offered the chance to portray a conflict between the static, synchronic narrative experience of cultural continuity (the usual subject of anthropology) and the disruptive, individual experience of narrative change, an experience anomalous to a discipline in which, as he later put it, "the group, not the individual, is always the primary concern."[109]

"An Eskimo Winter" does more than exemplify the affinity between fiction and ethnography, however. It shows how the written texts that most carefully address the difficulties and boundaries of the culture concept were often those that crossed the divide between the two genres. Boas's story did not initiate this practice, but rather punctuates an age in which the representation of group-based difference was the topic of frequent discussion, debate, and experimentation. In the chapters that follow, I focus on those figures of the late nineteenth century who worked at such generic intersections—anthropologists writing literary narratives, literary authors conveying ethnographic information—as well as on the manner in which works that more closely follow generic conventions wrestle with the problems of textualizing group-based difference. Only in this way can we comprehend how shifting definitions of culture produced new kinds of writing in the United States. Perhaps we have failed to appreciate many of these works because their writers encoded in them a sense of the limitations of their own methods and aims in documenting culture, a sense that restrains their optimism about what this emerging concept of culture could accomplish. "An Eskimo Winter" shows Boas's own profound awareness in this regard. Boas knew too well that culture, like any explanatory model of such scope, could be used to silence figures such as No-tongue as well as to give them voice.

2

American Literary Realism and the Documentation of Difference

> There is an affluence of bitter meaning hidden under these apparently nonsensical lines.
>
> —GEORGE WASHINGTON CABLE, "Creole Slave Songs" (1886)

> ... as the weeks wore on, and I observed the pleasure the Indians took in their own singing, I was convinced that there existed something which was eluding my ears.
>
> —ALICE C. FLETCHER, "Indian Songs" (1894)

During the last two decades of the nineteenth century, the years when Franz Boas became an anthropologist and began to define his version of the "culture concept," literary and scientific writing in the United States invited readers to value authentic, group-based difference. The two articles cited above, both published in the *Century* magazine, illustrate and rely upon this correspondence. George Washington Cable was an author already well-known by 1886, and was frequently mentioned as one of the "new school" of realists; Alice C. Fletcher was an anthropologist associated with the Peabody Museum of Harvard University and the Bureau of American Ethnology. In many respects, the methods and goals of Cable's "Creole Slave Songs" and of Fletcher's "Indian Songs" are similar. Both articles report the firsthand observations of a non-white group by a white professional; both incorporate literal transcriptions of vernacular lyrics; and both display the expertise of their authors by providing the translations of those lyrics as well as the musical scores that accompany them.[1] Cable and Fletcher give their readers the chance to grasp what makes their subjects distinct, through documentation of authentic difference.

For Cable and Fletcher, this comprehension comes through a careful, sustained engagement with verbal expression. In each passage cited above, the author describes progressing from an elementary understanding of such songs to a more profound one. Cable describes the lyrics as "apparently nonsensical" but actually full of "bitter meaning"; Fletcher states that over the course of weeks she learned that "there was something which was eluding my ears" beyond the "tumult and din" first heard. Through the objective distance of professional observation, Cable and Fletcher come to realize that the songs they are hearing contain an emotional complexity that distinguishes them from the merely curious or quaint. To put it slightly differently, implicit in each article is an argument that the accurate textualization of vernacular expression is worth pursuing because it contains the possibility of revealing the underlying, evasive complexities of group-based difference. Cable and Fletcher encourage their audience to read the songs that they have collected in search of authenticity, and suggest that this effort will be rewarded with pleasure most accurately described as aesthetic.

These two writers share more than the ethnographic idiom and an outlet for publication. Both were known as advocates for the political rights of the peoples about whom they were writing. Cable protested the post-Reconstruction descent of the South into Jim Crow, with articles such as "The Freedman's Case in Equity" and "The Silent South," which had also been published by the *Century*.[2] Fletcher was an active member of the "Friends of the Indian" groups denouncing the treatment of tribal peoples by the United States government and arguing for reforms that would lead to their Americanization.[3] In their attention to the power and the sophistication of African American and American Indian voices, Cable's and Fletcher's ethnographic writings about such vernacular expression roughly comport with their arguments against racial inferiority. In particular, these articles emphasize that the meaning of this expression requires an understanding of social setting, not biological essence. However, neither Cable nor Fletcher explicitly tie their discussions of these songs to political issues, nor do they plead for readers to empathize directly with the blacks and Indians who sing them.

Instead, the textualization of culture in which Cable and Fletcher are engaged requires a distance between the sources of the songs they record and the (most often white) readers of the *Century*. This distance encourages the aesthetic contemplation of authentic difference, and it is facilitated by the figure of the professional, outside observer, whether literary author or anthropologist, who stands between the reader and the ethnographic subject like an expert connoisseur. Yet the detached, objective pose of the recorder of culture also creates the possibility that a cultural text may be interpreted in a more chauvinistic manner by the ultimate reader. The illustrations accompanying Cable's article—produced by E. W. Kemble, best known today as the illustrator of Mark Twain's *Huckleberry Finn*— demonstrate just how slender the line between ethnographic observation and condescending caricature can be. Many of Kemble's drawings appear as neutral, even scientific portraits that emphasize the distinct features of his subject; others seem to slightly exaggerate those same features in a manner more typical of the supposedly humorous "coon" illustrations of African Americans that Kemble produced throughout his career (see Figure 4).[4]

The juxtaposition of Cable's text and Kemble's illustrations demonstrates the potential and the danger that the documentation of cultural identity represented at the end of the nineteenth century. Even though Cable's purpose and emphasis on mimesis were antithetical to Kemble's famous "coon" drawings, Cable's desire to describe songs and singers as emblematic of a larger population proceeded under representational logic similar to that of visual ethnic caricature, in which a broad ethnic identity overwhelms features of individuality.[5] In this way, the illustrated version of "Creole Slave Songs" prefigured the dilemmas facing the two African American writers, Paul Laurence Dunbar and Charles Chesnutt, discussed in the following chapter. By recording dialect, songs, and folk tales, Dunbar and Chesnutt situated their writing at the same convergence of literary realism and scientific ethnography as did Cable and Fletcher. Anthropology taught that the textualization of vernacular expression had scientific value with regard to understanding how groups took on different identities; simultaneously, literary realism instructed readers to prize authentic difference as conveying more than simple information. Even as the literary realists in the United States hoped to revitalize the major narrative form of the nineteenth century, the novel, they also fostered the publication of other literary forms, such as local color fiction, dialect tales, and folklore collections, that placed questions of difference at the center.

The shifting definitions of culture—culture in what E. B. Tylor called "the wide ethnographic sense"—shaped the production of this literature at both the thematic and formal level. The last two decades of the nineteenth century coincided with both the peak of American literary realism and the rise of institutions and publications crucial to the development of anthropology in the United States. While this moment preceded the full articulation of the Boasian culture concept that I described in the previous

Figure 4. E. W. Kemble, renowned for his illustrations of African Americans, produced these drawings to accompany George Washington Cable's "Creole Slave Songs" in *The Century Illustrated Magazine* in 1886. The first, titled "A Candjo," conveys objectivity by reproducing the posture and detail of a posed photograph; the second and especially the third drawings are more similar to the caricatures for which Kemble was well known. The second drawing, "A Nurse Mammie," evokes the plantation nostalgia popular during this period. In the third drawing, "Planter and Voodoo Charm," Kemble renders his black subjects absurd in their fear of the charm held by a more rational and collected white planter. Ethnographic writing like Cable's relied on a professional distance that left Kemble free to render visually the subjects through a variety of attitudes like those displayed here.

chapter, the practices and theoretical questions necessary to Boasian anthropology were already beginning to circulate. The questions that Boas would put forward about the possibilities and problems of documenting culture reverberated throughout American literary realism—both in the debates about the nature of its aesthetic and in the texts that attempted to execute its principles. These culturalist texts, in turn, prefigured the difficulty that Boas and his students would later encounter in attempting to make culture the cornerstone of a more egalitarian social order.

The Locked Room of Culture

Like the social sciences, literature in the United States was engaged in the process of professionalization during the final decades of the nineteenth century. Looking back on the previous thirty years, William Dean Howells stated in 1893 that it was "only since the Civil War that literature has become a business with us."[6] Howells championed what has come to be known as American literary realism, and the anxieties about the social and economic status of the author that he expressed in the essay just quoted, "The Man of Letters as a Man of Business," are telling. Even though many authors "live now, and live prettily enough" through the sale of their work, Howells claimed, they "do not live so nicely as successful tradespeople, of course, or as men in the other professions when they begin to make themselves names; the high state of brokers, bankers, railroad operators, and the like is, in the nature of the case, beyond their fondest dreams of pecuniary affluence and social splendor." Neither of the "classes" nor of the "masses," the serious artist, according to Howells, still occupied an "anomalous" position, though at least a more secure one than before the postbellum developments in publishing.[7]

Howells and his fellow realists in the United States tied this emergence of literary writing as a profession by which one could "live prettily enough" to their advocacy of realism as an aesthetic appropriate for the era. In this chapter, the discussion of American literary realism is as much grounded in what those who called themselves realists during these decades (as well as those who objected to the so-called realist trend in American literature) believed distinctive about realist works as in those works themselves. It is tempting to dismiss American realism as a sloppily theorized, absurdly applied critical term used by its champions to describe the works they admired for whatever reason; after all, the diversity of works to which the label was applied seems to render any guiding critical principles inconsistent. Urban novels, local color fiction, and utopian fantasies were all thought by American realist critics to be in the tradition of European realists like Tolstoy, Zola, and Balzac. Without claiming for realist critics the logical rigor that, with hindsight, one can easily find lacking in their discussions, one can still identify the features organizing late-nineteenth-century discussions of the realist aesthetic—features that played an important role in the literature of culture produced under the aegis of this movement.

Most obviously, late-nineteenth-century critics defined realism in opposition to sentimental and romantic literature. Sentimental fiction, realists argued, inflated human emotions to dangerous excess. Howells wrote in *The Rise of Silas Lapham* (1885), "The novelists might be the greatest possible help to us if they painted life as it is, and human feelings in their true proportion and relation, but for the most part they have been and are altogether noxious."[8] Sentimental fiction, in turn, "perverted" its audience, particularly female readers of novels.[9] Literary realists believed that they could correct such excesses by engaging more faithfully in the representation of smaller joys and sufferings, so as to prepare readers better for lives filled with neither spectacular romance nor terrible tragedy.[10] "If sentimentalism depended on characters who could transcend their environments," Kenneth W. Warren observes, "then realism would by definition highlight the obstacles to transcendence."[11]

This critical stance toward sentimentalism affected how realist texts would represent racial and ethnic diversity to a still largely white readership in the United States. As a literary and political strategy, the sentimental foregrounded the assimilative power of white domesticity to uplift the downtrodden, correct the wayward, and conquer the malicious.[12] The key emotion of sentimentality was a compassion usually centered in a presumed universal experience of femininity that could overcome differences of race, ethnicity, and class. The realist mode, conversely, sought to textualize those same differences and value authentic depictions of them. Sentimental literature had stressed the need to "feel right," in Harriet Beecher Stowe's famous formulation; realist literature would instead promote distanced, even professional, observation that necessarily moderated emotion.[13] To draw this distinction is not to claim that the realist textualization of difference always yielded a less essentialist account of identity than did the sentimental. Rather, with its derision of emotional excess, realism attempted to change the register of attitudes with which white readers would confront alterity on the page. Doing so, of course, would require that realist texts devise techniques of accurate representation.

One device through which literature could be certain of portraying "life as it is" was the reporting of firsthand experience. Ulysses S. Grant's *Personal Memoirs*, for instance, were a favorite of realist critics; Howells praised them for being "couched in the most unpretentious phrase, with never a touch of grandiosity or attitudinizing, familiar, homely, even common in style"—in short, not literary at all.[14] According to this brand of literary realism, the proper subjects for literature were the facts of everyday life, a stance that Frank Norris later derided as valuing "dramas of the reception-room, tragedies of an afternoon call, [and] crises involving cups of tea."[15] Yet the realist belief in the quotidian as a proper literary object went beyond the novels of manners to which Norris refers. A realist writer, Howells argued, "needs experience and observation,"[16] and those experiences and observations frequently occurred outside the urban centers of the eastern United States—in writing that often would fall under the "regionalist" or "local color" label today.

Regionalism, local color fiction, and dialect tales all flourished under the larger umbrella of literary realism because they emphasized how meaningful qualities of everyday life could be apprehended through the careful delineation of factual information. In his review of Sarah Orne Jewett's *Deephaven* (1877), Howells commented that he had "no doubt some particular sea-port sat for Deephaven" and went on to praise Jewett for holding her prose "far from every trick of exaggeration," for using verisimilitude to "vividly localize" her sketches of New England, and for using her "powers of observation" to find "the ideal within the real."[17] Fidelity to "local" reality, in other words, would give readers the opportunity to contemplate what was "ideal" in lives different from theirs. This line of reasoning led realist authors to produce writing that emphasized the variety of experience in the United States as having an aesthetic value. Hamlin Garland, a vocal champion in the 1890s of realism, began an 1888 article on "Boy Life on the Prairie" with the sentence, "The Middle Border has its poetry, its beauty, if we can only see it." What followed were descriptions of farm labor and prairie life in minute, almost ethnographic, detail.[18] Garland's point in beginning his article in this manner is to emphasize the "poetry" of this way of life, not for those who were living it, but for the distant readers who were not. As Nancy Glazener has observed, the "lowness or ordinariness of the materials of realism, considered either as the social status of its characters or the quotidianness of its actions, [became] the precondition for the transforming artistry of the realist writer and attests to the sophisticated perceptiveness of the realist reader by extension."[19] A work like Garland's succeeds on both counts Glazener names; it portrays figures of "ordinary" social status *and* shows their quotidian actions.

In part, what made these literary conventions so attractive to the realists was the ease with which they could be adapted and replicated. While local color sketches, dialect ballads, and ethnic traditions of folklore had been published throughout the nineteenth century, in the post-Reconstruction era these forms of writing appeared with greater frequency and attracted more widespread attention than before. Studies such as Richard H. Brodhead's discussion of regionalist literature and Gavin Jones's treatment of dialect literature show how these forms offered young writers the means of entry into newspaper, magazine, and then book publication.[20] Moreover, genres that represented group-based difference took on greater significance as the increasing immigration from central and southern Europe spawned fears about what former *Atlantic Monthly* editor Thomas Bailey Aldrich called, in his poem "Unguarded Gates" (1892), the "wild motley throng" of "Voices that once the Tower of Babel knew."[21] While groups such as the Immigration Restriction League, founded in Boston in 1894, advocated measures to "Stay those who ... come / To waste the gifts of freedom,"[22] realist critics emphasized that literature could represent the diversity of groups living within the United States in a way that could enable them to understand one another. "Men are more like than unlike one another," Howells wrote in a column discussing the regionalist fiction of Mary N. Murfree and Mary E. Wilkins; "let us make them know one another better, that they may be all humbled and strengthened with a sense of their fraternity."[23]

Even as realism responded to the dread of an unintelligible Babel, it reacted to growing concerns over increasing national uniformity generated by changes in the economy. Like ethnography, literary realism participated in a salvage mode that preserved, in the words of one literary critic, "local colors and local types fast disappearing."[24] Perched between the opposite fears of heterogeneity and homogeneity, realist critics frequently argued that some form of diversity was necessary for the success of American literature and, at the same time, held out the literary as a means of managing that diversity. Garland's *Crumbling Idols* (1894), his collection of essays advocating "veritism," exemplifies this trend:

> It is a settled conviction with me that each locality must produce its own literary record, each special phase of life utter its own voice.... The sun of truth strikes each part of the earth at a little different angle; it is this angle which gives life and infinite variety to literature.[25]

Literature, in Garland's formulation, not only needs "infinite variety" but becomes the means of making the benefits of this variety recognizable.

Garland's choice of the words "locality" and "special phase of life" is equally revealing. With the first, he seems to be calling for geographical represen- tation, but he supplements that aim with the second, more ambiguous phrase. While the "voice" that Garland wants may be tied to a particular location, it stands for more than a physical territory. The term that Garland reaches for, of course, is "culture"—a term that he does not seem to have at his disposal.

This conspicuous gap in Garland's lexicon matters because the tensions and contradictions created by the representation of culture within realist texts often result from a lack of adequate vocabulary. Writing concurrently with the emergence of social Darwinism, realist authors valued authentic difference but often remained undecided or divided about its ultimate significance. Realist writing frequently weighed the ethnographic appre- ciation of culture against a model of cultural evolution that emphasized progress from "primitivism" to "civilization" and that heavily relied upon the biological foundations of racial identity. Without the fully articulated vocabulary of Boasian anthropology, such writers faced the opposing par- adigms of culture without the conceptual resources necessary to untangle them.

An early, penetrating illustration of the prevalence and difficulties of this realist predisposition toward the culture concept was crafted by an author who rarely, if ever, figures in current discussions of American liter- ary realism. Frances Hodgson Burnett (1849–1924) is much better known today, as in her lifetime, as an author of children's romance than as a writer of literary realism for adults. Burnett secured her reputation with the publication of *Little Lord Fauntleroy* in 1886, and furthered it later with works like *A Little Princess* (1905) and *The Secret Garden* (1911), books that continue to enjoy the status of children's classics. During the 1870s and early 1880s, though, Burnett was visible within the arena of highbrow American literature; her stories were published in both *Scribner's* and *Harper's*, and her work was discussed alongside the efforts of Henry James, William Dean Howells, and Constance Fenimore Woolson.[26] Burnett, in sum, participated in the network of literary institutions that made realism possible. In reading her work during this stage of her career, Burnett's con- temporaries would have been reading *for* realism—to borrow Glazener's phrase for describing the predisposition of readers who recognized authors so aligned—just as we do with the works of figures better recognized as realists today.[27]

Published in 1880, Burnett's *Louisiana* foregrounds questions of the production of literary realism by making the practice of representing rural people and experiences through local color writing an integral element of its plot. The novel opens with Olivia Ferrol, a New Yorker who belongs to a family of authors and is an unpublished writer herself, vacationing alone at a North Carolina resort. "I am sure you will find a great deal of material here," she writes to her brother, Laurence, an accomplished professional author. "You see how I have fallen a victim to that dreadful habit of looking at everything in the light of material. A man is no longer a man—he is 'material'; a sorrow is not sorrow, joy is not joy—it is 'material.'"[28] *Louisiana*, the title of the book, evokes a geographic location with a history and ethnic composition that made it ripe "material" for realist writers, including George Washington Cable and Kate Chopin. In Burnett's novel, in contrast, "Louisiana" refers to a young woman, Louisiana Rogers, who embodies the local character that Olivia understands to be in vogue as "material" for representation.

Olivia Ferrol befriends Louisiana, who is the daughter of a wealthy local farmer and unaccustomed to the regimen of upper-class hotel life. Rather than writing about Louisiana, Olivia decides to remake her, by modifying her clothes, speech, and manners, into someone indistinguishable from the other ladies of the resort. Olivia treats Louisiana as literal "material," a raw substance to be transformed through a process that even includes her using another name than the one that titles the novel. When Laurence arrives, he is both charmed and captivated by Louisiana (now known as Louisa), who has been prompted by Olivia to refrain from speaking of her personal anxieties. As much as Louisiana wishes to reciprocate Laurence's interest, she also suffers from a guilty sense that her transformation is an insult to her father and her upbringing.

Culture figures in *Louisiana* in at least two senses. In the first sense, Olivia Ferrol hopes to make Louisiana Rogers "cultured"—to impart to her a body of knowledge that will cultivate her and somehow make her into a better person. How Olivia proceeds along this path and the conviction with which she does so subtly mocks the trappings and values of the educated upper class. At one point early in the book, Olivia quizzes Louisiana in a manner befitting E. D. Hirsch's *Cultural Literacy:* Has Louisiana read *The Scarlet Letter*? Does she know of John Stuart Mill? Michelangelo? No, no, no, Louisiana replies. The scene reaches its crescendo when Olivia realizes that Louisiana has not even heard of the dressmaker Charles Frederick Worth. "Oh," Olivia cries, "how—how you have been neglected!" (21).

Louisiana simultaneously draws upon the model of culture that motivates the documentary articles of Cable and Fletcher. The idea that people could be "material"—that they possessed a certain identity that could be recorded in such a way as to be instructive, even entertaining, to a consuming audience—derives from notions of cultural difference and authenticity central to late-nineteenth-century ethnography. Writing in the *Journal of American Folk-Lore*, for instance, Otis T. Mason compared cultural "specimens" to the data studied by natural scientists, and he noted that the ethnographer had the advantage of an infinite supply. "The folk-cabinet is like the piles of enumerators' atlases in the Census Office," he concluded. "The material is ever at hand to be considered."[29] Such "specimens" matter, whether they are tangible (such as dress) or intangible (such as songs), because they form a strand in the web of meaning that gives a group its identity. The drama of *Louisiana* emanates from the title character's growing comprehension that the Ferrols' interest in such markers of cultural alterity derives from their pleasure in manners different from theirs, a pleasure that occasionally slides into amusement. In this way, the novel uses the Ferrols to inquire into the conventions of the local color fiction that by 1880 had already launched figures such as Bret Harte, Sarah Orne Jewett, and the geographically relevant Mary N. Murfree. Indeed, Murfree's well-known story, "The Dancin' Party at Harrison's Cove," published in the *Atlantic Monthly* in 1878, begins at a Tennessee mountain resort and features, like *Louisiana*, interaction between white, upper-class visitors and their indigenous neighbors.[30]

In *Louisiana*, the two competing ideas of culture—culture as cultivation and culture as local identity—are not so very far apart. Both suggest a relationship between material things—dress, furniture, architecture— and an inner state of being. And both kinds of culture are the object of careful observation. Olivia begins the book by looking for representatives of rural culture in the ethnographic sense, seeking what the novel calls the "mountaineer 'type'" (6); in time, Louisiana watches Olivia's every move to discern the elements of dress and manners through which to become cultured, in the sense of *civilisation*. The book demonstrates, though, that these two versions of culture diverge in how they value group-based alterity. The notion of culture as achievement, of course, affixes a scale of worth that depends upon an individual's progress toward a fixed standard. But what about the other, ethnographic version of culture, the idea that all groups possess a cultural identity? Does that model of group-based difference create a sense of cultural equality in *Louisiana*?

Louisiana understands that, for Olivia and Laurence Ferrol, the answer is no. The recognition of cultural difference does not produce the egalitarian respect that American cultural anthropologists would hope to foster in the twentieth century. In fact, her unfulfilled desire for exactly that kind of tolerance creates the most dramatic scene in the novel. Circumstances lead the Ferrols and Louisiana into the latter's rural home, where she takes steps to ensure that the Ferrols do not learn of her affiliation with it or with the man who is her father. Laurence Ferrol then proceeds to confide in Louisiana his pleasure at witnessing this domestic setting (the same pleasure that motivated the widespread production of local color writing in the postbellum United States). In doing so, Laurence reveals how the quest for verifiable authenticity often presumed a condescending superiority to its subject. "Why, this is delightful!" he tells Louisiana. "These are the people we have read of. I scarcely believed in them before" (68). When Laurence later pokes fun at Louisiana's father—notably because Louisiana has pronounced a French author's name "François" as "Frankoyse"—the pressure becomes too much for her (76–78). She reveals herself to be Rogers's daughter and demands that the Ferrols leave without her.

The tension of this crisis results from Louisiana's contradictory desires to follow the path of culture-as-civilization *and* to have her cultural identity as a rural mountaineer recognized as equal to that of the society in which the Ferrols circulate. These desires conflict because, as in so many torn-between-two-worlds stories, the protagonist's effort to take on a new identity implies that her choice is of a better (not just different) manner of living from the one in which she was raised. Yet the shame that she feels when she must pretend not to be of rural origin, like the anger she displays when Laurence is amused by rural authenticity, suggests that she wishes to believe in cultural equality, to believe that although there are fundamentally disparate ways of life at the resort and at the farm, these cultural differences do not mark varying degrees of human achievement.

In the second half of this short novel, Burnett lays out for the reader how these competing ideas of culture might govern separate narrative trajectories. If Louisiana Rogers decides upon culture as a ladder of progress, she will change her way of life, marry Laurence Ferrol, and physically leave North Carolina; if she decides that the rural culture in which she was raised is equal to that of resort society, she will remain in her father's house without altering her lifestyle in any substantive way. While the plot of the novel tends toward the former course—Louisiana's father decides to redesign and redecorate the house, he then dies, and Laurence returns to marry Louisiana—it also attempts to enact a compromise between the two possible narrative resolutions. After moving to New York, Laurence and Louisiana continue to summer in the old Rogers home, redecorated to reflect a more sophisticated taste. Louisiana, however, has removed the original furnishings from the parlor and placed them in an unused room, where she arranges "everything as she remembered it" (152). Louisiana locks the room, and the final paragraph of the novel reminds the reader of this place that remains unseen by anyone except herself and her husband—"a little room, with strange, ugly furniture in it, and bright-colored lithographs upon the walls" (163).

Louisiana has made one room of her old home into a museum, a preservation of the material artifacts that represent a culture separate from the one in which she now resides. The lock on the door both maintains that separation and signals Louisiana's ambivalent relationship to this cultural archive, which conserves her former way of life and hides it from the urban, upper-class visitors who now make up her circle of friends. Rather than expose her parents' belongings to those who might not regard them as she does, Louisiana removes them completely from view. She has learned a lesson from her association with writers: putting cultural material into circulation risks the possibility of condescension instead of appreciation.

With its locked room of culture, *Louisiana* replicates something like the museum displays of tribal artifacts discussed at the beginning of the previous chapter. Indeed, the kind of exhibition that the novel places in that room is much more like those preferred by Franz Boas than those arranged by evolutionists such as Otis Mason. Rather than representing a progressive sequence, the parlor furnishings provide a snapshot of a fixed moment; they comprise something like "the complete collection of a single tribe" for which Boas hoped.[31] And like Boas's version of culture, the Rogers museum signifies a resistance to narrative change; Louisiana has shut it off entirely from the transformations that her life with Laurence Ferrol has brought. In doing so, Louisiana creates a physical barrier between herself and the culture into which she was born. She frames the "strange, ugly furniture" with the sealed room itself so that she may consider it anew each time she enters it. My point is not that she has transformed the sitting room of her youth into a work of aesthetically profound art—were that true, she would not need the lock on the door—but that the locked room enforces the distance that makes aesthetic contemplation possible and even likely.

In its canny dialogue with the obsession of literary realists with local authenticity, Burnett's *Louisiana* makes legible a struggle that would mark the relationship of realism to questions of cultural difference in the decades that followed. The conflict between two different concepts of culture—one that relies upon ideas of static, irreducible differences and another that offers the possibility of universal cultural development—was central to the debate surrounding the nature of literature in the age of realism, as well as to the products of literature in that period. As *Louisiana* demonstrates, the debates about literary realism involved matters of both the mimetic representation of the authentic, and the narrative patterns through which that "material" would be represented. At the center of late-nineteenth-century criticism, in other words, an argument raged over which model of culture was the proper subject for American literature. Equally important, the role of realism in conferring aesthetic meaning upon textualized ethnographic information emerged from the late-nineteenth-century disputes over the nature of realistic writing.

The "Time-Spirit" of Realism

In September 1889 the New York-based publication the *Critic* fielded a query. "Where can I obtain some work on realism in literature?" a reader asked; "I should also like to know who are considered the leading realists and realistic writers." The *Critic* editors replied that they knew of "no book devoted to the subject of realism in literature" and regarded William Dean Howells and Henry James as the writers in English who were the "chief exponents of what is known as realism in the treatment of fictional themes. But there are different qualities and degrees of realism, as of everything else."[32]

This written exchange illustrates the slipperiness of literary realism as an artistic movement in the United States. By the late 1880s, it was possible to speak of realism as a coherent thing and even to identify its chief proponents, particularly Howells, who in 1886–91 used the "Editor's Study" of *Harper's Monthly* to make the period's most sustained attempt to promote and explicate literary realism in the United States. The comment of the *Critic* about the differing "qualities and degrees of realism," on the other hand, points to an equally shared critical consensus that the principles of realism were more often discussed than practiced—that realism was much less an easily identified phenomenon visible among the works of a large group of writers than a subject for argument among critics. The influential *Century* editor Richard Watson Gilder suggested in 1887 that realism needed to be understood as something other than a carefully articulated set of rules for writing and evaluating literature: "Realism is, in fact, something in the air which even those who do not think it by name must necessarily feel. Its influence in America, as elsewhere, is not confined to those writers who proclaim themselves of the faith; it is the Time-Spirit."[33]

Gilder's characterization of realism as the *Zeitgeist* of his age explains how a writer like Frances Hodgson Burnett, hardly a consistent adherent to the kind of realism proposed by Howells and James, might produce such an elaborate riff on the realist representation of "material," the artistic process Howells would address in *A Hazard of New Fortunes* (1890) and James in "The Real Thing" (1892). Moreover, *Louisiana* shows how American literary realism resembled the emerging anthropological framework of culture in at least two key respects: its preoccupation with the representation of group-based differences, and its uneasy relationship to the narrative structures used to convey information. Not everyone liked this new "Time-Spirit," and the objections lodged against realism by the contemporaries of Howells and James show how this phase of American literature prefigured many of the questions that would be central to the Boasian era of American anthropology.

These related arguments against literary realism by American critics advanced in three directions: that realist works failed to offer the reader an adequate "story"; that realism was more akin to science than to art; and that the subject matter of realism was unnecessarily or inappropriately "common." Even those sympathetic to realism were willing to grant that American realists were less concerned with telling a compelling story than were the romanticists whom they imagined as their rivals. In 1886, James wrote of his friend Howells, the only writer and editor more consistently identified with realism in the United States at that time than James himself, "He hates a 'story,' and (this private feat is not impossible) has probably made up his mind as to what this pestilent thing consists of." Less jokingly, James continues by offering his own definition of "this pestilent thing": "Mr. Howells hates an artificial fable and a *dénouement* that is pressed into the service; he likes things to occur as they occur in life, where the manner of a great many of them is not to occur at all."[34]

Whether or not Howells's novels actually avoid such "artificial" resolutions, the recurring association of realism with an absence of the elements that made a traditional and attractive story is essential to understanding what literary realism represented in the late nineteenth century. What every undergraduate comes to recognize as characteristic of this period, the realists' "aversion to having a fiction end pleasingly,"[35] was both the subject of frequent commentary and recognized as part of a larger opposition between American literary realism and storytelling. In "The New Story-Tellers and the Doom of Realism" (1894), for example, William Roscoe Thayer laments the influence of realist editors and critics upon storytelling in literature. He writes, "'There shall never be any more plots,' was one of the edicts of the law-givers." Fortunately, Thayer ventures, the "horde of Realists, great and small" who "have been filling the magazines with their products and turning out an average of two novels a day" would soon face an uninterested public:

> [T]he knell of the Epidermists has sounded. The novels that are everywhere in demand are the novels with a story. Individually, they may be good or bad—it matters not: the significant fact is that the public taste has turned, and that that instinct which is as old as the children of Adam and Eve, the instinct for a story, has reasserted itself.

Thayer objects to realism because, like Boasian ethnography, it privileges description over narration. For Thayer, the deliberateness with which the realists thwarted the universal "instinct for story" was linked to the scientific prose of observation and analysis that had "enslaved" literary fiction.[36]

Georg Lukács makes an observation similar to Thayer's in "Narrate or Describe?" "The method of observation and description," Lukács writes, "developed as part of an attempt to make literature scientific."[37] Both Thayer and Lukács agree that descriptive prose resembles scientific writing, and Thayer makes this observation of realist writing at precisely the moment when one type of scientific writing, ethnography, is becoming even more descriptive and less narrative. Other, more sympathetic critics than Thayer also comment upon the resemblance between the careful description thought characteristic of literary realism and the methods of scientific endeavors. Richard Watson Gilder even goes so far as to contend that Benjamin Franklin "drawing down with his kite the lightning of Jupiter, was the first American realist."[38] George Pellew, in an 1891 review of "Ten Years of American Literature" suggests that this trend is the result of a democratic "curiosity" on the part of the reading public; "The scientific spirit of the age has popularized the love of accurate description, of 'human documents.'"[39]

Pellew could just as easily be describing the ethnographic monographs of the Smithsonian's Bureau of American Ethnology when he speaks of the "intelligent interest in the daily doings of and feelings of our friends and neighbors and, especially, of the poor and unfortunate and those who seem to be survivals and out of place in our civilization."[40] The language of "survivals" and "civilization" derives from the evolutionary anthropology of figures like E. B. Tylor, who suggested that superstitions and folktales often "survived" as a people progressed from an earlier stage of culture to a higher one. Moreover, Pellew's characterization of the desires of white, middle-to-upper-class readers to learn about the poor and the exotic—

the rurally remote as well as the recently arrived immigrants in urban centers—would also accurately describe those who funded anthropological research in the hope of understanding how to help indigenous peoples adapt to the ways of "civilization." Tellingly, Thayer's anti-realist polemic describes such motives as detrimental to both literature *and* science:

> It [realism] has been the logical outcome of our age, whose characteristic is analysis. Our modern science, abandoning the search for the Absolute, has been scrutinizing every atom, to weigh and name it, and to discover its relations with its neighbors. "Relativity" has been the watchword. Science literally knows neither great nor small: it examines the microbe and Sirius with equal interest....[41]

Thayer's concern is not, of course, about microbes or Sirius but about the human subjects fit for inquiry. In their turn away from storytelling and toward "modern science," he contends, realist authors (like their equally misguided scientific counterparts) have chosen to forego imagining the "Ideal" and concentrated instead upon the commonplace of the "Real." "The Realist frankly announced that the precise record of the humblest mind was just as important as one of Shakespeare's mind would be," Thayer complains.

Thayer's central objections to realism, its rejection of storytelling and its turn toward more pedestrian subjects, were not disputed by its advocates. Rather, realists praised the possibilities of careful observation and consequently hoped to forge a new alliance between literature and the scientific spirit. In his 1893 *Arena* article "Realism in Literature and Art," for instance, Clarence Darrow (decades before the *Scopes* trial) described how realist authors learned from scientists to be greater artists than their more romantic counterparts. "The real scientist," he wrote, "patiently and carefully gathers facts, and then forms a theory to explain and harmonize these facts."[42] And so, too, he argues, does the "real"—or realist—author.

While many "facts" gathered into realist texts derived from urban settings and forced readers to confront the economic divisions plaguing the nation, realist texts just as often brought to the cosmopolitan reader knowledge of rural, isolated peoples and their ways of life. These "facts"— how people dressed, behaved, and (especially) talked—were *cultural* facts, data that made tangible the differences between groups of people in ways beyond economic wealth. Hamlin Garland's *Prairie Folks* (1892), for example, described the "border life" of the village of Rock River by giving detailed accounts of religious rhetoric, a funeral, and a "donation party," as well as the texts of several songs.[43] This kind of ethnographic information

constituted one of the frequently employed strategies to "restore or construct a new sense of the real" that Amy Kaplan has described as defining
American literary realism. The framework of culture—in which a collection of carefully documented observations all pointed to a single, stable,
group-based identity—proved a way that realists could "use fiction to
combat the fictionality of everyday life."[44]

The complaint that realist texts were nothing more than reportage
and analysis of so-called minor people and incidents was a critique of this
culturalist turn in literature. Writing in the *New York Evening Post* in 1886,
James Lane Allen protested the parochialism of ethnographic realism by
lamenting the "little byway studies" that comprised the contemporary literature of the South. Citing the examples of "Miss Murfree's mountaineers,"
the African Americans of Joel Chandler Harris's *Uncle Remus*, and the
creoles of George Washington Cable, Allen took issue with the way these
realist texts prized "oddity": "The pursuit of the minor and remote is in a
measure the result of the premium that is set by the literary market upon
the peculiar, the strange, the exceptional, the fresh—of the predominant
demand for intense local color and extreme specialization of the field of
work."[45] Allen's grievance is that realism values local authenticity as culturally based, and that realist texts purport to define groups of people as
discrete entities. His worry is not simply that readers desire the "peculiar"
and the "fresh," but also that readers are taking such "byway studies" as
representative of the whole of Southern life.

As Nancy Bentley demonstrates in her study of the realist novel of
manners, the tendency to scrutinize the manners of a group so as to make
human behavior seem "fresh" and even odd was not confined to rural or
remote subjects; in *The Sacred Fount* (1901), for instance, James compares
an aristocratic villa to a museum and presents his characters as "exhibited
artifacts."[46] Yet the representative burden placed on realist texts about rural
and remote groups functioned differently than, for example, Howells's
writing about Boston's middle and upper classes or Wharton's about the
highest reaches of New York society. Fictions of manners in this more conventional sense frequently described their subjects—subjects who possessed
genuine power in American society—as undergoing processes of dramatic
change under the pressures of history. On the other hand, descriptions of
rural and ethnic peoples—usually people without power—were frequently
rendered as depictions of an inflexible, organic premodernity, static and
separate from the forces threatening to eradicate their cultural identity.
Moreover, in contrast to the satiric tone and exaggeration so frequently
recognized in James and Wharton's fiction, culturalist writing derived its

authority from the premise that it reported hard fact. The aim of un-distorted mimesis was crucial for portraying groups rarely represented otherwise in American social or political life. As June Howard puts it, local color (or regionalist) fiction has been "taken as a *representation* or even an *emanation* of a region that pre-exists it; therefore response to and evalua-tion of specific texts is persistently framed in terms of their accuracy or authenticity."[47]

Even though critics from Allen to Howard have disapproved of the way in which readers of realism imagined texts to stand in for groups, proponents of literary realism saw the mimetic possibilities of literary de-scription as a necessary counterpart to democratic recognition, and they habitually offered lists of regionalist authors and texts as a kind of map to a newly egalitarian literary geography. "Nothing could testify with more force to the fact that we have outgrown romanticism than this almost unanimous desire, on the part of our authors, to chronicle the widely divergent phases of our American civilization," H. H. Boyesen wrote in an introduction to one such list (which included more than twenty-five authors). "There are scarcely a dozen conspicuous States now which have not their own local novelist."[48] Mark Twain participated in and extended this tradition when he upbraided Paul Bourget in 1895 for generalizing about the United States. The American novelist, Twain contends, "lays plainly before you the ways and speech and life of a few people grouped in a certain place—his own place—and that is one book." Twain goes on to offer an extraordinary list of such groups, including a variety of regions, religions, ethnicities, and what might best be called stations of life (e.g., "the Idiots and the Congressmen"). "And when a thousand able novels have been written," he concludes, "*there* you will have the soul of the people."[49]

These descriptive lists of Boyesen and Twain point to a defining ten-sion within literary realism between the desire for unified nationalism, if not for a global universalism, and the reinforcement of social barriers. Realism celebrates and documents the fact of culture among a variety of groups, but for those cultural identities to be meaningful, they must also divide the groups from one another. The "middle border" songs and stories that Hamlin Garland prints in *Prairie Folks* have value, in part, because they differ from those that might be contained in *Cape Cod Folks* (Sarah Pratt McLean, 1881), *Bayou Folk* (Kate Chopin, 1894), or *Folks from Dixie* (Paul Laurence Dunbar, 1898). What Twain's list charts is the manner in which this division goes beyond simple regionalism to include something more vague and elusive, something that requires the "negroes," "Greasers," and "Mind Curists" to be documented in literature as well. Discussion of the varieties of language—dialect—followed this same logic during the nineteenth century. Linguists once understood variations of English as the product of geographical origin, but later began to consider dialect a "protean force" that encompassed "just about any form of cultural discourse from national languages and regional variations, to slang, trade jargon, and the distinct vocal style of women."[50] Like the literary realists, linguists were searching for a way to group Americans as disparate peoples and were engaging in an argument about the significance of this interpretation of the social world.

In *Crumbling Idols*, Garland links literary realism to a kind of Whitmanesque patriotism. He argues, "Provincialism (that is to say, localism) is no ban to a national literature."[51] But Garland is less successful in making this claim convincing than he is in showing how the presumed link between a literary text and a holistic culture may simply replace racial and class divisions with cultural ones. As Kaplan has shown, realists hoped to represent "an interdependent society composed of competing and seemingly mutually exclusive realities."[52] These discrete spheres, I have been suggesting, resemble the idea of culture that was developing in anthropology, and while this vocabulary of culture proved vital to the realists' effort to represent a diversity of experience, it also threatened to render those diverse elements living within the national boundaries irreconcilable to one another because of the cultural differences that divided them.

No realist fiction dramatizes this dilemma more painfully than Howells's novels, which often introduce characters from diverse social arenas only to have them separate by the book's end. *A Hazard of New Fortunes* may be the best-known example of this pattern. There, each character contributing to the magazine *Every Other Week* represents a different constituency: one is a German immigrant with socialist convictions, another is a Southern gentleman newly arrived in New York, a third is an Ohio farmer made rich by natural gas, and so on. A New York streetcar strike splinters the group and precipitates the demise of the magazine. The novel proceeds, therefore, from the possibilities of mutual sympathies to the dangers of insurmountable otherness.[53]

While the barriers that separate Howells's characters are largely rooted in economic class, his novels also suggest that the divisions may entail more than the distribution of wealth. In *The Rise of Silas Lapham* (1885), recognized in Howells's day as his most accomplished work of realist fiction, the plot revolves around the conflict between two families: the Laphams, arrivistes profiting from their rural paint farm, and the Coreys, a blue-blooded Boston family that has fallen upon hard economic times.

While money influences the relationship between the Laphams and the Coreys at every level, it is not a discrepancy of wealth that divides them. Rather, it is the difference in their social standing that separates them, and this disparity manifests itself in recognizable and measurable ways, such as in the fact that the Laphams do not have wine on their dinner table, in the "kneeling figures" representing "Faith and Prayer" that the Laphams have placed in their drawing-room window, and in the pleasure the Laphams take in middlebrow theater—all of which presumably compare unfavorably with the Coreys' more sophisticated tastes in literature, decor, and architecture.[54]

While such disparities ultimately result from the families' differing relationships to money, the Coreys having inherited it and the Laphams having worked for it, in *The Rise of Silas Lapham* Howells has converted incongruities of economic class into cultural ones. The novel legitimatizes class differences by figuring them to be the product of dispositions (including aesthetic ones) shaped by discrete cultural influences.[55] With its attention to social customs, tangible artifacts, dress, and speech, this novel portrays a conflict that is much less about literal wealth than about what E. B. Tylor called in *Primitive Culture* the "complex whole" of beliefs and habits that comprise culture. Moreover, in *Silas Lapham*, culture can be defined in either of the senses that I described regarding Burnett's *Louisiana*—either as a measure of cultivation or as a separate way of life. The book's title and the pains that Silas and Persis Lapham take to enter the Coreys' sphere (for instance, building a new house under the direction of an architect, ordering books with the help of Tom Corey, consulting an etiquette book to prepare for a dinner party) point to the possibility that the Laphams might "rise" into the arena of high culture. "It's a curious thing, this thing called civilization," says Bromfield Corey. "We think it is an affair of epochs and nations. It's really an affair of individuals" (117). As individuals, the Laphams hope to obtain the "civilization" of which Corey speaks.

The conclusion of the novel, in contrast, presents an alternative way of thinking about "civilization," a way of thinking about people not as standing upon various rungs of an ascending ladder but rather as inhabiting more equally situated, but distinct, spheres. As a resolution to the novel, Howells finally disperses his characters in a way that signals the deeper differences between the families. This separation occurs when Silas Lapham's business failure relegates him and his family back to rural Vermont and simultaneously leads the newly married Tom Corey and Penelope Lapham to exile themselves from the United States altogether. The geographical displacement of Silas Lapham represents more than financial misfortune;

the move brings him a satisfaction that he has not enjoyed previously in the novel. A Civil War veteran, he becomes "more the Colonel in those hills than he could ever have been on the Back Bay," and allows himself to become "rather shabby and slovenly," while, tellingly, still displaying "the statues of Prayer and Faith" that would have surely been banned from the new Back Bay home, which has been destroyed in a fire (363). Lapham returns, in other words, to the rural culture from which he came, and this final turn of events gives the title of the book yet another shade of irony. The financial ruin of Silas Lapham has given rise to something else, a kind of harmonious relationship between Lapham and his surroundings impossible for him in Boston. Contrary to Bromfield Corey's assertion, the novel tells its readers that "civilization" is not a matter of individuals, but of the settings and groups from which these individuals came—and to which they should return. In this sense, Howells's novel advocates a Boasian model of cultural interpretation based on the relationship of the individual object (or person) to its original contextual setting.

The ambiguity that characterizes the conclusion of *The Rise of Silas Lapham*—the mixed blessing expressed by the novel's ending—results from the difficult implications of this cultural solution to the Lapham-Corey conflict. If the two families must be divided into discrete geographic and aesthetic realms, then what becomes of the egalitarian goals that Howells would soon voice for fiction, the hope that literature can help men and women "know one another better, that they may be all humbled and strengthened with a sense of their fraternity"? Instead of realizing how they are "more like than unlike one another," the two families in this novel learn a new way of acknowledging and accepting their fundamental dissimilarities. Howells illustrates how well they have learned this manner of understanding difference through the reaction of the snobbish Corey daughters to their new sister-in-law's removal to Mexico. Nanny Corey hopes that "there is a chance that she will form herself on the Spanish manner, if she stays there long enough, and that when she comes back she will have the charm of not olives, perhaps, but *tortillas*, whatever they are: something strange and foreign, even if it's borrowed" (360). This hope that Penelope Lapham will, with time, acquire the strange and foreign "charm" of Mexico shows how the interest in the "picturesque" (the word one Corey daughter uses to describe a portrait of Penelope) is a way of appreciating the aesthetic qualities of alterity while still maintaining a separation between the observer and the object in question—whether that object is the archaeological ruins typically associated with the term picturesque, the artifacts displayed in a museum of anthropology, or a sister-in-law born in rural Vermont. The Lapham family, which had formerly attempted to join the ranks of Boston's upper class, has fractured into a panoply of characters inhabiting the topoi of local color sketches favored by Howells and his fellow realists.

In a review of *The Rise of Silas Lapham*, Hamilton Wright Mabie complained about its "unsatisfactory story": "No one is absorbed by it, nor moved by it; one takes it up with pleasure, reads it with interest, and lays it down without regret.... The novelist wrote it in a cool, deliberate mood, and it leaves the reader cold when he has finished it."[56] For Mabie, this condition made Howells's novel exemplary of the analytic dispassion that he associated with literary realism. What he neglected to mention was that the novel contained its own meditation on storytelling as a manner of making sense of otherwise senseless events. Near the end of the book, the Reverend Sewell visits Silas Lapham to see how the latter understands his own downfall. Lapham tells him that his "whole trouble" came from the way he had treated his original business partner, Milton Rogers, years before:

> It was just like starting a row of bricks. I tried to catch up, and stop 'em from going, but they all tumbled, one after another. It wa'n't in the nature of things that they could be stopped till the last brick went. (364)

Here is the "cool" and "collected" attitude that Mabie found so irritating in the novel as a whole. What Lapham describes is a narrative chain of events over which he has no control, and the deterministic language with which he describes these events—toppling like a row of bricks—neither enrages him nor suggests to him other actions that he might have taken. Howells has taken pains at the end of this novel to articulate, through Silas Lapham, a narrative pattern neither moralistic in its tone nor compelling in its explanatory power. Even as Lapham's words overtly invite Sewell and the reader to consider the story of his life—"I should like to know how it strikes you," he tells Sewell—the flat fatalism of this passage portrays a man not really concerned with finding a more meaningful way of understanding it.

This passage, with its simultaneous denial of and preoccupation with narrative explanations, distills what the anti-realist critics of the late nineteenth century found disturbing, a turn away from "storytelling." Silas Lapham realizes that his downfall comprises a narrative, a sequence of events that occurred in a logical order, just as "a row of bricks" topples when pushed in a particular way. However, he refuses to draw any moral lesson from this sequence, or to suggest that it has led him to any pronounced emotional response. To take either of those paths, for Howells, would be to engage in sentimentalism, which Howells believed to be produced by unrealistic and overly simplistic modes of narration. To put it another way, Silas Lapham knows the narrative of what has occurred to him, but he refuses to convert it into a "story" as the term was used by the literary critics of this period.

The compilations of local color sketches and stories that Howellsian realists vigorously promoted illustrate a different but equally important aversion to arranging sequences according to easily recognizable narrative structures. They do not usually offer a linked series of occurrences but rather a compilation of selected moments in time. The visual metaphor of the "sketch" reminds us of this chronological stasis, as does the other comparison of realist writing to the photograph, an analogy routinely articulated by anti-realist critics to suggest that such work was not sufficiently artistic.[57] Even volumes of linked sketches did not offer the kind of unifying story that such critics desired. Sarah Orne Jewett's *The Country of the Pointed Firs*, for example, relies upon the frame of an urban visitor to a remote Maine village, but the changes that this summer brings to the life of this narrator are, like her name, unspoken.[58]

The opposition between "storytelling" and "analysis" that played such a prominent role in defining literary realism was not the invention of anti-realist critics, but rather arose from their attempt to come to grips with a move in American literature away from more highly narrativized forms of fiction. In one of his "Editor's Study" columns, Howells wrote that to "spin a yarn for the yarn's sake, that is an ideal worthy of a nineteenth-century Englishman, doting in the forgetfulness of the English masters and groveling in the ignorance of the Continental masters; but wholly impossible to an American of Mr. Henry James's modernity."[59] That Howells rejects the "yarn for the yarn's sake" as being at odds with modernity as well as America dramatizes an anxiety about the power of narrative at precisely the moment when global narratives of biological evolution, historical progress, and industrial modernization were being deployed everywhere in the United States. Such narratives had a moral force to them, a presumption of optimism and inevitability, that had been extrapolated from the evolutionism of Charles Darwin and Herbert Spencer. The realist attack upon sentimental narrative became an outlet for the expression of skepticism about the preponderance of the progressive, evolutionary creed expressed throughout American society. In the last two decades of the nineteenth century, American literary realists turned away from unified, sweeping narratives of change and away from the global scale, to document the local, the particular, and the episodic.

The preoccupation of realist authors with evading the force of progressive narratives because of their moralistic optimism, which they considered sentimental, would later be rejected in the naturalist fiction of Theodore Dreiser, Jack London, and Frank Norris, who often turned the narrative structures suggested by evolution into a more pessimistic portrait of society than the boosterism of the day normally allowed. Before the emergence of naturalism in American fiction, however, the realists' concern about "storytelling" was tied to their efforts to describe the kinds of group-based differences expressed in the conclusion of *The Rise of Silas Lapham* or at the core of the countless collections of local color sketches, dialect tales, and other regionalist fiction. Their wariness about the importance of "storytelling" played a necessary and crucial role in creating new forms of ethnographic fiction, literature that documented the culture of a particular group and that reflected the changing definition of culture itself within American anthropology. During the same years that anthropologists were quarreling over whether museum artifacts should be arranged to convey an evolutionary progress, literary realists were devising forms of writing that similarly disputed the importance of narrative structure. That such efforts earned the realists the label of "scientists" should come as no surprise, for, like some scientists of their day, they were struggling to find new ways of understanding and documenting the group-based differences that they hoped to incorporate into their craft.

The limitations of the depiction of group-based difference in realist texts, in turn, often emanated from the contradictions and challenges produced by the emerging concept of *culture*, an idea that promoted the recognition of groups normally outside the center of highbrow literature but also stressed their separation from that center, an idea that granted those groups integrity yet enforced upon them a kind of stasis. The two articles cited at the beginning of this chapter, Alice Fletcher's "Indian Songs" and George Washington Cable's "Creole Slave Songs," illustrate the problems that this definition of culture raised. Both articles bridge the ethnographic and the aesthetic through the documentation of vernacular expressions that mark group-based difference. Yet the articles also share a limitation: neither is able to portray the people from whom these songs come as being of the modern moment in which the *Century* has published them. Fletcher ends her article by saying that "tribes as tribes are ceasing to exist"; therefore, "the expression of their emotions will hereafter be modeled on the lines of our artistic forms."[60] Cable, meanwhile, prizes the songs as the productions of an antebellum culture; he records, for instance, a song "said to be very old, dating from the last century. It is still sung, but the Creole gentleman who procured it for me from a former slave was not able to transcribe or remember the air."[61] In each case, even though the songs *are* being sung during the chronological time that their recorder publishes them, the language of professional observation leads the writer to treat the songs as relics from the past.

What neither the ethnographic model of culture nor the realist resistance to progressive narrative could provide was a way of imagining that such cultures could engage the modern present through innovation— while still maintaining the distinctions that conferred upon them cultural integrity. As a result, texts like Fletcher's and Cable's became the equivalent of the locked room of Burnett's Louisiana Rogers and of the rural paint mine to which Howells's Silas Lapham returns: closed off sanctuaries for preserving group-based difference and affording opportunities for others to regard their meaning by engaging in "analysis" rather than "storytelling." The following chapter demonstrates how the careers of two African American writers of the period were shaped by this realist absorption of ethnographic goals and practices. The success of both Paul Laurence Dunbar and Charles W. Chesnutt was fostered by the culturalist direction of literary realism in the United States. Both writers, in turn, were forced to contend with the problem of ethnographic culture demonstrated by the works discussed here—the privileging of synchronic description to the point of failing to provide a vocabulary for narrating cultural change—as well as an additional one, the persistent entanglement of cultural theories of identity with older ideas of biological race.

3

Between Race and Culture:
Paul Laurence Dunbar and
Charles W. Chesnutt

In 1880, at the age of twenty-one, Charles W. Chesnutt declared in his journal, "The Negro's part is to prepare himself for social recognition and equality; and it is the province of literature to open the way for him to get it."[1] Chesnutt's conviction that an artistic form, literature, could play a role in affecting the social and political goal of equality places him in step with the advocates of American literary realism, who took the transformative power of literature as a central tenet of their aesthetic creed. In the two decades that followed Chesnutt's journal entry, the realists' conviction that people "are more like than unlike one another,"[2] together with their pursuit of authentic, group-based difference yielded a proliferation of textual forms that relied on the ethnographic notion of culture—forms that a beginning writer could use to enter the world of professional letters. In this chapter we shall see how this realist interest in ethnographic culture shaped the production and reception of works by Chesnutt and another major African American author of the 1890s, Paul Laurence Dunbar. These two writers were published, reviewed, and acclaimed by figures associated with American literary realism, for whom Chesnutt and Dunbar represented the possibility that the literary sphere, by providing "social recognition and equality," could succeed where the larger society had failed.

That success enabled William Dean Howells, in a 1900 review of Chesnutt, to declare triumphantly that in the "department of literature ... there is, happily, no color line."[3] Chesnutt and Dunbar surely knew that the position of a writer of color was much more precarious. Through their adoption of the conventions of realism, each had deployed the vocabulary of culture to present African American experience in a way that was recognized as factually accurate as well as aesthetically pleasing by their largely white audience. Taken together, though, their writing reveals the limitations of that same vocabulary, and explains why Chesnutt would eventually find it wholly inadequate for addressing the problems of racial inequality that mattered so much to him.

These limitations emanate, in part, from the confusion that still surrounded the concept of culture during the period when Chesnutt and Dunbar launched their careers. In the early twentieth century the focus of Boasian anthropology would be to separate the studies of culture, physical race, and language: in fact, Boas gave to his retrospective collection of his scientific articles the title *Race, Language, and Culture* (1940), arranging the articles under these three headings as a way of effecting this division on his own work. In late-nineteenth-century thought, however, no theoretical model existed for distinguishing these three ontologies of group-based identity. Instead, many anthropologists and other social theorists were searching for a master key to link culture, race, and language into a single developmental history of humankind. Similarly, the texts of literary realists addressing group-based difference were frequently trapped in an epistemological confusion, for even as they inscribed cultural difference upon the page and conferred upon it aesthetic value, they often reproduced the incoherence of a theory of culture still yoked to biological racialism.

Nowhere did the relationship between anthropological notions of culture—with its emphasis upon first-hand observation, textual documentation, and the meaning of difference—and American literary realism become more complex than in texts addressing the racial divisions that plagued the United States in the post-Reconstruction era. The period in which realism was most prominent as a topic of debate and a principle of editorial selection was one in which African Americans suffered from the growing retrenchment of institutional, legal, and social racism. By the 1890s, poll taxes, literacy tests, and grandfather clauses had disenfranchised blacks throughout the South; Jim Crow laws had converted *de facto* segregation into *de jure;* and the lynching of African American men had reached record levels. While some realist figures, such as George Washington Cable, publicly argued the necessity of correcting such inequities, the depiction of

racial difference in realist literary writing rarely responded to this injustice
so directly. Realist writing, moreover, was less successful in its depiction of
African Americans than in taking on white, rural ethnicities: the mountaineers of Mary N. Murfree, the Moravians and French Canadians of
Constance Fenimore Woolson, the poverty-stricken New England farmers
of Mary Wilkins Freeman. Even though the rising rate of immigration
from eastern and southern Europe made issues of white ethnicity more
complicated each year, these rural groups could be presented through the
vocabulary of cultural difference in a way that did not immediately force
white, urban readers to consider the political inequities that marked the
"color line."

The regionalist works that represented such populations did not bring
to readers' minds a "rural problem" or an "agrarian problem" that was
the equivalent to the well-known "Negro problem." Even though a writer
like Hamlin Garland might strive to show the economic hardships facing
American farmers, his work was not regarded as taking up questions of
political import as were those works concerning African Americans.[4] Instead, most local color realism offered readers an opportunity to tour the
white ethnic communities that they believed would soon become (if they
had not already been) erased by a bland, homogenized modernity. Yet
African Americans did figure in literary realism, and not simply because
of the generally progressive stance of realist editors and writers on matters
of race. Rather, the ethnographic techniques favored by literary realism
to document group-based difference—the recording of local traditions,
the description of closed communities, and the textualization of distinctive
speech patterns and dialects of English—could easily be manipulated to
present the experiences of African Americans, under the rubrics of regionalism and local color writing. Each of these methods mattered to African
American realist writing, but the development with the greatest such influence during this era was the realists' preoccupation with the orthographically correct transcription of speech.

The Dialect of Difference

Dialect writing was situated at the intersection of scientific ethnography
and literary realism because it provided a literary vehicle through which
authentic difference could be textualized in tangible and accurate ways.
Dialect emphasized the ways group-based identities were made within a
community and could be observed by an outsider who spent time within
it. Dialect literature therefore positioned the author as a professional,

skilled observer of difference, akin to the scientific ethnographer charged with documenting the minutiae of a people's behavior and expression. On the one hand, the documentation of dialect employed linguistic difference in a way that occasionally evoked a characterization of cultural difference as socially constructed; on the other, the orthographic representation of vernacular English was mired in the older model of inherited, hierarchical racial difference.

The practice of marking the locally authentic by orthographically reproducing linguistic dialects began well before the ascendancy of literary realism in the United States. By the 1880s, this tradition already included James Russell Lowell's antebellum *Biglow Papers* (1848, 1866), Irwin Russell's enormously popular "Christmas-Night in the Quarters" (1878), and Edward Eggleston's *The Hoosier Schoolmaster* (1872), generally acknowledged as the first complete novel written in an American dialect of English. The dialect literature of the last two decades of the nineteenth century shifted the purpose of this strategy of writing. As Gavin Jones has observed in his study of dialect literature during this period, the post-Reconstruction "cult of the vernacular" differed from the comic political commentary that had appeared in newspapers and magazines since Lowell. The new dialect writing "was part of mainstream literature; it avowed realism, not humor; its political content sunk to a deeper, less overt level."[5] A remark by Howells on the dialect dialogue in Mary N. Murfree's fiction exemplifies the aesthetic qualities attributed to linguistic variety:

> As you read you feel sure that those people spoke as she has represented their speech, and that so much of their character dwells in their parlance that if she had made them speak otherwise or less faithfully to their usage, much that is precious would have been lost. A flavor, an aroma would have escaped in the translation that now enriches the reader's sense of them, like the breath of the woods and hills where their quaint, remote, pathetic life passes.[6]

For Howells, dialect conveys the "flavor" of the "remote," but only if it is convincing in its representation of the "parlance" of the actual people behind Murfree's fictional prose.

The reaction to and reception of writing in dialect during the realist era were dominated by such assessments of its accuracy. In 1884, when George Washington Cable wrote to complain about Thomas Nelson Page's "Marse Chan" (a story discussed below), he did so by pointing out that it was inaccurate and ludicrous for Page to represent African Americans as speaking in dialect and Southern white characters as not. Cable's complaint was clearly a larger criticism about Page's absurd caricature and its disastrous racial politics. However, instead of engendering a dialogue about the civil rights of African Americans, the letter merely created a debate about whether it would be accurate and authentic for black characters to speak in the "simple English" that Cable demanded.[7] The next year, Cable's friend Twain would poke fun at this obsession with linguistic exactness even as he exploited it. Twain's "Explanatory" note to *The Adventures of Huckleberry Finn* claims that the novel reproduces three different dialects, including four "modified varieties" of one, and that the "shadings have not been done in a hap-hazard fashion, or by guess-work; but pains-takingly."[8]

Twain's "Explanatory" satirizes the reliance of dialect literature upon claims of scientific precision in its mimetic reproduction of speech.[9] Dialect literature met the widespread expectation of the period that a text could and even should be both ethnographically valuable and aesthetically pleasing. Joel Chandler Harris's introduction to the first *Uncle Remus* volume (1880) illustrates how these two manners of reading could be brought to bear upon the same representation of dialect. Harris stresses his efforts to reproduce "characteristic" legends "without embellishment and without exaggeration" in "phonetically genuine" language, but he also writes that "if the language of Uncle Remus fails to give hints of the really poetic imagination of the negro . . . then I have reproduced the form of the dialect merely, and not the essence, and my attempt must be accounted a failure."[10] The terms of success and failure that Harris sets forward show how thoroughly American literary realism entered into the ethnographic project of reproducing cultures upon the page. These tales must not only be accurate—Harris is known to have corrected the orthography of the first edition[11]—but must characterize a whole group of people who speak in a manner similar to Uncle Remus. Just as the distance between the dialect of *Uncle Remus* and the standard, literary English of its introduction serves as a metaphor for the divisions between American blacks and whites, the expression of Uncle Remus himself must somehow synecdochically stand in for an otherwise inexpressible "essence" that defines a larger group.

To a certain extent, such a text, which shows how identities are socially made through language and which uses language to symbolize the texture of a discrete way of life, insists upon a version of group-based identity more cultural than racial. Harris shows the "poetic imagination" of Remus as being an actively creative force rather than a racial trait passively inherited. The cultural difference between Remus and the boy to whom he speaks, figured by the linguistic patterns, trickster plots, and animal characters of the stories in the volume, is something that is created anew in each framed narrative. For instance, Remus actually interrupts "The Wonderful Tar Baby Story" at the moment when Brer Fox realizes his trap for Brer Rabbit has been successful:

> Here Uncle Remus paused, and drew a two-pound yam out of the ashes.
> "Did the fox eat the rabbit?" asked the little boy to whom the story had been told.
> "Dat's all de fur de tale goes," replied the old man. "He mout, en den agin he mountent. Some say Jedge B'ar come 'long en loosed 'im—some say he didn't. I hear Miss Sally callin'. You better run 'long."[12]

Whether Remus pauses here because he wants the boy to reflect on Brer Rabbit's predicament, because he has yet to determine the resolution of the story, or simply because he wants to eat his dinner, the effect of his halting without telling the boy that he will later continue the story is an undeniable intensification of suspense. Harris forces his readers, here and elsewhere, to admire the mastery of Remus's storytelling. At the same time, he invites those whites who identify with the language of the book's introduction to indulge in an additional level of aesthetic pleasure, derived from the cultural difference symbolized by Remus's dialect.

The place of dialect in the "plantation tradition" of American literary history, a tradition invented to posit an antebellum harmony of whites and blacks living as masters and slaves before the terrible violence of the Civil War, reveals the problematic nature of such pleasure.[13] Thomas Nelson Page's "Marse Chan: A Tale of Old Virginia," first published in the *Century* in 1884, became a paradigm of this body of expression and one of the best-known works of literary prose of its day. Page's opening paragraph demonstrates how apologists for Southern slavery cannily deployed the ethnographic notion of a culture as a way of life distinct from others:

> The road I was travelling ... had just struck me as most significant of the character of the race whose only avenue of communication with the outside world it had formerly been. Their once splendid mansions, now fast falling to decay, appeared to view from time to time, set back far from the road, in proud seclusion.... Distance was nothing to this people; time was of no consequence to them. They desired but a level path in life, and that they had, though the way was longer, and the outer world strode by them as they dreamed.[14]

The narrator describes the Virginia plantation mansions as the archaeological ruins of an isolated people who belong to the past. The plantations evoke a set of customs and manners completely separate from those shared by the narrator or by the reader of the story, who both belong to the "outer world" that has passed by and left this one standing still. Crucially, when the narrator speaks of the "race" that inhabited this decayed landscape, he seems at first to mean those white Southerners who were the rulers of the plantation system. Who else would so vehemently defend this way of life as a "level path"?

Page answers this question through the character of Sam, the former slave of the story's hero, and the one who tells the story of his master to the narrator. Sam remains on the planation, looking after his master's dog and tending to the memories of bygone plantation life. While he is in many respects peripheral to the action of "Marse Chan"—a tale of thwarted love and filial duty—he is integral to the text as whole. Within the framed story, Sam demonstrates the depth of his loyalty to the plantation by going with his master to fight on the side of the South in the Civil War. Equally (if not more) important, Sam speaks in a dialect represented in deliberate contrast to the standard English of the narrator. In a letter to the *Critic,* an otherwise unidentified "Southern Matron" testified to the value of Sam's dialect in the success of the story; "coming from the faithful negro's heart," she wrote, the written representation of Sam's speech brought her to tears. The "Matron" continues, "One of the most interesting features of Southern life in the past will be obliterated when the old Negro dialect is forgotten."[15]

This reaction to Page's story clarifies the role of African Americans in this portrayal of the antebellum South. The significance of Sam's dialect is not in its representation of a separate African American identity, but in its evocation of a *culture of slavery.* Page's story attempts to ignore the gross injustice of slavery by recasting the antebellum plantation as a whole, functioning, discrete way of life—as a culture one may appreciate in its richness and isolation, just as the white, upper-class tourists of Frances Hodgson Burnett's *Louisiana* or Sarah Orne Jewett's *Deephaven* hope to appreciate the rural cultures they visit. In Page's text, the dialect that Sam speaks, shot through with a tone of affection for the events he recounts, serves as a linguistic symbol of this manner of living and of the integral place of African American slaves in it. Black slaves not only form an essential element of this culture, but are also portrayed as deriving personal well-being from their role in such a complete and well-regulated way of life. When, therefore, Page's narrator talks about "the character of the race" who inhabited the plantations, or when Page himself dedicates *In Ole Virginia: Marse Chan and Other Stories* (1887) to "My People," the text does not refer to biologically inherited whiteness but to a socially constructed way of behaving, a culture that Page believes necessarily to include both white masters and black slaves.[16]

As I have suggested, the most obvious effect of this way of speaking about the plantation economy is to ignore the brutality of chattel slavery and its aftermath through the aestheticization of culture. One of the means by which the text performs this feat is to portray plantation life as existing in a preserved moment in the distant past rather than as participating in the long history of contested race relations in the American South. "Marse Chan" is written so as to emphasize the distance of the antebellum past from the post-Reconstruction denial of African American claims to equality typified, for instance, by the Supreme Court's evisceration of the Civil Rights Act of 1875 in the year prior to the story's publication. The consequences of this strategy become even more transparent with its publication in Page's *In Ole Virginia*, where tales like "Marse Chan" are juxtaposed with "Ole 'Stracted," a story set in the present in which freed blacks suffer visibly from the cruelty of carpetbagger landlords. Tellingly, the black speech of "Ole 'Stracted" does not narrate the story, as in "Marse Chan." Instead of the colorful rhythms of Sam's storytelling, the vernacular language of African Americans in the post-Reconstruction tale is harsh and even incoherent at times. For Page, speech serves as an index for the demise of the culture he mourns, and the difference symbolized by dialect strengthens the aesthetic appeal of his claim to representing an antebellum culture of slavery with accuracy.

More than ten years after Harris's *Uncle Remus* and Page's "Marse Chan" were published—well after many American critics had noted their growing boredom with dialect literature—the poetry of Paul Laurence Dunbar gained a national audience because readers and critics could place it precisely at the intersection of the aesthetic and the ethnographic registers so vital to the response that Harris's and Page's work had received. The reception of Dunbar's work, both his poetry and his subsequent prose, illustrates how the relationship between these two manners of reading in realism—the admiration of artistic achievement and the search for scientific information—created the opportunity for African American authors to address the largely white audience of highbrow American literature. At the same time, the emphasis upon producing a recognizable, authentic difference, as well as the incomplete split between the concepts of biological race and socially constructed culture, circumscribed the range of expression available to African Americans connected to the realist network of writers and editors. While most critical studies of Dunbar's work have focused on the degree to which he was able to critique and satirize the plantation tradition ironically from behind what he called "the mask that grins and lies," my purpose in (briefly) discussing Dunbar is to show how the ethnographic concept of culture could create unresolvable difficulties for a young African American writer in the years surrounding the turn of the twentieth century. [17]

The shape of Dunbar's career resembles those of other young writers breaking onto the literary scene in the 1890s. Like Stephen Crane, for instance, Dunbar spent time writing for newspapers, enjoyed a brief span of literary celebrity, and died at a relatively young age. (Dunbar was born a year later than Crane, in 1872, and died six years later than he, in 1906.) Moreover, both Dunbar and Crane benefitted from the influence of Howells, who thought each produced the realist writing he advocated; the effect of Howells's favorable review of Dunbar's *Majors and Minors* (1896) should not be taken lightly. At the time that Howells's review introduced Dunbar to readers of *Harper's Weekly*, Dunbar had privately published a book of poetry (*Oak and Ivy*, 1892), contributed three poems to the *Century*, and performed readings to enthusiastic audiences in Dayton, Ohio, where he made his home.[18] Although he had gained enough reputation for Charles Chesnutt to have mentioned him in a letter detailing the achievements of "American colored writers" just months before the Howells review,[19] he was still largely unknown to readers in the United States. Howells's "Life and Letters" column praising *Majors and Minors* dramatically altered the trajectory of Dunbar's literary career, and presaged the terms of its reception.[20]

From its opening paragraph, Howells's review is concerned with the authenticity of Dunbar's expression as representative of a body of experience that extends beyond the poet as an individual. He notes, for example, the "pure African type" that Dunbar's photograph presents, and goes on to recount the achievements of two other writers of African descent, Booker T. Washington and Alexander Dumas, before even mentioning Dunbar's name.[21] By underscoring Dunbar's racial identity in this way, Howells conveys to his readers that Dunbar's "direct and fresh authority to do the kind of thing he is doing" rests upon his biological relationship to other blacks. Howells himself seems to have recognized how problematic might be this invocation of biology as the basis for poetic expression, for he dramatically altered it when he revised the column as an introduction to Dunbar's *Lyrics of Lowly Life* (1896). There, Howells begins by stating that he "should scarcely trouble the reader with a special appeal in behalf of this book, if it had not specially appealed to me for reasons apart from the author's race," even though he goes on to talk about Dunbar's race in much the same way as in the review.[22] As Marcellus Blount has pointed out, the combination of a supposedly color-blind assessment of Dunbar's literary merit and the certification of his racial membership means that the introduction to *Lyrics* "bears all the trappings of the authenticating preface to the typical slave narrative."[23]

Nevertheless, in both the review and in the later introduction, Howells emphasizes "the kind of thing [Dunbar] is doing" over the "type" of person Dunbar *is*—in other words, the value of Dunbar as a producer of texts rather than as a specimen of a biological race. In particular, Howells prizes Dunbar's ability to textualize cultural traditions through his dialect poetry; in contrast, Howells deems Dunbar's poetry written in standard English competent but "not specially notable." While one might think that Howells bases his praise solely on the "authority" that Dunbar has in writing "negro" dialect because of his ancestry, Howells's review is actually more complex in its evaluation of Dunbar's work. First, Howells emphasizes that Dunbar writes in both "the dialect of the middle-south negroes and the middle-south whites"; Dunbar "seems to have fathomed the souls of his simple white neighbors, as well as those of his own kindred," Howells writes near the end of the article.[24] In other words, Dunbar's ability to write dialect extends to groups with whom he does not share a biological tie. Second, the review stresses that Dunbar's achievement rests upon a particular relationship to his "material": "He is, so far as I know, the first man of his color to study the race *objectively*, to analyze it himself, and then to represent it in art as he felt it and found it to be" (emphasis added). Howells here assigns to Dunbar the complicated role of the so-called insider able to use the methods of "objective" analysis to present cultural material through a professional idiom. Howells therefore lauds Dunbar's poetry written in the dialect of "middle-south whites" because it shows that Dunbar's powers of observation and reproduction do not necessarily rely on his membership in the group he represents on the page.

Howells's appraisal of Dunbar's poetry proves contradictory; he calls attention to Dunbar's identification as an African American only to disavow its importance. Such confusion results from an incomplete and poorly articulated, but nonetheless significant, attempt to reorient the discussion of African American expression from biology to social construction. While Howells frequently refers to Dunbar's racial ancestry, he prizes the dialect poems because they constitute cultural documents, the tangible record of how a group (or groups, if we remember the poetry written in white dialect) imagines itself different from the highbrow literary culture to which

Howells belongs. Remarkably, Howells finds proof of "human unity" in these poems that employ orthography to render difference immediately recognizable—the difference that divides the "literary English" of the "Majors" from the dialect of the "Minors" of the book's title. Dunbar's highest achievement, in Howells's eyes, is to textualize that difference and do so in a way that he finds aesthetically rewarding.

In Frances Hodgson Burnett's *Louisiana*, Olivia Ferrol hopes that her rural protegé will become "cultured" and therefore "civilized." In contrast, Howells is working with something closer to a model of culture as a set of discrete spheres, and he therefore believes that Dunbar must remain *encultured* (and *not* "civilized") to continue to produce his finest art. The gap between the version of cultural achievement upon which Olivia bases her actions and the one on which Howells bases his encouragement is fundamental to his assessment of Dunbar. For Olivia Ferrol, culture is a ladder to be climbed; for Howells, it is a distinct identity that has aesthetic power when reproduced for outside connoisseurs. Instead of suggesting that Dunbar could possess the knowledge and manners that would enable him as a writer of "literary English" to become part of Howells's class, Howells stresses Dunbar's opportunity and ability to capitalize on his unique relationship to the cultural "material" of the African American experience. But in pronouncing this tie between Dunbar's artistry and his culture as emanating from his inborn "nature," Howells is unable to extricate his logic from a biologically-based understanding of racial identity:

> One sees how the poet exults in his material, as the artist always does; it is not for him to blink its commonness, or to be ashamed of its rudeness; and in his treatment of it he has been able to bring us nearer to the heart of primitive human nature in his race than any one else has yet done.[25]

The emphases on "commonness" and on thinking of group identity as "material" are features of what I call the culturalist orientation of American literary realism. Such an orientation suggests that group identities are discrete, socially constructed units that can be replicated in writing by the proper observer. In this case, though, Howells falls back on related ideas that emerge from the framework of social evolution and biological racialism: that the appropriate "poet" will be one who "exults in his material" because he shares a biological link to it, and that this same "material" is more "primitive" than that to which the readers of *Harper's Weekly* were accustomed.

Coupled to this limitation, the ideas about culture that Howells's review articulates—that culture characterizes a distinct group, that many of its features can be shared and recorded, and that it has an intrinsic value—governed both the production and the reception of Dunbar's books of poetry at this point in his career. *Majors and Minors*, for instance, divided the dialect poems from those in what Howells called "literary English," an arrangement that reproduced the separation of cultural spheres. The former poems, in fact, were printed in a section titled "Humor and Dialect,"[26] a physical arrangement signaling that the dialect poems represented something discrete and separate from those that preceded them. Little wonder that Howells organized his review around the disjunction between what seemed to him almost entirely unrelated bodies of work. When *Lyrics of Lowly Life*, Dunbar's first book with a major press, was published, reviewers followed Howells's lead, even though the dialect and non-dialect poems were no longer arranged in separate sections. The most dramatic extension of this logic appeared in *Bookman*, where the reviewer found the interspersal of the dialect "lyrics" and the "artificial 'literary' verses" so "irritating" that separate volumes were necessary; "Then we should have had a division that would accord with the two distinct traits of the African—one part illustrating how really clever and original he can be when he is thoroughly spontaneous and natural; and the other, how comparatively feeble and ineffective he will always show himself when he is merely imitating the Caucasian."[27] Such a comment argues that African American expression will be aesthetically successful ("clever and original") only when it evokes a culture that stands at a "natural" distance from the highbrow literary scene.

Reviews such as these replicate the separate-but-equal paradigm at the heart of Jim Crow, and they serve to remind us that the *Plessy v. Ferguson* decision of the U.S. Supreme Court formalized that doctrine in the same year that Howells published his review of Dunbar. However, this aestheticization of cultural difference marked a distinct departure from other accounts of racial identity. Thomas Nelson Page's *In Ole Virginia*, for example, suggests that African Americans can only form a part of a functioning culture so long as they have white masters; Page's free blacks either live in slavish deference to those masters ("Marse Chan") or in economic and spiritual poverty ("Ole 'Stracted").[28] In contrast, reviewers of Dunbar's dialect poetry felt that his work revealed a richness and depth of African American life portrayed in its own terms, and symbolized a cultural integrity of which they had been unaware. The praise for Dunbar, meanwhile, followed the realist trend of lauding those who could "portray men and women as they are" and "speak the dialect, the language, that most Americans know," to use Howells's phrases, rather than to transform them artistically.[29]

Dunbar's achievement, according to such logic, was "to transcribe into linguistic symbols" the essence of African American life rather than to invent from his own consciousness.[30] Dunbar himself cultivates his role as an observer and recorder of culture in several of his *Majors and Minors* dialect poems, including "An Ante-Bellum Sermon," "A Negro Love Song," and "A Banjo Song":

> Oh, de music o' de banjo,
>   Quick an' deb'lish, solemn, slow,
> Is de greates' joy an' solace
>   Dat a weary slave kin know!
> So jes let me hyeah it ringin',
>   Dough de chune be po' an' rough,
> It's a pleasure, an' de pleasures
>   O' dis life is few enough.[31]

The dialect speech of this poem represents a speaker who has heard "de music o' de banjo" as a slave, and who is reporting how the music is played and what effect it has on those who belong to this culture. At the same time, the "pleasure" enjoyed by the readers of the poem, presumably outsiders to this world of the slave, derives not from the music itself, but from this act of cultural reportage marked as the recollection of a first-hand observer. To late-nineteenth-century readers of dialect, the speaker of this poem embodies the possibility that cultural difference could be reliably documented, and that the results would have aesthetic appeal from their very dissimilarity to the world of white, middle-to-upper-class Americans.

The presumption that Dunbar's writing would be an accurate transcription of African American culture dominated the critical reception of his work throughout the rest of his career. His first novel, *The Uncalled* (1898), centered upon a young white male Ohioan struggling to decide whether to pursue a career as a preacher. The novel was neither critically nor commercially successful, quite likely because its subject matter did not comport with what white readers expected of an African American dialect poet. In contrast, the collection of short fiction Dunbar published that same year, *Folks from Dixie* (1898), enjoyed better reviews and sales.[32] As the title suggests, *Folks from Dixie* offers short, regionalist sketches of southern African American life, including black characters speaking in dialect; with the exception of "At Shaft 11" (a fascinating story about the role of race in a rural labor strike),[33] the work gives the impression that rural black life in the postbellum South is stagnant, satisfactory, and disentangled from the history of slavery and Reconstruction. Near the end of his career and his life, Dunbar even came close to a Page-like nostalgia for the antebellum

South in *In Old Plantation Days* (1903), a collection that does little to dispute the absurd proposition of Page and others that slaves were happier on the pre-war plantation than following emancipation.[34]

The trajectory of Dunbar's career shows how the culturalist texts of literary realism could be pressed into the service of a primitivism that had more in common with the evolutionary scheme of a ladder of cultural stages than with cultural pluralism—in part because these two models of culture had not been adequately articulated as competing definitions. Therefore, African American culture, or any culture, could be easily relegated to premodern inferiority; in the case of Dunbar, this possibility meant that his dialect poetry and regionalist fiction was always in peril of devolving into an evocation of the plantation culture, with its presumption of natural hierarchy between civilized whites and primitive blacks. The illustrations that accompanied Dunbar's poetry and prose, like those used by the *Century* for George Washington Cable's "Creole Slave Songs" (see chapter 2), make this danger clear. In fact, *Folks from Dixie* was illustrated by E. W. Kemble, the artist whose drawings had accompanied Cable's earlier article. In the case of Dunbar's volume, some illustrations clearly exaggerate the features of Dunbar's African American characters for obvious effect; others plainly do not; and just as many fall in between these two extremes (see Figure 5). The author of a document of a culture might insist upon the integrity of that culture, as Dunbar usually did, but the reader, particularly when so guided by an illustrator, might impose a less generous interpretation upon such texts.

In outlining how the ethnographic notion of culture influenced Dunbar's literary career, I am not trying to suggest that he was a passive victim, forced by a white establishment into a pre-fashioned role of "recording angel" of African American life. Although on one occasion Dunbar complained that Howells's review of *Majors and Minors* did him "irrevocable harm in the dictum he laid down regarding my dialect verse," Dunbar also continued to write, read, and enjoy a literary career based upon dialect writing.[35] The very first letter that Dunbar wrote to his future wife—then Alice Ruth Moore—in 1895, on the eve of his success, shows that he questioned whether "preserving" the "quaint old tales and songs of our fathers which have made the fame of Joel Chandler Harris, Thomas Nelson Page, Ruth McEnry Stuart and others" was a wise course for an African American writer.[36] Such a letter offers evidence that Dunbar at least partially understood the risks as well as the rewards of producing materials that purported cultural authenticity. He entered the American literary scene at a moment when the textual documentation of culture had been redefined

Figure 5. These illustrations by E. W. Kemble accompanied Paul Laurence Dunbar's
Folks from Dixie, published in New York in 1898. The original captions to the drawings
read (a) "Why'n't you git me somp'n to fix myself up in?"; (b) "Wha'd you catch?"; and
(c) "I see possum grease in you' mouf." The first (5a) does not caricature its subject, but
the third (5c) obviously exaggerates the features of its subject for comic effect. Dunbar's
writing, which insisted on accurate representation of African American life yet often
did so in an idiom that rendered its subject quaint and humorous, was vulnerable
to such divergent interpretations.

as a literary enterprise, but racial theories of group-based identity had not yet been discarded for social ones. Therefore, while some white readers were eager for Dunbar to describe to them through the accented language of dialect how African Americans imagined their world, most still believed that he possessed insight into this world only because of his biological race. While Dunbar might "mouth myriad subtleties" with his poetry, as he suggests in "We Wear the Mask," his readers were more interested in the "pleasure" generated by poems like "A Banjo Song," a pleasure derived from the belief that definitive, unsubtle group-based differences could be inscribed upon the written page.

From Cultural Documentation to Racial Narrative

The image of the author as a figure standing between a highbrow, cosmopolitan audience and the remote subject of ethnographic literature had become a sturdy convention, with several variations, by the advent of Dunbar's literary career in the 1890s. Harriet Beecher Stowe's *Oldtown Folks* (1869), often named as the text that initiated the steady stream of postbellum regionalist fiction, begins with a preface in which the author's persona, "Horace Holyoke," asserts that he has tried to make "his mind as still and passive as a looking-glass" so that he could "maintain the part simply of a sympathetic spectator" and record the stories in the volume directly from reality.[37] In works like Burnett's *Louisiana*, the presence of the metropole is embodied in a character traveling to a rural enclave as an outsider, a pattern also followed by Dunbar in his story "The Ordeal at Mt. Hope," in which a Northern black preacher wonders what connection he might have with his ignorant Southern parishioners. Alternatively, works such as *Uncle Remus* and "Marse Chan" split the process of cultural interpretation through two mediating narrators, one indigenous to the culture in question, the other from outside it.

The presence of these mediating figures gave authors an opportunity to embody the conflict central to the realist representation of difference. On the one hand, the ultimate goal of depictions of otherness was to assert a baseline of humanity that could be the foundation of what Howells, Garland, and other realist critics hoped would be a more democratic literature. On the other, the realist critique of sentimental sympathy required that group-based differences be attended to, that they be recognized in order to be rendered manageable rather than invisible. The pairing of the young boy and Uncle Remus, for instance, places the reader at three removes from the framed tale; readers recognize at least a small distance between themselves and the white boy, another marked by race and age between the boy and Remus, and even a third between Remus—an older, experienced raconteur who has mastered the storytelling traditions of his community—and the world of Brer Rabbit. As a result, Harris's text allowed white readers to maintain an interval between themselves and the culture that gave rise to Remus's stories, while at the same time sympathetically appreciating both the stories and their teller. Harris's framing device proved so effective, in fact, that it not only was revisited by Dunbar in his story "A Family Feud," but proved crucial to the career of Charles W. Chesnutt.[38]

When Chesnutt published "The Goophered Grapevine" in the *Atlantic Monthly* in 1887, he received his first exposure to the national audience that the magazine commanded. This tale, like the six others that eventually comprised Chesnutt's first book, *The Conjure Woman* (1899), revolves around an African American man, "Uncle" Julius McAdoo, recounting stories of plantation life to an educated white Northern couple who have come to North Carolina for both the climate and the economic opportunity of refurbishing a plantation into a vineyard. The journals and letters of Chesnutt, who spent much of his childhood and a short teaching career in North Carolina, demonstrate that he believed the documentation of rural African American life might offer him a chance toward a professional life in letters. His journal from 1880 reveals his reflections upon the best means of pursuing a literary profession:

> I have thought, during the great revival which is going on, that a collection of ballads or hymns which the colored people sing with such fervor, might be acceptable, if only as a curiosity to people, literary people, at the North. Though these songs are not of much merit as literary compositions, they have certain elements of originality which make them interesting to a student of literature, who can trace, in a crude and unpolished performance, more of the natural ability or character of the writer than in the more correct production of a cultivated mind.[39]

Though the journal shows that Chesnutt quickly passed over this idea in favor of presenting "vivid pictures of Southern life and character" in prose—a decision prompted by learning that Albion Tourgée had sold his Reconstruction novel *A Fool's Errand* for $200,000—the manner in which the future writer considers publishing "a collection of ballads or hymns" indicates how pervasive the notion of culture here discussed was during this period.[40] Chesnutt recognizes that these verbal works ("ballads or hymns") would not be regarded by the audience of the book in the same way as by the "colored people" who sang them "with fervor." Such a collection would instead be received as a "crude and unpolished performance" appealing to the reader by affording a direct window into the "natural ability" of the group from which it originates. The reader would therefore have access to something at once foreign and recognizable—just like the dialect in which such songs might be recorded.

With such astute recognition of how the "literary people" of the North desired the "curiosity" of texts marked as culturally exotic, it seems nearly inevitable that Chesnutt would eventually hit upon the appeal of vernacular tales of supernatural conjure and use them, as he did in "The Goophered Grapevine," to break into national publication. As Kenneth M. Price has pointed out, the *Atlantic Monthly* "conveyed mixed signals on racial issues" during the late 1880s.[41] The magazine retained some sense of its abolitionist origins in the 1850s, but it also printed favorable reviews of nostalgic memoirs of the antebellum South and more overtly offensive pieces like those of Nathaniel Southgate Shaler, the Harvard-trained "purveyor of science to the nation" who argued that racial segregation and discrimination were scientifically justified.[42] Chesnutt's Julius stories published by the *Atlantic Monthly* in the late 1880s—"The Goophered Grapevine," "Po' Sandy," and "The Conjurer's Revenge"—may have sent mixed signals as well. Although these stories dramatize the injustice and violence of slavery, they also extend the plantation tradition of writing, which readers had been trained by authors such as Page to recognize as a form of nostalgia. Chesnutt had undoubtedly realized the limitations of the form when he wrote to Tourgée in 1889 that he had "about used up the old Negro [Julius] who serves as the mouthpiece, and I shall drop him in future stories, as well as much of the dialect."[43]

Nearly a decade later, however, Chesnutt returned to both the mouthpiece and the dialect when Walter Hines Page, the new editor of the *Atlantic*, indicated that Houghton Mifflin might be willing to publish a book of "'conjure' stories" rather than the more diverse collection that Chesnutt had submitted to him. Eager to finally secure book publication, Chesnutt quickly proceeded to compose six new tales featuring Julius narrating to John and Annie, the new Northern owners of a former plantation. Four of these six would soon be published in *The Conjure Woman*, together with three stories Chesnutt had previously published in the 1880s.[44] In the letter that he later sent to Page, accompanying the new stories, Chesnutt lamented the "despairing task" of writing dialect once again, and showed he understood it to be a fiction, created for the "curiosity" of "literary people" that he had noted long before. "The fact is, of course," he wrote, "that there is no such thing as Negro dialect; that what we call by that name is the attempt to express, with such a degree of phonetic correctness as to suggest the sound, English pronounced as an ignorant old southern Negro would be supposed to speak it, and at the same time to preserve sufficient approximation to the correct spelling to make it easy reading."[45] In the final version of *The Conjure Woman*, Chesnutt crafted a collection that he knew would meet the expectations of the same audience that had applauded Paul Laurence Dunbar's dialect verse but that remained un-moved by Dunbar's "literary" English. *The Conjure Woman*, in fact, rede-ploys nearly all the conventions central to the literary realist's fascination with culture: a regionally-remote people hesitant to change, the recording of dialect speech, and an educated outside narrator who records what he sees and hears.[46]

The formula of *The Conjure Woman* remains consistent throughout each of the seven tales. John and Annie, the Northerners, discuss some question or problem regarding the management of the plantation-cum-vineyard with Julius, who ventures an opinion that usually runs contrary to John's inclination. Julius then tells a story about the antebellum plan-tation that involves the magic of "conjure" and that provides an easily understood lesson to support his position. At the conclusion, John usually becomes convinced that Julius had some ulterior motive for his advice. In "Po' Sandy" (44–54), for example, John mentions that he is thinking about using the boards of an old schoolhouse for a new kitchen. Julius then tells a story of a slave named Sandy who is turned into a tree by his wife to prevent their separation. Julius's tale ends tragically when the tree (Sandy) is cut into lumber for a kitchen; since the kitchen seemed haunted, those very boards were removed from the plantation house and used to build the schoolhouse that John is thinking of dismantling. Upon hearing this story, Annie decides that she would rather use freshly cut lumber for her kitchen, a wish to which John grudgingly complies. Later, John dis-covers that Julius plans to use the old schoolhouse for a new branch of the "Sandy Run Colored Baptist Church," thereby learning Julius's practical reason for recounting the tale of "Po' Sandy."

The frame—John's narration—surrounding each of Julius's stories draws the reader into a complicated dispute about the proper method of inter-preting them.[47] At his least sympathetic, John describes the action of the tales as "absurdly impossible" (53); at other times, he responds to the tales as he would to a crude amusement: "some weirdly grotesque, some broadly humorous," and all containing "the shadow . . . of slavery and ignorance" (96). Equally important, John's narration reminds us that he suspects

Julius of crafting the stories to advance his self-interest. While Annie likewise reacts to the tales as entertainment—at one point John even thinks that hearing them improves her health—she does so in a manner that consistently underscores what the tales reveal about the brutality of plantation life. "What a system it was," she says after Julius finishes telling her and John about Sandy, "under which such things were possible!" (53). She later admits that the transformation of a man into a tree is "absurd," but her appreciation of the violence that slavery inflicted on Sandy and his wife has convinced her that she would not "ever be able to take any pleasure in that kitchen if it were built out of that lumber" (53). Craig Werner has persuasively argued that Julius's interaction with this divided audience is integral to understanding how Julius has participated in the "mask" of the signifying tradition, by which the critical, satiric commentary of the disempowered remains hidden beneath more literal interpretive possibilities. By making his stories available to two different kinds of reading—one based on economic self-interest (John's), the other on the sentimental tradition (Annie's)—Julius prefigures "the doubly conscious Afro-American modernist writer" and "manipulates his audience through his awareness of the structure and limitations of Euro-American oppositional thought."[48]

The pairing of John and Julius also enables Chesnutt to articulate an awareness of the shifting definitions of culture and to do so in an ultimately provocative manner. On the one hand, Julius's conjure tales obviously participate in the "folk" traditions prized for their authentic alterity by readers of both highbrow literary magazines and such scientific journals as the *Journal of American Folk-Lore,* first published in 1888 (the same year the *Atlantic* printed "Po' Sandy"). Even though these highly imaginative vernacular narratives, full of animal characters and supernatural occurrences, could hardly be called directly mimetic in the way that realist fiction was, the publication of folk literatures was aligned with the goals of literary realism by gesturing toward literary diversity and offering tangible markers of group-based distinction. Usually written in dialect, folk tales extended the realist project of textualizing "natural" speech and embodying in verbal forms the essence of discrete, holistic group-based identities. Chesnutt, for instance, later wrote that all but one of the tales were his own invention and that the collection was deliberately modeled upon Harris's *Uncle Remus,* but reviews of *The Conjure Woman* suggest that most readers in 1899 assumed (as, indeed, Harris claimed for his tales) that the conjure stories had been taken directly from the African American oral tradition.[49] Undoubtedly, this presumption of authenticity played a role in the positive reception the book received.

In contrast to the trappings of the folk culture that Julius bears, *The Conjure Woman* emphasizes that John is cultured in the sense that Olivia Ferrol of *Louisiana* is, by reminding the reader of John's education, his appreciation for learning, and his desire to be "enough of a pioneer to start a new industry" in the South (32). This text, in other words, repeats the pattern seen throughout this chapter of pairing an indigenous example of ethnographic culture and an elite, cultivated purveyor of that culture. However, Chesnutt enriches this pattern in a crucial way by reiterating John's skepticism toward these stories of curses, blessings, and transformations.[50] The doubt that John voices at the end of nearly every story, as well as his arguments with Annie about the tales' meanings, force the reader to ponder the value of the texts as one might not in another collection. We ask: Are the stories true? Does Julius believe them true? Do they really only serve Julius's self-interest? The audience of *The Conjure Woman* has been trained to read these stories as cultural artifacts, but Chesnutt's volume raises a dilemma about the utility of such traditional texts in the life of someone like Julius. In other words, this book asks us to consider what exactly culture—the accumulation of customs, beliefs, rituals, songs, and tales of such interest to ethnographers and literary realists alike—is *for*.

Consider the lead story, "The Goophered Grapevine," among the first that Chesnutt composed. In its frame, John and Annie meet Julius for the first time as they are contemplating purchasing the old McAdoo plantation, where untended grapevines are a visible reminder of an antebellum attempt at a vineyard. Julius, who was "bawn en raise' on dis yer same plantation" attempts to dissuade the couple from buying the land by telling them that a curse (a "goopher") has been placed upon the vineyard due to the actions of a greedy planter eager to make as much money from his slaves and his grapes as possible. John ignores the warning, and later learns that "Uncle Julius had occupied a cabin on the place for many years, and derived a respectable revenue from the product of the neglected grapevines. This, doubtless, accounted for his advice to me not to buy the vineyard, though whether it inspired the goopher story I am unable to state" (43). While recent readers of *The Conjure Woman* have commonly commented upon John's inability to share "Julius's secular faith in magic," they have less frequently asked whether John's final suggestion might be correct, whether Julius may have invented the story to thwart John and Annie.[51]

The volume itself never resolves this issue; although John repeatedly displays interest in Julius's creative process. In "Tobe's Tribulations," a story that Chesnutt composed for *The Conjure Woman* but published in *The*

Southern Workman, John ruminates further on the relationship between Julius and the "raw material" of his storytelling:

> He had seen life from what was to us a new point of view—from the bottom, as it were; and there clung to his mind, like the barnacles of a ship, all sorts of extravagant beliefs.... But from his own imagination, I take it—for I never heard quite the same stories as anyone else—he gave to the raw material of folk-lore and superstition a fancifulness of touch that truly made of it, to borrow a homely phrase, a silk purse out of sow's ear.[52]

While John praises Julius for his ability to transform folklore with a "fancifulness of touch," this passage illustrates that what John actually values is Julius's unique relationship with the body of work he relates. The metaphor of barnacles clinging to a ship implies that Julius's mind is acted *upon* by the force of cultural tradition rather than acting in any original way as an individual, creative agent.

John enjoys the cultural authenticity of Julius's tales, and Annie is educated by them about slavery. But what does Julius get from telling them? He does not, for instance, dissuade John from buying the vineyard. The practical lessons of his stories, as in "Po' Sandy," so blatantly serve his own interests that his landlords can frequently recognize those interests immediately and, if they choose, dismiss them; his is hardly an effective strategy. One might suggest that "The Goophered Grapevine" has a second significance, that it is a story about the demise of a bad master told by a prospective employee to his new employer. Yet if John and Annie are unable to understand this deeper meaning, then it is hard to say that the tale has been successful. In pursuing this line of inquiry, I am not suggesting that Julius is without verbal resources, or that his jostling with John over how to run the vineyard is without consequences. Rather, *The Conjure Woman* repeatedly invites the reader to inquire with care into what exactly those consequences are. Late-nineteenth-century critics of realism complained that realist texts prized descriptive, even scientific, "analysis" to the detriment of narrative "storytelling." Through the frame of these tales, Chesnutt has crafted a volume that offers a meditation upon the process through which realist texts offered the ethnographic product of culture to an audience for analysis. Regardless of the respect and sympathy the reader might gain for Julius over the course of *The Conjure Woman,* the very form of the book reinforces the distance between the stories that he tells and the actions in which John and Annie are engaged.

On the one hand, Chesnutt shows that verbal works such as Julius's offered victims of racism the opportunity to redefine the identity of their group as something other than biologically inferior; Julius, after all, is able to enter into an extended conversation with John and Annie because they want to hear "a new point of view—from the bottom" that they think Julius can provide. He is also able to use this method to secure a place (though a marginal one) in the new economic order, and even to preserve institutions such as the church in "Po' Sandy." Nevertheless, the same aesthetic stance of John and Annie that creates Julius's opportunity to speak also limits what they will hear. As Ben Slote has argued, by stressing that John and Annie are interested in Julius's stories only as connoisseurs of an entertaining alterity, *The Conjure Woman* "predicts and even indicts" the trivialization of the post-Reconstruction experiences of African Americans that would deepen after the turn of the century. The stories of the volume cannot arrest this process, in turn, because they participate in a framework that marks them as subjective interpretations of the world and separates them from "objective" observers like John and Annie; a figure such as Julius—like Remus, an elder who has mastered the craft of storytelling— stands somewhere in between. The very division that creates the distance necessary for John, Annie, and most of Chesnutt's readers to regard the culturally other in an aesthetic manner also prevents them from presuming a shared social history.[53]

The shape of Chesnutt's writing career suggests that he felt these limitations of the ethnographic culture concept and its place in the literary depiction of African Americans. While *The Wife of His Youth and Other Stories of the Color Line* (1899) could be characterized as depicting the culture of a particular stratum of society, none of the novels he composed in the years that followed took up the documentation of culture—of songs, stories, beliefs particular to a group—in the way that *The Conjure Woman* did. When Chesnutt tried to write a novel that would rival *Uncle Tom's Cabin* in popularity and political impact, he produced *The Marrow of Tradition* (1901), a work much more conversant with the concept of biologically inherited race than with the idea of socially constructed culture.[54] In describing events modeled on an 1898 race riot in Wilmington, North Carolina, *The Marrow of Tradition* centers upon what Chesnutt called "the fate of the child of a proud old family related by an unacknowledged tie to the family of a colored doctor."[55] The etymological roots of the word "race" are entangled with those of the word "generation," an overlapping of meaning that becomes visible in *Marrow*, both a racial and a generational drama.[56] Biological ties govern the narrative of the novel from its opening episode, in which the white Olivia Carteret lies ill after being profoundly disturbed by seeing her mulatta half-sister, the wife of the "colored doctor," walking along the street, to its closing scene, in which Olivia begs the half-sister for forgiveness so that her husband will attend to Olivia's ill child. In contrast to the stories of *The Conjure Woman*, this novel relies upon the biological connections between parents and children to tell the story of what it means to belong to a particular group.

In arguing that *The Marrow of Tradition* can be characterized as placing biological race at the center of its narrative logic, I am not claiming that the book is complicit with the racial prejudice and violence that it clearly deplores. Rather, my contention is that by making genealogy and inheritance so central to the plot, Chesnutt has largely abandoned the vocabulary of culture, with its emphasis on tangible phenomena that attach aesthetic value to group-based differences, for the vocabulary of race. Howells's *Rise of Silas Lapham*, for instance, seems very much about the genealogical division between the Lapham and Corey families, as I described in the previous chapter. However, Howells's novel in fact recasts the difference as a product of culture, of social and aesthetic forces rather than biological ones. The characters and narrator of *Marrow*, on the other hand, do not attempt the same compromise between biological identity and the social construction of culture; they rely upon race exclusively to explain group difference. Chesnutt's characters and narrator repeatedly invoke the importance of "blood" as a metaphorical way of speaking about the biological divisions that form the cornerstone of racist ideology. They speak of "the value of good blood" (29), the fact that "blood would tell" (102), the aphorism that "blood is thicker than water" (66 and 262). Chesnutt has crafted the novel to show the flaws of such race-based manners of speaking about heritage—"blood" does not "tell" anything about the superiority or inferiority of a character—but he does so by deploying racial theories of group identity in an ironic manner rather than by articulating an alternative to race.

In the transition from *The Conjure Woman* to *The Marrow of Tradition*, a shift that includes his novel of miscegenation and racial passing, *The House Behind the Cedars* (1900), Chesnutt's writing moves away from the synchronic description associated with the documentation of culture and toward diachronic narration. Or, in the terms of realism's critics, Chesnutt rejects "analysis" and embraces "storytelling." *The Conjure Woman* contains the storytelling performances of Julius and, through its frame, encourages an analytic engagement with them. The result is a volume that does not rely upon a single, overarching narrative structure but rather upon a series of problems resulting from two different manners of perceiving the world.[57] *The Marrow of Tradition*, in contrast, is a heavily plotted novel oriented

around a social history of the "Wellington" race riots. It begins by expli-
cating the genealogical and historical background of the families at its center, then develops several plot lines that intersect (helped by an occasional
Dickensian coincidence) with increasing frequency as the book proceeds
toward a unified narrative of the white supremacist coup and the subsequent climactic violence. This plot, moreover, depends upon biological
genealogy as a device for uniting a diversity of characters and illuminat-
ing the political context in which the suppression of African Americans
occurred. The novel relies upon ideas about race, in other words, as the
foundation of its narrative structure.

Notably, the one scene in which Chesnutt returns to the ethnographic
mode of describing difference reveals the depth of his dissatisfaction with
it. In the chapter entitled "The Cakewalk," Chesnutt describes the visit of
Northerners who have come to "Wellington" to find, like John and Annie
of *The Conjure Woman*, both outlets for economic investment and information about the "social conditions" of the South. Before they leave the
city, the management of the hotel in which they are staying decides to offer
them "a little diversion, in the shape of a genuine negro cakewalk," so that
the visitors will leave with "a pleasing impression of Southern customs,
and particularly of the joyous, happy-go-lucky disposition of the Southern
darky" (115–16). Eric J. Sundquist's extended analysis of this incident in
Marrow explains how, by the time Chesnutt wrote *The Marrow of Tradition*, the cakewalk—a promenade of couples executing elaborate steps to
music—had come to be considered an artifact of "genuine" plantation
culture and had achieved widespread popularity in performances by both
black entertainers and white ones in blackface. Like Harris's popular dialect stories, the cakewalk at once afforded African American expression the
opportunity to gain a wider audience and provided whites the chance to
reinscribe "the forms and hierarchies of a clearly defined racial order."[58]

In his depiction of the cakewalk, Chesnutt takes pains to show how the
production of ethnographic culture, instead of being a vehicle to promote
cross-racial tolerance and understanding, could be staged in the service of
apologists for racial inequality. Equally notable, Chesnutt's white character
Tom Delamere not only participates in the cakewalk, in stolen clothes and
a blackened face, but wins the competition. This role-playing calls into
question the valorization of the authentic at the core of the predisposition
of literary realism for ethnographic description. Tom's impersonation of
a black man, Sandy, results first in Sandy's expulsion from his church
and later in Sandy's arrest. This chain of events demonstrates one risk of
recording group-based identity through the observation of culture in the

absence of well-defined standards of equality. An enterprise at the heart of literary realism and ethnography, the documentation of complex cultural forms—stories, songs, religion—could be satirized, simplified, and impersonated, to make these social markers of group-difference a way of not just identifying groups, but also of evaluating their relative worth.

This danger explains why a figure like Paul Laurence Dunbar has occupied such a precarious position within the criticism of African American literature over the last century; his dialect poetry treads the line between a complex aesthetic engagement with vernacular traditions and the caricature of those same traditions.[59] In his autobiography, *Along This Way* (1933), James Weldon Johnson encapsulated a century of Dunbar criticism by presenting him as an unfortunate casualty of the dialect tradition that prevented him from writing what "he really wanted." Though Johnson writes that Dunbar had brought to dialect poetry "the fullest measure of charm, tenderness, and beauty it could hold," he stresses that it was a "limited medium" with its tradition of painting "humorous, contented, or forlorn 'darkies' in standardized colors against a conventional Arcadian background of log cabins and cottonfields," a picture similar to what the "Wellington" whites in Chesnutt's *Marrow* hope their northern visitors will see.[60]

Dunbar continues to puzzle his readers, but he undoubtedly holds a less prominent position in the current study of American writing than does his contemporary, Chesnutt, even though Dunbar enjoyed at least equal regard in his own day.[61] These disparate critical fortunes may result, in part, from the differing roles that culturalist documentation played in the corpus of each author. Dunbar was rewarded in his own time when he offered cultural material in a way that could be interpreted through an emerging culturalist paradigm, but readers have since been made uneasy by the degree to which this paradigm was still dependent on hierarchical measurements of group-based difference. Chesnutt, meanwhile, has been installed into the canon of American letters because he more visibly displayed ambivalence and even skepticism toward the project of textualizing culture. Dunbar, for instance, purports to reproduce "An Ante-bellum Sermon" in the frequently reprinted poem of that name; Chesnutt portrays the northern tourists of *Marrow* being led to hear an African American preacher who regularly attracted white audiences with "an oft-repeated sermon intended to demonstrate that the earth was flat like a pancake" (116). Although Dunbar's poem illustrates the difficulty of reproducing vernacular traditions for a mainstream audience, Chesnutt's sharp indictment of the way that whites could shrewdly cast certain strands of African American expression as "authentic" compels greater attention.

The cakewalk episode in *Marrow* not only continues that indictment, but even more dramatically demonstrates how models of group-based difference can have widespread and even violent repercussions for the groups in question. Tom Delamere's masquerade nearly costs Sandy his life and contributes to the tension that erupts at the conclusion of the novel. By using the cakewalk to set such events in motion, Chesnutt signals his ultimate preference for engaging the logic of biological race to risking the descriptive vocabulary of culture. His efforts to uncover the fiction of racial identity, though, were not entirely dissimilar from the efforts of anthropological proponents of the culture concept. Like Chesnutt, Franz Boas devoted concerted energy during the first decade of the twentieth century to wrestling with popular beliefs about racial inheritance. Just as Chesnutt used *Marrow* to show the dangers of relying on the logic of "blood," Boas and his students conducted studies of Indian, immigrant, and African American head forms to show that long-held anthropological truths about the stability and importance of physical race were not valid.[62] Both Chesnutt and Boas suggested at least once that racial prejudice in the United States might be resolved by a future of "complete race-amalgamation" (to use Chesnutt's phrase) that would render racial discrimination impossible.[63] What Chesnutt did not finally share was Boas's optimism that culture "in the wide ethnographic sense" was a useful and necessary alternative to the racial theories that bring the white characters of *Marrow*—like their real-life counterparts—to injure and kill those they think different from themselves.

Chesnutt employs the description of the carefully-staged cakewalk in *Marrow* to ironically reinscribe the old master-slave hierarchy—showing that he understood the crucial limit of the cultural concept, its inability to incorporate change. The disjunction between the antebellum past and the post-Reconstruction present that appeared in the works of Page, Harris, and Dunbar was not simply nostalgia; rather, it was also the product of a descriptive framework capable of producing only an episodic history. As this chapter and the previous one suggest, those who employed the ethnographic model of culture often did so because it could serve as a distinct alternative to the developmental narrative of racial and social evolution. But what ethnography, whether in literature or in social science, sacrificed was an alternative narrative structure capable of articulating historical transformations in a compelling way. For Chesnutt, this shortcoming played a role in his leaving behind the descriptive techniques related to culture, even though the ethnographic imperative had been crucial to the establishment of his writing career.

Chesnutt's corpus illustrates how authors of realist literature employed the vocabulary of ethnography in a confusing and even contradictory way, but the fact that they so often returned to the observation, description, and analysis of verbal artifacts to illuminate group-based differences demonstrates the power of the culture concept in an age trying to reconcile ideals of equality with a frequently disturbing diversity. Ethnographers were likewise forced to wrestle with these questions of narrative and meaning as they documented the complexity of Native American cultures on the written page during the last two decades of the nineteenth century. These social scientists laboring in the field of cultural anthropology were confronted by the same problem that Chesnutt faced: how to incorporate change while simultaneously articulating an integrity essential for a group identity. The mass violence of *Marrow* indicates the enormity of the stakes in these debates about identity, something that the ethnographer James Mooney, the subject of the following chapter, understood all too well.

4

Searching for the "Real" Indian: Ethnographic Realism and James Mooney's *Ghost-Dance Religion*

"Whatever else an ethnography does," states James Clifford, in a well-known discussion of the discipline of anthropology, "it translates experience into text."[1] The treatment of ethnography as a practice of writing has become a critical reflex since Clifford and other anthropologists drew upon post-structuralist literary theory in the 1980s to reexamine the methodology and practice of their field. Clifford's comment, in fact, appears in a book that makes this point by spelling out the etymological roots of "ethnography" itself in its title, "Writing Culture." By inquiring into the place of writing in their profession, the anthropologists contributing to this volume aimed to address the historical constraints of ethnography as a textual activity claiming to represent scientific fact. In his essay, Clifford argues that one such set of constraints has arisen from the conceptualization of ethnography as a salvage project (an imperative shared by those literary realists documenting culture in the late nineteenth century). The textualization of culture, he writes, too often proceeds from the unquestioned assumption that cultures must be recorded in an archive because their existence is endangered; ethnography becomes, therefore, the representation of a "disappearing object"—culture—presumed to vanish at the moment of its inscription on the page.[2]

The insight that Clifford offered in this essay has been foundational to my discussion of ethnographic texts, yet it raises the possibility of dismissing the textual history of ethnographic writing in the late-nineteenth-century United States as a hegemonic gesture devoid of any meaningful intellectual engagement. To ignore these works for being produced with the ultimate goal of salvaging a "disappearing object," however, would be to lose a crucial and complicated chapter in the history of writing that attempts to address the diversity of lived experience in the United States. This textual history, moreover, extends across disciplinary boundaries. Ethnographic writing occurred without, as well as within, professional anthropology; ethnographic texts published under the aegis of literary realism can help us to understand better the nuances of the attempts at "writing culture" within anthropology. In particular, literary realism foregrounds the pivotal role of narrative in the documentation of culture. The narrative organization of knowledge affects how we interpret cultural difference, whether an ethnography relies upon a highly narrativized model of cultural evolution or upon the more static, less narrativized model of Boasian particularism.

In the second half of this chapter, I focus on a single work of late-nineteenth-century ethnography, James Mooney's *The Ghost-Dance Religion and the Sioux Outbreak of 1890* (1896), to show the narrative complexity of a text that follows neither the evolutionary nor the Boasian model precisely. Mooney's work demonstrates that it was possible for the narrative structure of ethnography to index the dissonance that results from a confrontation with the disciplinary paradigm described by Clifford: the formulation of culture as a "disappearing object." For even while the salvage imperative structured the enterprise of ethnography, a work of ethnographic writing itself could register the perseverance—what Gerald Vizenor calls the "survivance"—of indigenous peoples living within the borders of the United States.[3] Writing culture was a widespread activity in the late nineteenth century, and while it often made silent judgments that reflected the inequities of power within American society, it also fostered the creation of texts that questioned those same inequities in nuanced ways.

Mooney's *Ghost-Dance Religion* came at the end of a century in which the ethnographic description of American Indians was a widespread endeavor. But the writing of culture as a scientific practice had entered a dramatically new phase in 1879, when the United States Congress appropriated $20,000 for a national Bureau of Ethnology, the first professional institution in the United States devoted to the textual documentation of cultural diversity. The Bureau, later renamed the Bureau of *American Ethnology*, was charged with the task of "completing and preparing for publication the *Contributions to North American Ethnology*, under the Smithsonian Institution," and the texts that it produced represented the most thorough and painstaking effort to detail the minutiae of the lives of indigenous North American peoples to date.[4] Under the direction of John Wesley Powell, a Civil War veteran and geologist, the period of the Bureau's greatest influence and achievement coincided with both the literary movement of American realism and the successful advocacy of a policy agenda known as "Indian reform."

The implications of the relationship between the research produced by the Bureau, literary realism, and the so-called "Indian Question" were perhaps most dramatically presaged in 1882, when the first of a series of articles announcing the arrival of a new ethnography appeared on the pages of the *Century*. Frank Hamilton Cushing's "My Adventures in Zuñi," published in three parts over the next year, was the first work to bring before the general public the efforts of the new government-sponsored effort to reproduce Native American life upon the page. The flamboyant Cushing (1857–1900), a Smithsonian scientist in his mid-twenties when these articles appeared, had lived among the Zuni Indians for more than two years, and his "Adventures" were part of a public relations campaign to win support for extending his stay even further.[5]

Similar to John of Charles Chesnutt's *Conjure Woman*, or to the unnamed narrator of Sarah Orne Jewett's *Country of the Pointed Firs*, Cushing's narrative persona stands as a reporter and interpreter of a social world that does not wholly include him. "My Adventures," in fact, is as much about the struggles of the scientist to record knowledge as it is about the people of the Zuni (or A:shiwi) pueblo themselves. The stakes of this process, and how much they resemble the tenets of American literary realism, become apparent in an exchange between Cushing and the Zuni "governor," his host. When Cushing explains that he wishes to remain at the pueblo "to write all about his children, the Zuñis, and to sketch their dances and dresses," the governor expresses frustration and bewilderment:

> "Hai!" said the old man. "Why does Washington want to know about our *Kâ-Kâ* [a sacred society]? The Zuñis have their religion and the Americans have theirs."
>
> [Cushing replied,] "Do you want Washington to be a friend to the Zuñis? How do you expect a people to like others without knowing something about them? Some fools and bad men have said 'the Zuñis

have no religion.' It is because they are always saying such things of some Indians, that we do not understand them. Hence, instead of all being brothers, we fight."[6]

Cushing's answer recalls William Dean Howells's guiding maxim that realist literature should show how "men are more like than unlike." The ethnographer argues that the future survival of the Zunis depends upon his ability to render the differences between their religion and that of "Washington" in terms that Washington will understand. He must not only make the "fools and bad men" there realize that the Zunis *have* religion, but must do so in a manner that makes Washington accept the continuance of Zuni religious practices. Yet it is necessary for him to perform this task only because Zuni culture appears so "unlike" Washington's. This simultaneous reassurance of human similarity and emphasis on group distinction typifies not only the ethnographic work of figures like Cushing, but also the regionalist and local color literature of writers like Burnett, Jewett, Cable, and Dunbar. The writing of culture—the sum of what Cushing observes and records about the Zunis—creates the possibility of asserting these two apparently contradictory principles, and this discursive project, according to "My Adventures," is most profitably undertaken by the professional ethnographer trained to see and interpret the mysterious details of a foreign way of life.

The appearance of "My Adventures" in the *Century* illustrates how this profit was not entirely scientific. Brad Evans has persuasively argued that Cushing's publication in the *Century*, as well as the contemporary publication of articles by and about Cushing in the *Atlantic* and *Harper's Monthly*, places Cushing firmly within the late-nineteenth-century tradition of connoisseurship of the rural and the exotic by urban, primarily white, upper-class readers.[7] While the Zunis' survival, according to Cushing, might be contingent upon letting Washington (as well as New York and Boston) know about them, what the readers of these magazines received in exchange was entertainment in the form of specialized scientific knowledge. In other words, the articles were the print equivalent of the trip by several Zunis to Boston and Washington that Cushing arranged during this period, a trip with performances that delighted upper-class purveyors of culture and garnered support for the Zunis and Cushing's work among them. In both the *Century* articles and the tour, Cushing presented pieces of scientific information about Zuni culture as aesthetic objects for the pleasure of his audience, all with the purpose of winning further support for his research. The visits of Cushing and the Zunis to institutions of higher learning and

philanthropy was a highbrow version of the more sensationalist performances by Indians that P. T. Barnum had once provided in his American
Museum, as well as of those that William F. Cody, at nearly the same
moment in the 1880s, was beginning to stage in his Wild West shows.[8]
Charles F. Lummis, who would later play a pivotal role in promoting the
U.S. Southwest as a tourist destination, recalled Cushing's ability to strike
the right balance between education and amusement: "Never was [a] tour
more skillfully managed. Perhaps never was another quite so curiously
mixed between genuine scholarship and the arts of the showman."[9]

Efforts like Cushing's conveyed appreciation for the complexity and
integrity of Native American ways of living, but also made it difficult for
most Americans to understand how these ways of living could be viable
in their own modern industrial age except as a quaint reminder of a distant past. Cushing's writing contributes to this difficulty by relying on
two competing paradigms for understanding culture, a framework of cultural particularism similar to the Boasian model that dominated American
anthropology in the 1920s and 1930s, and the model of cultural evolution
that still held sway in the late nineteenth century.[10] As Joan Mark has
observed, Cushing referred to the plural "cultures" even before Boas did,
suggesting that, like Boas, Cushing did not see "culture" as a single, unilinear process of development through evolutionary stages but, instead,
hoped to interpret each culture in its own terms.[11] However, Cushing also
argued in the 1880s that the ancestors of the Zunis were, "with slightest
variation of detail and background," the same as "the progenitors of every
civilization on the globe today"—one of several comments that employ
the logic of cultural evolution.[12] While the sheer quantity of ethnographic
data about Zuni culture that Cushing recorded and published in the
1880s demonstrates the necessity of regarding cultures as separate and
particular entities, Cushing could not resist characterizing the Zunis as
simply belonging to an earlier stage of cultural development than those
who would read about them in the *Century*.

This confusion about culture in Cushing's public writings mattered
because these were not solely scientific questions related to the professional
production of knowledge. During the late nineteenth century, the notion
of culture as an evolutionary ladder also fit perfectly with the conviction of reformers that Indians could "progress" from lowly "barbarism" to
the achievement of "civilization."[13] These East Coast based, mostly Protes-
tant "Friends of the Indian" made accurate observation the cornerstone
of their efforts to solve the "Indian question" and to integrate Native
Americans into their version of American citizenship.[14] As a leading figure

in the movement for "Indian reform" put it to his colleagues, "Perhaps our work ... might be epitomized in the phrase letting go the Indian of romance, and learning what the *real Indian* is" (emphasis added).[15] Like literary realists and scientific ethnographers, reformers inveighed against the inflated emotions, those too hateful and those too compassionate, engendered by the "entertaining" misrepresentations of the past, and contended that a factual, unsentimental mimesis produced by dispassionate scrutiny would be necessary to solve the problems raised by the diversity of the nation.

In the United States, the most articulate and influential proponent of the evolutionary version of culture so important to the reformers was Lewis Henry Morgan, whose 1877 book *Ancient Society* incorporated his previous work on Iroquois social organization. Like E. B. Tylor, Morgan worked from a developmental model of human history, and his work delivered what its subtitle promised: "researches in the lines of human progress from savagery through barbarism to civilization."[16] Morgan spelled out what each of his stages (savagery, barbarism, and civilization) entailed and divided them further until he was satisfied that he could pin tribal groups with a particular classification. "The Australians and the greater part of the Polynesians when discovered," for example, were at the "Middle Status of Savagery"; on the other hand, "the Grecian tribes of the Homeric ages, the Italian tribes shortly before the founding of Rome, and the Germanic tribes of the time of Cæsar" could all be confidently placed in the "Upper Status of Barbarism."[17]

In spite of the global implications of the book, among the most attentive members of its audience were those who, like Morgan himself, were primarily devoted to the study of American Indians. Bureau of American Ethnology director Powell, for example, suggested that he would take it on all his future trips into the field.[18] This final work by Morgan—he died shortly after *Ancient Society* was published—also found favor among the Indian reform organizations beginning to take shape. While it is doubtful that all, or even most, reformers actually read *Ancient Society*, the book established the fundamental principle that their organizations took as their premise: "barbarous" or even "savage" peoples could progress along the same path toward "civilization" that Europe's ancestors had travelled. As Gail Bederman has shown, this late-nineteenth-century rhetoric of civilization could be used both to reinscribe biological categories of difference and to undermine them by emphasizing patterns of behavior essentially social in nature.[19] In an age that presumed that certain races had greater potential for achievement than others, Morgan's claims about the uniformity of culture as a process encompassing all of humanity could not be made easily or taken lightly. Although it relied on older ideas of inherited racial difference, this developmental model of progress opened the door to a kind of cultural constructivism, an idea that groups are malleable in their social identities. This notion that culture could be remade, and could remake people, was precisely what inspired the Americanization strategies of the Indian reform organizations.

The desire for a new understanding of assimilation flourished during this era, as a result of concerns that extended well beyond indigenous America. The last two decades of the century were years in which Americans increasingly voiced fears about the nation's ability to assimilate the "rising flood of immigration" from southern and eastern Europe, which one statistician likened to "an invasion in comparison with which the invasions under which Rome fell were no more than a series of excursion parties."[20] Against such a backdrop, the Americanization of indigenous peoples became something of a test case, and the reservation a laboratory in which reformers could conduct experiments of assimilation.[21]

Reformers often emphasized the relatively small number of "reservation Indians" to suggest that the "Indian Question" ought to be easier to solve than either the "Negro Problem" or the "Immigrant Question":

> I suppose it to be true that the number of Indians in this country does not vary to-day very much from what it was when our fathers landed at Plymouth Rock—300,000, I think, or thereabouts—in a land in which more than 50,000,000 of people have sprung up speaking the English language, rejoicing in a civilization that otherwise was irresistible, ready to sacrifice life or any amount of treasure or enjoyment for the accomplishment of its purpose, and yet struggling with the question, What will you do with 300,000 Indians? and yet unable to answer it.[22]

During the 1880s, the decade these remarks of Senator Henry L. Dawes were published, 5.2 million immigrants would arrive in the United States, nearly double the immigration total of the previous decade.[23] The nation was simultaneously struggling to come to terms with a free African American population estimated in 1880 to be more than 6.5 million.[24] If the country could not cope with 300,000 Indians, how would it be able to deal with these millions? While, on the one hand, reformers always considered the Indians a "special" case—possessing particular claims as the original inhabitants of the continent, and, like African Americans, racially distinct from Americans of European ancestry—the broader question about the ability of the nation to attend to and manage difference always lurked beneath the surface efforts of Dawes and his fellow Indian reform advocates.

The solutions that Dawes and others proposed in the last two decades of the nineteenth century consisted of a series of legislative reforms revolving around land, law, and education. Through this agenda, organizations like the Indian Rights Association and the Lake Mohonk Conference of Friends of the Indian hoped to erase the historical and cultural differences that separated indigenous peoples from white, native born Americans. What may be most remarkable about the Indian reform groups of the late nineteenth century is the success they enjoyed in pursuing their legislative goals. The crown jewel of these victories was the General Allotment Law of 1887, commonly referred to as the Dawes Act in honor of its Senate sponsor. The act empowered the president to select unilaterally those reservations to undergo "allotment," a practice whereby communal land would be divided into individual parcels, generally 160 acres to heads of families, 80 acres to single persons, and 40 acres to other family members. The land was to be held "in trust" by the U.S. government for twenty-five years, after which the allottees or their heirs would receive the fee simple title to the land. The surplus reservation land would then be sold to others, thereby satisfying both Westerners and railroad companies eager for new land and those Indian reformers who believed it beneficial for Indians to intermingle with whites regularly.[25] The General Allotment Law was the culmination of a trend in American Indian policy that began in the first half of the century and that included several treaties granting allotments to individual tribes.[26] Between 1887 and 1934, when Congress formally recognized allotment as a failure and passed the Indian Reorganization Act, nearly 90 million acres of the 138 million acres of the reservation land in the United States passed into non-Indian hands.[27]

Enthusiasm for allotment began to wane slowly at the turn of the century, though it remained widespread for another twenty years. (The government allotted the most land during the years between 1900 and 1921.)[28] In the 1880s, however, reformers believed that individual land ownership could teach Indians to be "civilized" Americans, and they took this pedagogical quality of land ownership as an article of faith. Morgan's *Ancient Society* had focused on the evolution of ideas surrounding property and inheritance as crucial to the development of modern society. "It is impossible to overestimate the influence of property in the civilization of mankind," he wrote.[29] Reservations, conversely, were believed by Indian reform organizations to perpetuate "the ancient social organization of the Indian tribes," to subject individual Indians to the tyranny of tribal chiefs and

Indian Office agents, and to prevent "the establishment of the family, with its legal rights over property."[30]

Indian reform simultaneously memorialized and erased the presence of Native peoples within the United States during a period when certain ways of life regularly were marked as necessary sacrifices to the progress of the nation. The perceived innocence of American Indians as victims of a "century of dishonor" was crucial to this figuration, for it enabled the reformers to lament the passing of Native peoples into history while placing this event in a frame of inevitability.[31] Through the documentation of their cultures, Indians could be enshrined as part of the premodern past of the nation, the first stage of its evolution toward industrial civilization. The violence that Native peoples suffered was regrettable but part of that historical narrative; in such a formulation, Indians *as* Indians had no future. The actions of the Friends of the Indian coalesced as national narrative acts of remembering and forgetting.[32] For although the reformers hoped to Americanize the Indian, to "forget once and forever the word 'Indian' and all that it has signified in the past," they simultaneously reinscribed the figure of the Indian as part of a history of conquest, exploitation, and degradation.[33] In the narrative gap between the "blind, helpless, ignorant" Indians of the past (to use Henry Dawes's description),[34] and the successfully Americanized Indians-who-are-Indians-no-longer, fell, of course, actual people of indigenous ancestry who were unrepresented and unrepresentable except insofar as they engaged these stories of the nation's past and present.

Yet the professional writers of culture during this period sought precisely this goal of accurate representation, the portrayal of American Indians in a painstakingly complete manner that rendered all the complexities of tribal life. Many of these ethnographers, unsurprisingly, rearticulated the narrative model I have been describing by casting tribal cultures as inevitably "disappearing" and preserved only on their pages. In fact, several anthropologists—including Cushing, Powell, and Alice Fletcher—openly supported the reformers' agenda of Americanization.[35] Not everyone working in ethnography, though, wholeheartedly accepted the project of assimilation, and the ethnographic texts produced during this period could also employ the realist detachment of professional observation to document tribal life in a way not wholly conforming with a narrative of unavoidable vanishing. Such works may not have ultimately prevailed in diverting the allegiance of ethnography from the salvage paradigm; however, in changing the narrative structure of their documentation, these works insisted that their readers apprehend Native cultures in more challenging and provocative ways than usually allowed by the principles of cultural evolution. In so doing, ethnographies could shift anthropology toward a more pluralistic definition of culture and herald new ways of reading Native American oral expression transcribed to the written page.

The Ethnographic Imagination and the Bureau of American Ethnology

In spite of the approbation they sometimes received from members of the scientific establishment, proponents of Indian reform took a dim view of anthropologists, whom they generally dismissed as a sentimental, romantic lot preferring "the Indian kept in his original paint and feathers" for the sake of scientific curiosity.[36] Reformers believed that social scientists had failed to come to grips with the necessity of assimilation for Native Americans. "I am not at all sure that . . . the scientific desire to preserve the Indian animal for study, is not a further impediment to his civilization," a speaker at the 1886 Lake Mohonk Conference of the Friends of the Indian remarked.[37] Sixteen years later, Richard Henry Pratt attacked the existence of the Bureau of American Ethnology by ridiculing its research goals: "What particular benefit would it be if we knew their [the Indians'] origin? And what possible influence upon the welfare of the country or of the Indians themselves could it have if we knew all the music and all the modes and methods and every feature of the old Indian life?"[38]

John Wesley Powell recognized the necessity of being able to answer such questions, and he promoted a government-sponsored anthropology more attuned to the reformers' goals than someone like Pratt probably realized. Powell was a largely self-trained geologist who became a national hero after his exploration of the Grand Canyon in the late 1860s. During the 1870s, Powell gradually shifted his interest from the study of the lands of the western United States to the study of their indigenous inhabitants.[39] In 1879, Powell lobbied Congress for the creation of a new kind of government survey, one that would measure and record the qualities of the indigenous peoples of the nation and that would, like the geological surveys he had directed, produce a series of published volumes. The resulting institution, the Bureau of American Ethnology, was Powell's creation, and he would oversee it until his death in 1902.

Powell conceived his geological and geographic studies so that they would yield conclusions with immediate policy implications, and he wanted his work related to Native American peoples to be no different. Throughout his tenure at the Bureau, Powell stressed the importance of producing "results that would be of practical value in the administration of Indian affairs."[40] Although these results included information on population size, habits, and language of use to the military, Powell also believed the Bureau's work could play a role in the project of assimilation pursued by the "Friends of the Indian" reformers. Heavily influenced by Lewis Henry Morgan's evolutionary, stagist narrative of cultural history, Powell believed in what Frank Hamilton Cushing would later call "the need of studying the Indian in order to teach him."[41] Powell wrote in an 1880 letter:

> If we are to conduct our Indian affairs wisely and induct our barbaric tribes into the ways and institutions of civilization that the red man may become completely under our government and share in its benefits, the first step to be taken is to acquire a knowledge of Indian tribal governments, religion, sociology and industrial institutions.[42]

Like the reformers, Powell believed that "letting go the Indian of romance, and learning what the real Indian is" was the first step in effecting American Indian social betterment. Powell chided those inclined "to overlook aboriginal vices and to exaggerate aboriginal virtues. It seems to be forgotten that after all the Indian is a savage, with the characteristics of a savage, and he is exalted even above the civilized man."[43] Sentimentality, according to Powell, would help neither "the Indian" nor the ethnographer.

For Powell, the most crucial component to discovering what he referred to as "the laws of acculturation" was the study of language.[44] When the Bureau was founded, Powell acquired for it a collection of more than six hundred linguistic vocabularies that had been in the possession of the Smithsonian, and he emphasized the acquisition of still more language manuscripts. The collection became the most important physical item held by the Bureau.[45] Powell shared the belief that motivated the literary realists' interest in dialect and became a crucial principle of early-twentieth-century Boasian anthropology as well, a belief in the importance of the exact reproduction of language and in the possibility that this reproduction could convey the precise sense of how groups differed from one another.[46] He wrote in one early Bureau report that language could provide "the key to [the] most interesting and otherwise undiscoverable anthropologic facts," including the development of Native American institutions, the history of their migrations, and their psychology.[47] Linguistic classification, according to Powell's longtime assistant and eventual successor WJ McGee,[48] could even yield insight into a group's prospects for assimilation:

[Linguistic] classification affords a means of measuring the susceptibility of the various tribes to civilization, to education, and to arrangement on reservations in harmonious groups. The classification is thus essentially practical.[49]

A language-based theory of identity seemed to run counter to a biologically-based one, and it also provided a more tangible way of defining the essence of group identities. In the late nineteenth century, language manuscripts were much easier to physically possess and to examine than were genetic markers of ancestry; vocabularies could be collected, measured, and analyzed just as physical anthropologists had been doing with skulls and skeletons for more than half a century. Powell and McGee did not change the paradigm of descent-based identity (biological race) to a behaviorally-based one (socially-constructed culture), but rather conflated the two by mapping the newer model onto the older. Thus language signified biological racial difference in almost the same way that skin color did, as an imprecise marker of biological history and differentiation. Language became the most important item of cultural property that a people could possess; it was the ethnographer's job to gather it, to categorize it, and to interpret how to use it to elevate that people to a "higher" state of culture. One of Powell's major achievements as Bureau director, in fact, was a linguistic map of North America, published in 1891 and exhibited at the 1893 World's Exposition in Chicago.[50]

The project of correlating languages and "civilizations" would do more than help anthropology determine where the "real" Indians stood on the culture ladder. As David Murray points out, the study of indigenous languages in the nineteenth century presumed that they offered a window into the "pure" and "natural" state of uncivilized humanity writ large—humanity before the advent of artifice. As a corollary, these languages could reveal what barriers remained to the incorporation of American Indians (and their land) into the "civilization"of the United States.[51] Language could enable anthropologists to delineate what made Indians "Indian," and could therefore demarcate the cultural attributes that indigenous peoples would need to be divested of to stop being "Indian" and start being "American."

The documentation of linguistic difference in the hopes of discovering deeper patterns of group-based difference marks one point of contact between ethnography and literary realism in the late nineteenth century. The growing importance of professional observation in anthropology is another. At the Bureau's inception, anthropology operated under a deductive model that articulated the laws of human history and then applied those laws to collected data. The major theorists of anthropology (figures like Tylor and Morgan) were "armchair" anthropologists; they drew their conclusions by reading the reports of others who had actually come into contact with the peoples in question. Powell attempted to enact a comparable division of labor in the Bureau, similar to that employed in his earlier geological surveys. In this tradition, Curtis M. Hinsley writes, "the generalizing savant stood apart from the mass of data-collectors, whose labors constituted only the essential first stage of science." Despite this model of organization, the widespread popularity that Cushing, the young star of the Bureau's roster of fieldworkers, enjoyed in the early 1880s foreshadowed how those engaged in the "first stage" of scientific "exploration, observation, and collection" would soon displace those who limited their activities to "the higher tasks of synthesis."[52] Cushing's "My Adventures in Zuñi" positions the ethnographer as a figure with widespread appeal in an age that prized the experience of coming into contact with the remote and exotic: a scientifically-informed reporter uniquely qualified to comment upon the foreignness he (and occasionally she) witnessed. Moreover, the media in which Bureau ethnographers published their work—long Bulletins and even longer Annual Reports—meant that Bureau ethnographers had room to report observations on a single subject in impressive detail. This large-scale documentation of tribal life shifted the emphasis from deductive application of laws to inductive reasoning from the mass of data accumulated through fieldwork. The result was that the Bureau, in an unforeseen transition, gradually moved nearer to the Boasian disciplinary model of intensive efforts toward gathering ethnographic information from a single culture, and away from the generalizing, comparative approach used to formulate narratives of universal cultural evolution.

The career of James Mooney (1861-1921) unfolded in the midst of these changing expectations about ethnographic practice. Mooney's work provides an invaluable corpus through which to unravel the implications and variations of disciplinary methodology because, at the beginning of his career, Mooney's orientation neatly complemented Powell's own. Yet by the time that Mooney began to write *The Ghost-Dance Religion and the Sioux Outbreak of 1890*, the monograph that constituted the Bureau's fourteenth *Annual Report*, he had lost full confidence in Powell's evolutionary assumptions—and also, perhaps, in the methodology developed to accompany it. His writing reveals a deep awareness of the problems of documenting culture during a period in which the theoretical questions of cultural identity itself were at once unsettled and immediate in their political consequences. Though he could not transcend these questions, his ethnography makes them legible.

Mooney, the son of Irish immigrants, was born and raised in Indiana and had an affinity for collecting and designing taxonomic schemes long before he came to Washington to work for Powell's Bureau. In June 1882, as a twenty-two-year-old newspaper reporter, Mooney wrote to Powell asking for either work at the Bureau or a similar government position. What may have caught Powell's attention was the odd sort of experience that Mooney offered in place of more conventional training. In his letter, Mooney stated he had been studying the "local names, tribal relations and boundaries, linguistic affinities, and general histories of Indians of North and South America" for "about ten years." He had even begun compiling a synonymy, a list of variations of tribal names; he claimed he had collected synonymous names for over two thousand tribes. "I feel confident my ten years of preparation would enable me to do the work intelligently," he wrote.[53]

It took several more letters and two trips to Washington before Mooney was able to land a place in the Bureau. While the Bureau still predated a thoroughly professionalized discipline with uniform requirements in experience or academic training—only one of the early group of Bureau ethnologists had a university degree—most of its staff had some background in either science or government work.[54] Mooney had neither, save the volumes of notes he had written with youthful enthusiasm. When he started at the Bureau in 1885, it was as a volunteer. But he quickly proved his diligence and talent for detailed research by playing an important role in the completion of a project close to his personal interests—a fifty-five page synonymy, *A List of Linguistic Families of the Indian Tribes North of Mexico, with Provisional List of the Principal Tribal Names and Synonyms.* By August 1886, he received a full appointment as a Bureau ethnologist and was ready for fieldwork.[55] Over the next several years, Mooney conducted research among the Cherokees of North Carolina (often referred to by Mooney and others as the "Eastern Cherokees"), a tribal people in whom he had expressed interest in 1882 in his first letter to Powell. These efforts led to Mooney's first major publication, "The Sacred Formulas of the Cherokees" (1891).

Dramatic developments in the western United States would interrupt Mooney's efforts to extend further his research on the Cherokees. In November 1890, reports began to circulate in the national press about widespread, frenzied "ghost dancing" among the Western Indian tribes. According to such stories, Ghost Dance adherents preached that the return of the buffalo, the resurrection of Indian dead, and the restoration of Indian land were all imminent. The attention of the press throughout the United States quickly focused on the Sioux, who loomed large in the national imagination as a particularly bellicose, unregenerate people.[56] The Army feared that the religious revival, said to be connected to a "messiah" from the Far West, would lead to an armed uprising among the Lakotas, many of whom were dissatisfied with recent land cessions that the government had negotiated with them.[57] Rumors spread that Sitting Bull, whose notoriety had not diminished despite his tours with Cody's Wild West Show, would use the Ghost Dance as a cover for organizing a final military stand against the certainty of white incursion into Lakota territory. In 1890, many Americans were already beginning to view the western frontier with nostalgia; the U.S. Census pronounced it "closed" that year, a fact that Frederick Jackson Turner would popularize soon after with his "Frontier Thesis." The events on the Sioux reservation were therefore frequently cast in the popular press as the final act in the national melodrama of the vanishing Indian.[58] As one book capitalizing on the notoriety of the Ghost Dance put it, "The Indians are practically a doomed race, and none realize it better than themselves."[59]

The reporters who flocked to the reservations of South Dakota in the hopes that the Ghost Dance would be followed by a clash between the U.S. Army and the Sioux were not disappointed.[60] On December 15, 1890, an Indian policeman killed Sitting Bull during an attempt to arrest the leader on behalf of the United States government; the New York Times referred to Sitting Bull the next day as "the most unrelenting, the most hostile, the most sagacious, the most cruel, and the most desperate foe of the whites of any chief of modern times."[61] His death, however, did not bring the conflict to an end. The army continued to round up groups of Lakotas considered hostile. On December 28, troops from the Seventh Cavalry, Custer's former division, intercepted a band of Miniconjou Lakotas led by Big Foot on its way to the Pine Ridge Agency in South Dakota. The soldiers ordered the Miniconjous to halt and camp near Wounded Knee Creek. Tired and hungry, Big Foot's followers had long evaded the soldiers before accepting what had seemed a hospitable government offer to come to the agency; Big Foot himself was suffering from pneumonia and spent that night attended by a government physician. The next morning, with four Hotchkiss guns and hundreds of rifles trained on the Lakota camp, the soldiers began systematically seizing the Miniconjou weapons, and a scuffle broke out when one man refused to give up his rifle. That gun went off—probably inadvertently—and the ensuing bloodshed left, Mooney would later write, nearly three hundred Lakotas dead, including dozens of women and children trapped in a nearby ravine.[62] While twenty-five Army soldiers were also killed, even the New York Times, usually unsympathetic to Indians, remarked that "it would be an abuse of language" to refer to the encounter as a "battle."[63]

When the massacre at Wounded Knee occurred, James Mooney was on his way to the Indian Territory from Washington. He had originally intended to go there to conduct fieldwork among the Cherokees in the hope of corroborating his findings from North Carolina. He also planned to begin a study of the Kiowa language at Powell's request. News of the Ghost Dance and the Wounded Knee massacre, however, increased his Bureau research assignments. The Cheyennes and Arapahos of the Indian Territory were among the most devoted practitioners of the Ghost Dance, and Powell wanted Mooney to investigate.

Hunting Jack Rabbits: *The Ghost-Dance Religion and the Sioux Outbreak of 1890*

The eventual result of this research was Mooney's most prominent work, the most widely read publication of the Bureau of American Ethnology and one of the lasting contributions of nineteenth-century ethnography. First published in 1896, *The Ghost-Dance Religion and the Sioux Outbreak of 1890* still stands as the most complete ethnographic account of the Ghost Dance and its historical practice and, in the recent words of one eminent anthropologist, as "one of the greatest studies of an American Indian religion ever written—perhaps the greatest such."[64] It is a massive text, with nearly 650 pages of description, detail, and analysis. As an ethnographic work, *The Ghost-Dance Religion* demonstrates the possibilities of professional observation even as it illustrates the shortcomings of a methodology that derives its authority from its practitioners' attempts to represent the "real" Indian through a specific set of writing practices. Equally important, this ethnography makes it possible to understand the difficulty of describing group-based difference in an age in which the relationship of culture to narrative was the subject of an intellectual dispute with direct political repercussions.

Like many of the literary authors working to produce records of cultural difference, Mooney developed an apparatus for his text that addresses the need for both historicist structures of interpretation and the exact, detailed results of his own labors of observation. He divided *The Ghost-Dance Religion* into two sections, "the narrative" (comprising two-thirds of the work) and "the songs" (the other third). The first section uses the causal pattern of chronological narrative to explicate the Ghost Dance. The second, smaller section relates the particulars of the Ghost Dance songs as entities observed as though frozen in time. The story of the Ghost Dance, in other words, is followed by an effort to reproduce its components as accurately as possible through the medium of a written text.

Mooney's use of narrative in the Ghost Dance, moreover, presents a complex and remarkable innovation in late-nineteenth-century American ethnography. Within "the narrative," Mooney actually attempts to emplot (to use Hayden White's term) his subject inside several stories that fit together and resemble one another like the nesting dolls of a Russian *matrioshka*.[65] At the center of the narrative is the recent Lakota Ghost Dance; outside and homologous to that narrative are accounts of increasingly distant—both geographically and temporally—instances of similar prophetic leaders and religious revivals. Mooney includes among his examples the anonymous Delaware prophet of the eighteenth century who played a key role in Pontiac's pan-Indian military resistance (662–69), the birth of "Mohammedism" in the seventh century (930–32), Joan of Arc's "hallucinations" that led to her being burned at the stake in 1431 (932–35), and, closer to Mooney's time and place, the "epidemic of religious frenzy" among white and black Protestants in 1800, known as "the Kentucky revival" (942–44). In *The Ghost-Dance Religion*, Mooney does more, that is, than describe the recent events among the Sioux leading to the massacre at Wounded Knee; he documents the rise of the Ghost Dance within the larger scope of the various Western tribes who took it up; he provides a history of Native American prophecy and resistance to which he believes the Ghost Dance belongs; and, perhaps most interestingly, he tells a universal story of messianic vision and religious fervor that cuts across cultural and racial lines.

This narrative form, in which larger, more global narratives encircle smaller, more local ones, constitutes a careful strategy on Mooney's part to resist the evolutionary version of human history put forward by Lewis Henry Morgan and John Wesley Powell. To Morgan and Powell, the Ghost Dance would have been better described as a marker of a particular phase of cultural development, perhaps a last gasp of "barbarism." Evolutionary narratives move definitively *forward*. Mooney's work, with its circular narrative structure, has very little to say about progress. Mooney places the Ghost Dance of the North American Indians within the context of other religious movements in order to reject the widespread belief that the movement must necessarily be the result of something less than "civilization." On the one hand, Mooney's approach is not that of Boasian particularism, which would stress the necessity of interpreting the Ghost Dance, independent of these other religious movements, as the product of the individual cultures that practiced it. On the other hand, Mooney's narrative organization rejects the progressive model that Boas also repudiated, and so comes close to creating the kind of engagement with the Ghost Dance that the Boasian anthropologists might have called for.

This strategy comes at a price. While Mooney's account resists casting Ghost Dance adherents as ignorant barbarians and refuses to see the Wounded Knee massacre as the acceptable destruction of a backward race, the work's circular emplotment does not conceive of the people about whom he writes, either the Ghost Dancers or the government agents and soldiers who reacted so fearfully to them, as conscious, historical agents. In general, *The Ghost-Dance Religion and the Sioux Outbreak of 1890* can be characterized as a form of tragic realism—tragic because the text makes it difficult for the reader to see the suffering of the Lakota Ghost Dance worshippers as anything but inevitable. As in tragedy, the divide between the Lakotas and the U.S. government has but been widened through a series of terrible misunderstandings.[66] At the same time, the tone of the description and the narrative structure enforce a distance between the reader and these events that, as described in previous chapters, is characteristic of the realist documentation of group-based otherness. As in the classic works of American literary realism, the text treats the suffering of the protagonists as an unavoidable outcome and discourages the reader from moralizing about the resolution or responding with excessive emotion.[67] Mooney's monograph is engaged in a careful balancing act between the sympathy we must have with the Ghost Dance adherents to be interested in them as ethnographic subjects, and the dangers of the sentimentalism (in the form of either excessive sympathy or disdain for the victims of the massacre) against which his contemporaries inveighed. As a result, although the nature of the identity that the text fashions for its Native American differs from Tylor's race-inflected "culture," it presents other limitations. While Mooney refuses to place the Ghost Dance singers on a particular rung of the culture ladder, he also makes it difficult for the reader to imagine how these peoples might change their own cultures at all, for they seem caught in a web of cultural forces forever beyond their control.

Mooney's first chapter, "Paradise Lost," gestures toward the largest narrative frame of the text:

> The doctrines of the Hindu avatar, the Hebrew Messiah, the Christian millennium, and the Hesûnanin of the Indian Ghost dance are essentially the same, and have their origin in a hope and longing common to all humanity. (657)

As Cushing's "Adventures in Zuñi" demonstrates, one of the purposes that ethnography and literary realism shared during this period was the documentation of fundamental similarities between dissimilar groups; Mooney's comparison of the Ghost Dance to these other religious phenomena is akin to Cushing's desire to show "Washington" that the Zunis have a religion. However, anthropology (like literary realism) was also predicated upon the necessity of demonstrating how groups are *unlike* one another, and, during the 1890s, equating the Ghost Dance with early Christianity (or *any* Christianity) was sure to spark controversy. The so-called "Friends of the Indian" advocating the Americanization of Native peoples would have never hazarded such comparisons. In 1891, reformer Merrill Gates said that "the Dakota disaster shows that we shall not need to have taught us again the lesson of the difference between savagery and civilization.... We saw that for one brought up in the atmosphere of Christian civilization to enter the consciousness of the savage at such a time is almost as impossible as it is for us to get behind the great, blue, limpid eyes of the ox as he chews his cud in the pasture, and know how the world looks to him."[68] For Gates, the Ghost Dance dramatizes an inferior alterity that both necessitates the project of assimilation and embodies its ultimate challenges.

Gates's reaction reflects the stagist approach to human history that Mooney's transhistorical statements contravene. As one might expect, John Wesley Powell was skeptical of Mooney's position, and the Bureau director expressed his doubts in the introduction to the Annual Report that included *The Ghost-Dance Religion.* "It may be observed," Powell wrote, "that caution should be exercised in comparing or contrasting religious movements among civilized peoples with such fantasies as that described in the memoir; for while interesting and suggestive analogies may be found, the essential features of the movements are not homologous."[69] Despite Powell's disagreement with Mooney, he characterizes Mooney's emplotment accurately; *The Ghost-Dance Religion* does suggest a homology between what Powell refers to as the "fantasies" of the Sioux and other Ghost Dance adherents and the "more definite religious movements" of the Old World. The final chapter of the "narrative" section of the monograph, like the first chapter, is dedicated to just this purpose. "The human race is one in thought and action," Mooney observes before going on to discuss parallels among the Ghost Dance, "the biblical period," "Mohammedism," "Methodists," and others (928). To Powell, such a narrative must have smacked of naive romanticization resulting from excessive sympathy for the Indians; in the age of Indian reform, it seemed necessary to both reformers and ethnographers to take for granted certain inequalities between indigenous and "civilized" peoples. These inequalities, like the inequality of property relations within capitalist society, represented the difficult truths the recognition of which separated shrewd realists from soft sentimentalists. Powell's introduction accuses Mooney of just such sentimentalism.

Though *The Ghost-Dance Religion* does strive for cross-cultural homology, it does not rely on an appeal to universal emotion. Rather, its anti-sentimental bias stresses an alternative conception of what constitutes the genuine basis of culture—a conception that valorizes the comparison of material practices across cultural lines but downplays the individuality and power of religious spirituality. Powell and Gates believed Christianity not only the product of a sophisticated civilization, but also a civilizing influence. Mooney, conversely, suggests that all religious movements are equally deluding, that they all share the "fantasies" of the Ghost Dance. In this formulation, religion itself becomes part of the romance that the scientific monograph dispels. Mooney's innovation lies not in abandoning the differentiation between the real and the sentimental, but in relocating the site of that differentiation. In this way, the sentimental project of reaching across racial divisions to assimilate racial and cultural others to a white Christian domesticity gives way to an alternative form of cross-cultural symmetry, one that begins by recognizing that all peoples have been equally susceptible to religious delusion. Simultaneously, such logic reifies the method through which scientifically verifiable "reality" becomes distinguished from religious "illusion."

Like John in Chesnutt's *The Conjure Woman*, who constantly questions both the veracity of Julius's tales and the motivation for telling them, Mooney repeatedly underscores his narrative role as someone qualified to differentiate between what is true and what is not. Ethnography, like realist fiction, becomes a record of this process. Moreover, Mooney makes this differentiation an authoritative act by emphasizing his own investigative presence in the field as the purveyor of the real. This thread of personal narrative takes on a different, although still professional, tone from his distanced, impersonal reportage of the sweeping narrative movements situating the Lakota "outbreak" in larger and larger contexts. Like Cushing's description of his stay at Zuni, the chapters in which Mooney narrates his own experiences meeting the leading figures in the Ghost Dance movement stress that the discipline of ethnography is predicated upon the ability of the scientist to recognize what is worth recording and to interpret the data he or she observes firsthand. In such portions of the monograph,

Mooney articulates how ethnography functions and how ethnographic observation leads him to conclusions about culture that guide the organization of the work.

Nowhere is this personal narrative more powerful than in Mooney's depiction of his meeting with the originator of the Ghost Dance, the "Indian Messiah" Wovoka. Mooney's conversations with Wovoka were important to the ethnographer's understanding of the Ghost Dance; they function even more crucially in the text, providing the first moment in which readers feel themselves in the presence of an actual living American Indian. Wovoka, also known as Jack Wilson, was a Northern Paiute, or Numu, living outside the Walker Lake reservation in Nevada. During the height of the Ghost Dance, rumors about the Messiah, his abilities, and his teaching were rampant. Mooney writes, "He [Wovoka] has been denounced as an impostor, ridiculed as a lunatic, and laughed at as a pretended Christ, while by the Indians he is revered as a direct messenger from the Other World, and among many of the remote tribes he is believed to be omniscient, to speak all languages, and to be invisible to the white man" (766). Mooney's depiction of his encounter with Wovoka, which the monograph recounts after a one-hundred-page history of Native American prophets but before any direct discussion of the Ghost Dance itself, puts both sets of rumors to rest. As a realist text, *The Ghost-Dance Religion* repeatedly emphasizes its ability to overcome such exaggerations and to replace them with more reliable and precise information. Mooney is careful to point out, for example, that no other chronicler of Wovoka or the Ghost Dance "had undertaken to find the man himself and to learn from his lips what he really taught" (766). The meeting with Wovoka provides an opportunity for Mooney to demonstrate his abilities as a realist ethnographer, someone willing to go to great lengths to distinguish fact from fiction and someone able to make the reader feel the authenticity of a scene through the conventions of representational realism.

Traveling with Wovoka's uncle and a guide, Mooney meets the Messiah en route to his camp:

> Dyer [the guide] looked a moment and then exclaimed, "I believe that's Jack now!" The Indian [Wovoka's uncle] thought so, too, and pulling up our horses he shouted some words in the Paiute language. The man replied, and sure enough it was the messiah, hunting jack rabbits. (768)

Mooney's description of Wovoka proves quite different from what the popular accounts of Wovoka would have led Mooney's contemporaries to expect. Rather than introducing the reader to an insurgent plotting violent uprisings or a mystic spouting cryptic wisdom, Mooney shows a Wovoka engrossed in one of the day-to-day activities of physical existence, rabbit hunting. Wovoka, according to Mooney, "disclaimed all responsibility for the ghost shirt," a garment some Sioux wore in the belief that it would stop bullets; he disavowed any claim "to be Christ, the Son of God, as so often has been asserted in print"; and he "earnestly repudiated any idea of hostility toward the whites, asserting that his religion was one of universal peace" (772–73). Wovoka is even, unexpectedly, something of an assimilationist in Mooney's account, wearing "white man's clothing" and telling the ethnographer that he thinks it would be "better for the Indians to follow the white man's road and to adopt the habits of civilization" (772). Wovoka inverts Cushing's paradigm of the ethnographer adopting Native dress and habits, for he has already absorbed what he finds useful in Euro-American manners.

As Michael Hittman's recent biography of Wovoka attests, Mooney's claims about the prophet's beliefs were accurate.[70] Yet Mooney's portrayal has an ironic quality. Throughout this discussion, Mooney demonstrates an awareness of the two characterizations of Wovoka most often found in popular accounts (Wovoka as inassimilable "barbarian", Wovoka as scheming, opportunistic con-artist) and attempts to maneuver his own discussion of the Numu prophet away from such misinterpretations. He does so, though, by employing a dichotomy between "traditional" and "assimilated" Indians, a dichotomy that still leaves Wovoka, the leader of a revivalistic religious movement who appears in many regards to have taken up non-Indian ways, difficult to place. Consider how Mooney's description of Wovoka's lodge repeatedly registers the absence of "Indian" artifacts:

> There were no Indian beds or seats of the kind found in every prairie
> tipi, no rawhide boxes, no toilet pouches, not even a hole dug in the
> ground for the fire. Although all wore white men's dress, there were no
> pots, pans or other articles of civilized manufacture, now used by even the
> most primitive prairie tribes, for, strangely enough, although these Paiute
> are practically farm laborers and tenants of the whites all around them,
> and earn good wages, they seem to covet nothing of the white man's....
> It is a curious instance of a people accepting the inevitable while yet
> resisting innovation. (770)

On the one hand, the Numus are not hostile to interacting with Euro-American culture; on the other, they resist "innovation." Mooney does not allow, however, that they will be able to do so indefinitely. Even though he neither suggests that the change will be positive nor hints at how or when the change may occur, he states that Wovoka and his people recognize and accept the "inevitable"—which must be read as an "inevitable" substitution of "white man's" ways for Numu ones. The Numus, by this account, are in a kind of cultural limbo between tradition and assimilation—one that reads today like a strategy of tribal survival, yet which did not correspond with any of models of culture that Mooney had at his disposal.

Mooney's description of the Northern Paiutes as "accepting the inevitable while yet resisting innovation," suggests a way of approaching Wovoka's teachings that, with typical realist equanimity, considers them neither a wild hoax nor a fully vibrant and persuasive belief system. By recalling the inflated claims that have been made about the Messiah, Mooney has set the reader up to be, if not disappointed, at least surprised by the Wovoka that he describes. The text does not reconcile the humility and simplicity of his characterization of Wovoka's teachings with the tremendous social and political upheaval that the Ghost Dance engendered elsewhere.[71] Mooney admits that he takes Wovoka's testimony "with several grains of salt" because "no Indian would unbosom himself on religious matters to a white man with whom he had not had a long and intimate acquaintance" (773), but the ethnographer offers no speculation at all as to what details he might have missed. Further, although Mooney does not consider Wovoka a sham or fraud, he does not provide a serious explanation of why this man might be worthy of the respect he has received from tribal peoples across the western United States. Rather, the tone of journalistic, realist objectivity of this section of The Ghost-Dance Religion flattens the claims of the Numu prophet and the significance of his teachings.

Mooney writes that while Wovoka is sincere in his belief that he has received a "divine revelation" leading him to instruct others in the Ghost Dance and its doctrines, one can "explain the whole matter":

> It appears that a short time before the prophet began to preach he was stricken down by a severe fever.... While he was still sick there occurred an eclipse of the sun, a phenomenon which always excites a great alarm among primitive peoples.... It was now, as Wovoka stated, "when the sun died," that he went to sleep in the daytime and was taken up to heaven. This means simply that the excitement and alarm produced by the eclipse, acting on a mind and body already enfeebled by sickness, resulted in delirium, in which he imagined himself to enter the portals of the spirit world.... To those acquainted with the spiritual nature of Indians and their implicit faith in dreams all this is perfectly intelligible. (773–74)

Mooney's account of Wovoka's revelation is not an attempt simply to enhance the reader's knowledge of cultural details. Rather, the ethnographer's realist logic attempts to explain Wovoka's vision, to demystify it, by showing that its roots lie in material, not spiritual, causes. Mooney does not show how the fever and eclipse set the stage for the revelation; he suggests that they were its direct causes. The fever and the eclipse "resulted" in a "delirium"; Mooney's text considers Wovoka's agency only in connection with the possibility of self-delusion: Wovoka might have "imagined himself to enter the portals of the spirit world," but could not have actually done so. After all, Mooney implies, everyone can assume that the sun has not "died."

It would be easy to reduce Mooney's interpretation of Wovoka's prophecy as the paternalistic gesture of the civilized toward the so-called primitive, but if we keep in mind the universal parallels that Mooney draws at the beginning and end of the narrative text, the passage becomes more complicated. By rendering Wovoka sincere, benign, but mistaken— "His weather predictions are about as definite as the inspired utterances of the Delphian oracle," Mooney later remarks (782)—*The Ghost-Dance Religion* locates the central focus of its study of culture outside the realm of belief and creativity and inside more material forces. Mooney does not want us to judge Wovoka either positively or negatively on the validity of his spiritual teachings. Instead, the ethnographer hopes we will see those teachings as the necessary outcome of a series of events over which Wovoka has had no control. Significantly, the same sense of inevitability that propelled the Numu prophet into the spotlight later, according to Mooney, retired him from it: "As for the great messiah himself, when last heard from Wovoka was on exhibition as an attraction at the Midwinter fair in San Francisco. By this time he has doubtless retired into his original obscurity" (927).[72]

This version of Wovoka and of his status as a Numu prophet responds to the evolutionary paradigm of culture described by the likes of Tylor, Morgan, and Powell. On the one hand, Wovoka does seem, in this account, to belong to an earlier age; he therefore must accept the "inevitable" even if he does resist it. At the same time, Mooney wants to characterize Wovoka as a recurring type, an intelligent man acting under psychological pressures that could affect anyone regardless of race or culture. In the process of crafting such an identity, however, Mooney devalues Wovoka's own role in effecting his own religious and political identity. In other words, Mooney's account does not treat Wovoka as the product of one of Morgan's cultural "stages," but it does create a new kind of cultural determinism that diminishes the agency available to a figure like Wovoka to influence events.

Mooney's devotion to inevitability and determinism prevents him from seeing a connection between sincere religious consciousness on the part of

Wovoka and other Native Americans and the massacre that ultimately unfolded at the Sioux reservation. When Mooney does turn to Lakota participation in the Ghost Dance, he uses the voice of careful, detached observation so common to realist writing. Mooney cites three main causes for the popularity of the religion among the Lakota: "(1) unrest of the conservative element under the decay of the old life, (2) repeated neglect of promises made by the government, and (3) hunger" (823). What of the Ghost Dance itself? What of Wovoka's prophecy that, if the Ghost Dance were followed, the buffalo would return and the Indian dead would return to earth? "The Ghost [D]ance itself, in the form which it assumed among the Sioux, was only a symptom and expression of the real causes of dissatisfaction.... It is significant that Commissioner [of Indian Affairs T. J.] Morgan in his official statement of the causes of the outbreak places the 'messiah craze' eleventh in a list of twelve" (828).

Mooney had taken a certain risk by suggesting that Native peoples were similar to Christians in their susceptibility to religious excess, but his downplaying of the repercussions of the religious movement has the effect of shutting down discussion of the possibility of a widespread Native resistance that might extend beyond simple reactions to material deprivation. Mooney's version of culture participates in what William James referred to in an 1884 essay as "soft determinism," a framework in which the predetermination of events limits but does not preclude the consideration of moral issues.[73] Mooney's efforts to place the Ghost Dance in a global, historical pattern suggests that such revivals of religious sentiment are inevitable under certain circumstances. Even the soldiers' actions at Wounded Knee become nearly inescapable, for the "brave regiment" included many "new recruits fresh from eastern recruiting stations" who "were probably unable in the confusion to distinguish between men and women by their dress" (870). In the end, Mooney's cultural forces leave little room for conscious decision-making. He decides that "on the fatal morning of December 29, 1890, no trouble was anticipated or premeditated by either Indians or troops; ... that the Indians were responsible for the engagement ..., but that the wholesale slaughter of women and children was unnecessary and inexcusable" (870). In the framework of soft determinism, it is possible to view these events without assigning blame, just as it is possible to characterize Wovoka's original teachings of peace and honesty as useful (which Mooney does) without crediting him as a fully original figure. Most of all, such an interpretive narrative structure circumvents the most troubling questions about Indian-white relations raised by the Ghost Dance and the Wounded Knee massacre. Mooney shows the reality of the

Lakota suffering, but ignores the possibility that the teachings of the Ghost Dance—the cultural phenomena at the heart of his study—could have been part of a solution to the problems facing the Lakotas rather than, as the U.S. government understood it, the problem.

This missed opportunity means that Mooney's monograph fails to address the Ghost Dance as constituting, or at least related to, a political statement on behalf of its participants in favor of greater tribal self-determination. In this manner, *The Ghost-Dance Religion* illustrates how the culturalist turn in late-nineteenth-century writing could be used to deemphasize the relation between inequities of power and contemporary practices of legal and social institutions. At the same time, Mooney's desire to remove Native American histories from the evolutionary context of progress creates a new imperative to document tribal phenomena as having meaning only within the context of the cultures that produced them, a move that resonates much more powerfully with Franz Boas's model of culture than with John Wesley Powell's. For this reason, Mooney's turn away from cultural evolution invites an engagement with the meaning of Indian verbal expression as situated within particular tribal settings. These seemingly contradictory commitments—to separate Indian voices from contemporary politics and to read them with care—are at the heart of Mooney's struggle to represent, upon the page, indigenous Ghost Dance practices. On the one hand, Mooney wants us to see the practices as no less valuable than (what Powell would call) their "civilized" counterparts; on the other, Mooney does not want the Ghost Dance religion judged as a set of possibly valid beliefs. We are somehow to accept these performances as markers of authentic difference without considering the equally genuine consequences of the political uprising with which they were connected.

"There is nothing new under the sun," Mooney writes in the final chapter of "The Narrative" (928), and given the failure of his monograph to entertain the possibilities of transformation articulated by this religious movement, there never will be. Nonetheless, he wants his readers to appreciate the importance of these cross-cultural patterns by paying close attention to the voices that emerge from them. His circular narrative structure may limit the imagination of indigenous political change, but it produces an alternative to the evolutionary sequence of Powell and Morgan, to demand that American Indians be heard as equal representatives of humanity's spiritual impulse. The unevenness of Mooney's success in trying to effect this equality throughout *The Ghost-Dance Religion* speaks to the extent to which he grappled with the methods and theories of his profession.

This conflict becomes even more apparent in Mooney's treatment of the Ghost Dance songs that comprise the second section of the work. Rather than incorporate these songs into the "Narrative" section, Mooney organizes them, by tribal affiliation, within a separate section. Through this arrangement, the texts of the Ghost Dance songs become ordered and catalogued as cultural artifacts, linguistic museum pieces that provide synchronic description rather than the diachronic narration of the first part of the monograph. At the same time, Mooney's organization gives the songs a separate textual arena in which they can articulate their own political and spiritual visions. In this practice, Mooney demonstrates a belief in language as a signifier of meaning that cannot be adequately translated—the same belief that prompted literary realists to employ dialect as a marker of deeper group-based differences. In other words, like the collections of dialect tales and other vernacular traditions promoted by the advocates of literary realism, the Ghost Dance songs are presented, by Mooney's ethnography, as objects that can be regarded as having both aesthetic and scientific significance.

The "Songs" section brings together a collection of works from more than a dozen different tribal groups. Here, Mooney's dedication to textual representation paradoxically confirms his skills as an ethnographer even as the indigenous voices he brings to the page threaten to displace his narrative authority by raising matters that he does not adequately address. For if Mooney employs these texts, these songs, to bring tribal life to the page with detail and precision, he does so in a way that evades the troubling questions of Native American survival and resistance to which the Ghost Dance attests. Introducing the voices of others makes certain kinds of dialogue possible, but, as Marc Manganaro writes, "polyvocality has to be read in a fuller context of power relations" by addressing the forces that compel the expression of ethnographic informants.[74] Mooney's commentary avoids precisely this issue, even though what he has left on the page opens up the possibility of examining it.

In *The Ghost-Dance Religion*, the songs serve dual tasks of ethnographic description. First, they tell us about the practice of the Ghost Dance; second, they tell us about cultural life outside the Dance and its religion. Mooney repeatedly stresses this latter value of the songs, using textual explication to position them as loose threads that can unravel the social totality of the people who sing them. For example, an Arapaho song, "Ha'ti ni'bät—E'he'eye," that Mooney translates as "the cottonwood song," offers him the opportunity to discuss at length the properties of the cottonwood admired by Arapahos, the ways in which they use its juice and its bark, and the fact that the "tree is held almost sacred" (967–68). The subsequent song refers to "A'-baha' ni'esa'na,'" the "young thunderbirds," providing an occasion to discuss thunderbird mythology (968–69). In this way, Mooney foreshadows the cultural particularism of the Boas school by using the Ghost Dance song to provide what Clifford Geertz would later describe as "thick description."[75]

The songs of the Sioux present a more formidable challenge to Mooney. The Lakota songs that he has collected often speak to the collective resistance to Euro-American incursion that fermented during the events leading up to Wounded Knee. Mooney attempts to differentiate between what he believes are the older, more "authentic" cultural practices of the Sioux and the religious, politically inflected sentiment that became well-known through the popular press. He devotes extensive discussion to the "vivid picture of the old Indian life" evoked by a song about jerking pemmican (1065–67), thus privileging the synchronic portrait of culture that was a widespread feature of cultural documentation.

In contrast, he provides only perfunctory summaries of songs with explicitly political content, such as one beginning with the lyrics, "The whole world is coming / A nation is coming, a nation is coming" (1072). And some of the most prophetic songs receive no commentary at all:

> Michinkshi'yi twea'qila che—Ye'ye'!
> Michinkshi'yi twea'qila che—Ye'ye'!
> Oya'te-ye i'nichagha'pi-kta che—Ye'ye'!
> Oya'te-ye i'nichagha'pi-kta che—Ye'ye'!
> A'teye he'ye lo,
> A'teye he'ye lo.
> Haye'ye' E'yayo'yo!
> Haye'ye' E'yayo'yo!
>
> I love my children—*Ye'ye'!*
> I love my children—*Ye'ye'!*
> You shall grow to be a nation—*Ye'ye'!*
> You shall grow to be a nation—*Ye'ye'!*
> Says the father, says the father.
> *Haye'ye' Eyayo'yo'! Haye'ye' E'yayo'yo'!* (1065)

What the Sioux might have meant by "growing" into a "nation," and how they believed they would accomplish this, were two of the most disturbing questions that the Ghost Dance raised in the minds of non-Sioux. This song and others raised the possibility that the Lakotas would soon assert a nationalism independent of United States jurisdiction. Notably, the "father" mentioned here seems to bear no relationship to the "great white father" so often referred to in nineteenth-century U.S.-Native negotiations. If the Lakotas had come to recognize the prospect of becoming a national entity no longer dependent on the United States, but based on some other authority, then the political landscape would be altered indeed. These were the possibilities that brought the U.S. Army to Sioux land, ready to put down an armed uprising.[76] This song, as translated by Mooney, would seem to suggest that the Lakotas did not see themselves in any of the ways that the competing notions of culture prescribed; they were neither on the verge of cultural extinction nor mired in an anachronistic, static way of life. The song emphasizes the future of the Lakotas and their growth as a "nation"; it suggests that the Lakotas may be able to restore their traditional kinship relation as "children" of the divinity. These characterizations make sense only if one takes seriously the claim that the Lakotas were capable of creating social change, in ways that deliberately contradicted the models put forward by Merrill Gates, Lewis Henry Morgan, and John Wesley Powell.[77]

I will not (and indeed cannot) put forward a complete interpretation of this song here, that would require attention to the Lakota cultural context and to its language that is outside the scope of this book.[78] I do, though, wish to suggest that the song raises serious questions about the nature of the Lakotas' world view in relation to the Ghost Dance, questions that Mooney was not able or willing to address. In the textual arrangement of Mooney's investigation, the dilemmas and excitement of Lakota nation formation are relegated to the background; the practice of jerking pemmican and the use of the juice of the cottonwood tree exemplify the type of tangible but static cultural phenomena that constitutes the main object of ethnographic description—and that would continue to do so when Boas's model of culture became widely influential. Mooney's methodology appears, in other words, to leave no place for a direct confrontation with a philosophy of political resistance.

Mooney's dedication to textual reproduction, however, makes it possible to apprehend more than the discrete data he uncovers in the texts, particularly for a reader disposed to regard such transcriptions of vernacular expression as aesthetic objects and not only repositories of scientific information. The glaring absence of commentary on a song like "I love my children" calls the reader's attention to it. Moreover, when Mooney writes about the "vivid picture of old Indian life" recalled by jerking pemmican, he helps the reader to understand how songs that, upon a first reading, appear so different can be integrally interconnected. The Lakota songs that Mooney reproduces attest to a connection between past, present, and future alien to those non-Lakota observers who became alarmed by the Ghost Dance. Even if Mooney's commentary implies that the pemmican jerking might be more traditional than the Ghost Dance as a cultural practice, the way in which he has woven these texts together offers the reader a glimpse of how the world might look if the pemmican song, as a marker of cultural reality, were placed on an equal footing with the description of the "nation" and the "buffalo" returning. A reading of Mooney's ethnography that interpreted the songs as pieces of an integrated, aesthetic work would lead the reader back to the political content that he slights.

No one in Mooney's day, though, engaged the Ghost Dance as a legitimate form of religious and political activity. Those who came closest may have been those representatives of the U.S. government, including members of the Army and the Office of Indian Affairs, who attempted to repress it. To take the Ghost Dance seriously, for the majority of Americans, was to take it as a threat to the power of the United States, a threat that produced the violence of Wounded Knee. No wonder Mooney did not treat the songs as representative of genuine political resistance, even though the Ghost Dance songs demand precisely such treatment. While it might be true that no non-Native intellectual interested in Indian affairs could accept the Ghost Dance as an arena in which a religious and political vision of indigenous peoples was articulated, Mooney's contact with the Ghost Dance songs and his dedication to their textual reproduction made such an interpretation feasible. The issue at stake in reading Mooney's ethnography is not whether he is "guilty" or "innocent" of being able to see certain things now apparent to students of Native American cultures. Instead, his monograph illuminates the ways in which the realist mode of observation imposed a set of limitations on the comprehension of the group-based differences that he and others worked so assiduously to document. The orientation against sentimental sympathy among social scientists and authors adhering to realism prepared them to accept unequal relationships among groups adhering to distinct ways of living, among cultures. The Lakotas could join the modern nation-state, or they could continue making pemmican, but few would have found it conceivable that they could do both.

For Mooney to have made the narrative connections between pemmican and a Lakota national revival would have run directly against Powell's evolutionary outlook and Powell's endorsement of the Americanization agenda of the Friends of the Indian. More important, these connections would have run counter to an ethnographic strategy that stressed the cross-cultural commonality of suffering against any historical particularity. In his effort to resist the pervasive evolutionary impulse of the period,

Mooney erected a narrative structure that derived authority from its ability to distinguish between false cultural divides and real cultural inevitability. This approach enabled him to penetrate the cloud of hysteria that surrounded the Ghost Dance but left him unable to cope with the persistence of cultural difference that could not be explained by cross-cultural historical forces.

Consider the conflicting comments in the monograph about the continuation of the Ghost Dance. At the close of the "Narrative" section, he writes that "[a]mong most of these tribes the movement is already extinct, having died a natural death" (927). In the introduction, in contrast, he states that "the dance still exists (in 1896) and is developing new features at every performance" (653). This contradiction may be the result of nothing more than a simple oversight, a failure to correct an earlier draft. However, I take this inconsistency to mark Mooney's own recognition of the limitations of his discursive strategies. According to his narrative structure, in which prophets regularly rise and fall in all cultures, the demise of the Ghost Dance is a fitting and proper conclusion. By leaving this discrepancy in such an obvious position—the two statements open and close the "Narrative"—Mooney signals the limitations of his answer to evolutionism. He met the needs of the day by developing a narrative structure in which the Lakotas and other groups are encircled and dominated by the sweep of history. Yet within that circle, he attempts to represent tribal voices with clarity and force, even if he cannot adequately respond to what they say. Mooney's offering of two mutually exclusive resolutions to the story of the Ghost Dance signals his inability to come to terms with his own narrative form and opens the possibility for his audience to read it more critically than otherwise.

If Mooney recognized the discursive blindnesses of his ethnography, he was unable wholly to overcome them. The Native Americans whom he describes emerge on balance as peoples static in their culture, temporarily deluded by the false hopes of a religious revival. One could extend this textual logic to its extreme and infer from Mooney's interpretation of the Ghost Dance songs that such Indians do not actually change, only their anthropologists do—a conclusion that would have rung false for Mooney himself.

This judgment about the cultural stasis of Native peoples was even more potently at work in the ethnography of Mooney's contemporary, Frank Hamilton Cushing. The widely circulated pictures of Cushing in his Zuni dress shows a scientist capable of moving across cultural boundaries in ways that his informants are not. For instance, there is no illustration accompanying Cushing's writing from the 1880s, or the vast majority of late-nineteenth-century ethnography, equivalent to the portrait of Wovoka in "white man's clothing" that Mooney includes in *The Ghost-Dance Religion*—an illustration of an Indian man who refuses to accept that indigenous cultures were incapable of both material and spiritual adaptation. That Mooney chose to insert this portrait that resisted the ethnographic paradigms of his day speaks to his courage as an observer of culture. Equally telling, there is no extant picture of Mooney in indigenous dress to correspond with the iconic portraits of Cushing that culminated in the 1895 painting by Thomas Eakins (see Figures 6 and 7). The complexity and even difficulty of Mooney's monograph reveal a man who did not share Cushing's confidence that a social scientist could apprehend the full intricacy of a Native culture and comfortably assume its trappings.

Figure 6. This drawing of Wovoka, made from a photograph, appeared in James Mooney's *Ghost-Dance Religion and the Sioux Outbreak of 1890*, published in 1896. The portrait emphasizes Wovoka's position as someone who has adopted "white man's clothing" but has not assimilated into Euro-American culture, as evidenced by the armbands and feather.

Cushing's ethnographic project, particularly "My Adventures in Zuñi," might be interpreted as an extension of the portraits made of him in Zuni costume, just as the struggles of Mooney are encapsulated by his difficulty in confronting the markers of cultural innovation that the picture of Wovoka bears. In an 1896 address to the U.S. Board of Indian Commissioners, Cushing described his "feeling of love and admiration for the Zunis." But he also emphasized his belief that he and his fellow Euro-Americans

Figure 7. This portrait by Thomas Eakins of Frank Hamilton Cushing presents a picture of the ethnographer as a culture-crossing hero. When Cushing's friend Stewart Culin curated an exhibit on the Zuni Indians at the Brooklyn Museum in 1905, this portrait was placed at its focal point. Thomas Eakins, *Frank Hamilton Cushing* (1895), from the collection of Gilcrease Museum, Tulsa, Oklahoma; reproduced by permission.

needed to instruct "the Indian" so as "to aid him to overcome in his sadly unequal struggle with an advancing and alien civilization so that he may be fitted to survive among us and not be further degraded or utterly destroyed."[79] The contrast between his own triumph in entering into Zuni society and the difficulties that he describes facing American Indians is striking. Even though Cushing suggests that they must do so, he cannot see how the Indians whose costume he has adopted will leave behind the spiritual, ethical, and material practices that Americanization requires. The only hope for the continuance of the cultures of American Indians, therefore, will lie in the anthropologists who know how to wear its costumes appropriately. Little wonder that when Cushing's friend Stewart Culin staged a major exhibition on the Zunis at the Brooklyn Museum in 1905, five years after Cushing's accidental death, the Eakins portrait formed its centerpiece.[80]

Mooney, in contrast, responded to his own "love and admiration" for indigenous cultures by rejecting the assimilationist rhetoric of Gates, Dawes, and Pratt, and he later clashed with the "Friends of the Indian" over the status of the Peyote Church in the early twentieth century. Nevertheless, he could not do that which, seen from within late-nineteenth-century notions of culture, appeared impossible: he could not fashion a text in which the indigenous peoples of the North American West stood ready to meet the challenges of the modern age while maintaining tribal sovereignty. Indeed, Mooney's work demonstrates why this idea of sovereignty was not an available strategy in the realist age, either to ethnographers like himself or to Indian writers such as Charles A. Eastman, Zitkala-Ša, and Francis La Flesche who were politically active in the first two decades of the twentieth century.

Even though Mooney's work precedes the full articulation of the Boasian culture concept, it reproduces a dilemma that would be crucial to twentieth-century studies of culture. How can one write culture in a way that resists retelling a narrative of inevitable evolution without rendering the people at the heart of ethnography into static museum objects? Mooney's efforts to fit the phenomenon of the Ghost Dance into an alternative narrative structure reminds us that the path taken by Boas—to emphasize synchronic description almost entirely—need not have been the only one. Yet Mooney's circumlocutions and difficulties in describing the Ghost Dance also make apparent why Boas made such a sharp turn away from narrating laws of human development. In an age in which Indian Reform and the Wounded Knee massacre represented two applications of the racially inflected theory of cultural evolution, detaching biological race from socially constructed culture might have necessitated removing culture from the frame of historical narratives altogether.

What the ethnographic notion of culture did for the late nineteenth century was to provide a vocabulary for describing indigenous peoples that was uneasily balanced between the "love and admiration" mentioned by Cushing and the pose of scientific objectivity important to Mooney and Boas. If ethnographic documentation did not furnish the means for depicting sustained engagement between cultures, it did offer the possibility of arguing for a kind of group-based identity not determined by a biological hierarchy. In this way, ideas of culture circulating in ethnography could not only generate a body of work by ethnographers *about* American Indian ways of life; it could provide textual forums in which American Indians could represent their experiences—even if, as Mooney's monograph so dramatically illustrates, their words were framed by a set of textual practices that limited how such words might be read. This project forced Indian writers to borrow from the formal traditions of both literary realism and scientific ethnography, a conjunction that is the subject of the next chapter.

5

Culture and the Making of
Native American Literature

In the summer of 1899, the anthropologist Alice C. Fletcher wrote to her aide and collaborator of over fifteen years, Francis La Flesche, declaring that the two would resolve the tension that had crept into their professional labors by devoting themselves to separate disciplines. "I stand for science, rather than letters ... letters will, I trust, be your avocation in the future," she wrote.[1] This proposal that La Flesche, an Omaha Indian, enter the world of professional authorship distinguishes the world of "letters" from the world of "science." However, in suggesting that La Flesche could easily make the transition from one to the other (a plan that may have originated with La Flesche himself) Fletcher also presumes their affinity. La Flesche, in fact, would try to stand at precisely the intersection between the documentation of Native American culture through "science" and through "letters," and the result would be a lightly fictionalized memoir of his own experiences at a Presbyterian boarding school on the Omaha Reservation. This book, *The Middle Five*, not only demonstrates the generic overlap between descriptive ethnography and narrative literature, it shows how this same convergence could enable someone like La Flesche to address his own formation as an observer of cultural difference.

The Middle Five (the subject of the second half of this chapter) stands as a culmination of the culturalist turn in the age of literary realism by offering a compelling meditation on the concept of culture itself. La Flesche, however, was not alone as a Native American writer making a foray into the world of "letters" in English at the turn of the twentieth century. Like him, Charles A. Eastman (Ohiyesa, Santee Sioux) and Zitkala-Ša (Gertrude Bonnin, Yankton Sioux) situated works at the convergence of ethnography and literature. These three figures were hardly the first Native Americans to write in English, but they represent the beginning of an intellectual tradition of using the vocabulary furnished by the culture concept to describe Native American experience for non-Natives. Though I will not detail their careers completely, I will attend to these writers, particularly La Flesche, to show how this moment in American literary history afforded American Indian writers discursive opportunities. Ethnography fueled a widespread interest in group-based difference that such writers were well-equipped to meet, and the textual forms that had flourished under literary realism furnished the arena and idiom through which their writing could be channeled. The genres of local color writing, dialect literature, and scientific ethnography all played a role in creating the possibility for written texts that could invite their readers to regard otherness in complicated ways. The works produced by La Flesche, Eastman, and Zitkala-Ša under these rubrics demonstrate how these modes of textual documentation could function as a commentary on the future of Indian cultures within modernity, even though the same texts illustrate how these culturalist forms of writing limited the content and the accessibility of that message.

The extent to which Native American writers could document culture in ways that engaged modernity was crucial, for all publication of traditional Indian verbal expression in the late-nineteenth and early-twentieth centuries occurred within the larger context of the salvage imperative, the drive to preserve cultural phenomena on the presumption that the same cultures would soon vanish. Under this set of assumptions, social scientists recorded volume after volume of narratives, songs, chants, and ceremonies—work that complemented the simultaneous push to collect significant physical objects for the collections of museums like the Smithsonian Institution and the American Museum of Natural History. At Zuni pueblo, for example, the place where Frank Hamilton Cushing conducted his famous experiment in tribal immersion, the Smithsonian expedition that brought Cushing to the Southwest collected over 12,000 artifacts between 1879 and 1885, an average of more than six objects per person living at Zuni.[2] The oral texts collected and published by Boas, Mooney, and their fellow ethnographers have seemed to many the literary extension of this history of removing cultural artifacts from their tribal contexts and ensconcing them in Western institutions.[3] Daniel G. Brinton's 1883 pamphlet, *Aboriginal American Authors and Their Productions*, articulates precisely this connection between physical objects and printed texts while relegating American Indians to the past tense:

> Time and money are spent in collecting remains in wood and stone, in pottery and tissue and bone, in laboriously collating isolated words, and in measuring ancient constructions. This is well, for all these things teach us what manner of men made up the indigenous race, what were their powers, their aspirations, their mental grasp. But closer to very self, to thought and being, are the connected expressions of men in their own tongues. The monuments of a nation's literature are more correct mirrors of its mind than any merely material objects.[4]

The formidable, olive-green volumes of reports and bulletins from the Bureau of American Ethnology became the answer to Brinton's plea; taken together, these volumes do resemble textual "monuments"—or perhaps museums—in which "the connected expressions of men [and women] in their own tongues" have been neatly arranged and displayed for inspection. But the parallel between cultural texts and physical artifacts also suggests how a written work could function simultaneously as a repository of scientific information and as the realization of aesthetic achievement. Steven Conn has shown how anthropological museums during this period frequently struggled to occupy a position "between science and art." Even though understood to have scientific importance, ethnological exhibits shared as many similarities with the works of sculpture and painting to be found in, say, the Metropolitan Museum of Art, as with the stuffed mammals and dead insects housed in museums of natural history.[5] The correspondence between viewing artistic and anthropological exhibits in a museum, moreover, encouraged viewers of the latter to place themselves in the disinterested stance still described by philosophers and critics as necessary for aesthetic judgement. This "museum effect," Svetlana Alpers has argued, turns "cultural materials into art objects."[6] The transformation she describes, though, was never complete in the anthropological exhibitions of the late nineteenth and early twentieth centuries, since a patron could respond to an artifact according to aesthetic and scientific registers simultaneously.

In like manner, the intersection of literary realism and scientific ethnography meant that written texts could be understood by readers both as sources of factual data about cultural difference and as pleasurable works of beauty. This convergence, in turn, enabled the Native American authors discussed in this chapter to use narrative forms of literature to inquire into the limits of culture as a model for understanding group experience. For if ethnography gave these authors a vocabulary for describing that experience to non-Native readers, it also forced them to become aware of how the culture concept more often treated Native Americans as scientific objects than as historical agents. No textual development better illustrates this dilemma, as well as how Indian writers could use the alignment of aesthetic and social scientific manners of reading to respond to it, than the explosion of folkloric and vernacular texts that dominated this new literature of Native American cultures.

American Indian "Folklore" in the Age of Realism

The study of folklore represents a point of connection between the two disciplines central to this book, literature and ethnography, and therefore offers an opportunity to understand how these written discourses applied the theories of culture that they shared. Historians of the study of folklore in the United States describe its emergence in the late nineteenth century as an interdisciplinary enterprise poised between these two approaches.[7] The first membership list of the American Folk-Lore Society, founded in 1888, makes this point clear. Franz Boas as well as the leading figures from the Bureau of American Ethnology, including John Wesley Powell, James Mooney, and Frank Hamilton Cushing, appear on the list. But so do names associated with dialect literature and American literary realism, including Samuel Clemens, Joel Chandler Harris, and Edward Eggleston, as well as the names of professors of English and other modern languages, including Francis James Child, appointed the first chair of English at Harvard University in 1876.

The efforts of Bureau ethnographers to collect, translate, and publish Native American oral tales represent one type of folklore studies during this period; Child's scholarship stands for quite another. Instead of focusing on culturally distinct peoples of North America, Child represents the branch of folklore studies that sought to take up "the remnants of the unlettered European tradition."[8] Child's most accomplished work, for instance, is the five-volume collection *English and Scottish Ballads* (1882–98). His choice of subject, the oral traditions of European peasantry, was not necessarily as important as was the difference in disciplinary goals between the literary and anthropological scholars of folklore. For a literary scholar, the hope was to establish an aesthetic text that had value and meaning *separate* from the people from whom it was gathered.[9] For those scholars coming from anthropology, the value of folklore lay in its ability to yield insight about the culture *to which it belonged.*

What both literary and anthropological folklorists did agree on was the urgency with which vernacular texts needed to be recorded and published. Late-nineteenth-century ethnographers shared the salvage imperative with their counterparts in literary folklore studies. Both feared that literacy and industrialization would erase the remaining traces of ballads, fairy tales, and the like.[10] The first year of *The Journal of American Folk-Lore* indicates how wide a range of materials such texts could encompass. While articles most frequently addressed the verbal expression of Native Americans, contributions also included "The Counting-Out Rhymes of Children," "Louisiana Nursery Tales," "Brer Rabbit and Brer Fox," and "English Folk-Tales in America." The vernacular materials contained both in the *Journal* and in the American Folk-Lore Society's series of "Memoirs" parallel the reach of works being published during the same years under the rubrics of "dialect literature," "local color writing," and "regionalism"—forms associated with American literary realism.

The publication of vernacular materials corresponded with the realist agenda of ushering into print so-called natural productions, free of artifice and sentiment, and it provided to the urban, middle-to-upper-class reader a diversity of peoples and manners of expression. Like literary realists, folklorists focused on the manner in which linguistic accuracy could stand as a marker of a deeper group-based identity. The first publication in the "Memoirs" series, to name one example, was a volume of *Louisiana Folk-Tales* in both French dialect and English translation, collected and edited by Alcée Fortier, a professor of Romance languages at Tulane University. This collection appeared in 1895, only one year after the publication of Kate Chopin's *Bayou Folk*—a book that, like Fortier's work, assembled narratives presumed particular to this region of the United States that possessed a recognizably unique linguistic and ethnic history. Although Chopin presents her dialogue as having been spoken in a dialect of English, she too conveys the authenticity of her stories by emphasizing the process of translation necessary to bring them before the reader. Her story of "La Belle Zoraïde," for instance, ends with an exchange in English followed by the same lines in untranslated French dialect to show how the characters "really talked to each other."[11] At such moments, the same principle governs Chopin's prose as Fortier's collection; exposing the process of translation verifies the linguistic accuracy of vernacular texts and thereby confers upon them greater value as indices of otherness.

Even though the Boasian school of anthropology eventually came to dominate both the American Folk-Lore Society and its *Journal*, the affinities between the publication of folklore and literary realism in the United States remind us of the multiple agendas active in collecting and reading such texts in the realist era. The complications of such disciplinary variety are visible in works such as Charles Godfrey Leland's *Algonquin Legends* (1884), a book published before the actual founding of the American Folk-Lore Society but just as the Bureau of American Ethnology was reaching prominence. Leland's career as an amateur folklorist had much more in common with literary scholars like Child than with the ethnographers who more frequently produced American Indian texts. Over the course of his career, Leland authored multiple volumes of German and German-American ballads, collections of Italian tales, several works on European gypsies, and even a volume on the hybrid language of *Pidgin-English Sing-Song, or Songs and Stories in the China-English Dialect*.[12] For him, the traditional narratives of northeastern, Algonquin-speaking Indians collected in this volume represented an extension of his scholarship both in European folklore and in North American varieties of language.[13] Moreover, the publication of the book by a non-scientific, trade publisher like Houghton Mifflin, as well as the appearance of Leland's two articles in the general interest *Century* and *Atlantic Monthly* magazines, show how the appeal of such work extended beyond scientific circles.[14]

In *Algonquin Legends*, Leland positions himself as both a social scientist and a literary aesthete. He takes pains throughout the book to annotate and comment on the tales in the manner of an anthropologist who may use them to discover something new about the group from which he collected them. Leland provides notes on the original language, on the tribal customs to which the tales refer, and on the people from whom they are gathered. Meanwhile, *Algonquin Legends* also articulates a connection between such ethnographic study of these indigenous narratives and the history of European literature. Leland calls Goolskap (also known as Kluskap), protagonist of many tales reproduced in the volume, "by far the grandest and most Aryan-like character ever evolved from a savage mind ... more congenial to a reader of Shakespeare and Rabelais than any deity ever imagined out of Europe."[15] Such comparisons are aimed at establishing evidence for the status of these Algonquin works as achievements of the imagination. Leland concludes his introduction by remarking that, "while these legends of the Wabanki are fragmentary and incomplete, they still read like the fragments of a book whose subject was once broadly and coherently treated by a *man of genius*" (emphasis added).[16] Though these legends might have much to offer to the anthropologist in explaining Algonquin *culture,* Leland saw the folklorist's purpose as the restoration of such tales to their status as aesthetically powerful verbal *art.*[17]

Algonquin Legends was not the first book-length work of Native American stories written for a broad audience, but it was a harbinger of the sharp increase in publication of such material in books and general interest periodicals at the end of the nineteenth century and continuing into the twentieth. Such works benefited from the more scholarly work being conducted by the Bureau of American Ethnology and other professional organizations in two ways: first, the growing stature of anthropology fed the perennial fascination of Euro-Americans with Indians and thereby fostered the audience for such works; second, ethnographic scholarship produced documents that could be mined for the purpose of creating derivative works, making publication in this field relatively easy. Editors of Native American narratives who aimed for a general audience could (and still can) choose from a wealth of already translated texts—then make them shorter, more lively, and free of the scatological and sexual episodes that often punctuated Native American oral narratives. *Forest and Stream* editor George B. Grinnell, for example, published not only tales that he had collected himself but also new versions of Chinook stories originally transcribed by Boas.[18]

The publication of Native American verbal expression relied upon the same antimodernist pleasure generated by authentic difference that played such a large role in the popularity of dialect tales and local color fiction. As Charles L. Briggs has argued, the folkloristic practice of distinguishing between the "folk" and those capable of collecting their verbal expression played a part in the complicated process of articulating a division between the "modern" (or "civilized") societies and the pre-modern, a division that, in turn, contributed to the "more general process of creating, sustaining, and naturalizing social inequality."[19] By recording and interpreting oral expression, writers intrinsically emphasized the progress of technology (in the form of printed texts), as well as the influence of scientific method, even though these works sometimes evinced a nostalgia for the imagined holism of oral cultures.

As others have shown, the interest in such texts, thought to provide non-Indians with access to a kind of primitive aesthetics, would later play an important role in the twentieth-century history of modernism in the United States.[20] In particular, the perceived "passing" of American Indians made their stories especially suitable for transformation into the nationalist texts that formed the history of the United States, much as the Grimms had looked to folklore to establish a nationalist history of Germany earlier in the nineteenth century.[21] Once their texts were recorded as the legacies of a supposedly vanishing group, Indians could be claimed as literary ancestors—the first Americans—by "modern" artists who believed indigenous groups to have a unique relationship to the geographical landscape of the United States but who had little interest in confronting actual, living tribal peoples.[22] Ethnographic texts, both those published through professional ethnography and those such as Natalie Burlin Curtis's popular volume, *The Indians Book* (1907), facilitated this process by purporting to provide what Curtis called the "direct utterance of the Indians themselves." Her book, she claimed, "reflects the soul of one of the noblest types of primitive man—the North American Indian."[23]

The valorization of the primitive so obvious in twentieth-century modernism was at work during the late nineteenth century as well. Yet during this earlier period, these texts had additional kinds of value for readers. Just as Joel Chandler Harris's work was intended to instruct his readers as to the "mind and temperament" of African Americans,[24] the reproductions of Indian stories and songs were of interest because they presumably revealed something new about the identity of Native peoples. And as in the dialect collections purporting to depict African Americans, these works often cast Indians as childlike in their reasoning and imagination, a characterization directly related to the evolutionary model in which "civilization" was understood to be the maturity of humanity and "barbarism" its youth.[25] Just as important for the history of this sub-genre, such works were frequently targeted at children because of their presumed affinity with indigenous peoples as "undeveloped" and as yet "uncivilized" beings.

In this way, folklore could demonstrate the complexity and accomplishments of groups that had been grossly misunderstood throughout U.S. history, but it could also replace the old caricature of Indians as mindless savages with a new one: Indians as child-like purveyors of Aesop-like fables. Equally damaging, the popular publication of folklore often reproduced the tendency of scientific ethnography to ascribe the achievements of Native American cultural imagination to an imagined past unconnected to the actual lives of Indians living in the United States. The ahistorical temporal frame of these works left writers and readers ill-prepared to explain how Native peoples might continue the cultures represented by traditional narratives and still participate in the modernity of "civilization."

The publication of American Indian oral texts for non-scientific audiences might have replicated the dilemmas of ethnographic writing, but it also afforded a new opportunity to write about culture in a way that, unlike more straightforward ethnography, made use of popular interest in aesthetic properties of the vernacular. The transcription of such materials was shaped by what has come to be a major theoretical problem in the study of oral indigenous expression: translation.[26] While contemporary readers of collections of vernacular materials from the late nineteenth and early twentieth centuries have often found these translations of Native sources wanting, the very fact that such works engaged in complex acts of translation—translation from the oral to the written, from the everyday to the scientific, and (most literally) from an indigenous language to English—can call attention to the complexity of studying culture through such verbal artifacts. Even as ethnographers attempted to carry a diversity of tribal experience into a uniform framework of textual production and interpretation, they could articulate for a nonscientific audience the difficulty of transforming cultural difference into universally accessible texts.[27]

Zuñi Folk Tales (1901), a trade volume collected, translated, and arranged by Frank Hamilton Cushing before his death in 1900, shows how the publication of such material could foreground this process of translation in ways that illuminate the overlap between the cultural and the aesthetic in the wake of literary realism. Although Cushing, as the previous chapter described, made his mark by publishing articles in a variety of general interest magazines in the 1880s, *Zuñi Folk Tales* was his first attempt to address the non-scientific audience through book publication. The tales are presented in English translation, with only a scant sprinkling of footnotes for scholarly apparatus. The volume does, however, include an introduction by Bureau of American Ethnology director John Wesley Powell, who used the opportunity to articulate his belief in the universal development of human intellect, the belief so central to his evolutionary model of human history.[28] Since all of humanity passes through the same phases of savagery and barbarism on the path to civilization, Powell reasons, the "ancient mythology" of a group like the Zunis can be of use to science "for the purpose of discovering stages of human opinion."[29]

One of Cushing's selections for the volume offers the reader the chance to see that there could be an altogether different purpose in studying vernacular narratives such as these. In 1886, Cushing brought three Zuni men with him to the East coast for a tour; during a session of storytelling that occurred during this trip, the Zunis requested that Cushing tell a tale of his "own" culture. Cushing responded by reading "The Cock and the Mouse" from the collection *Italian Popular Tales* (1885), by Cornell professor of Romance languages Thomas Frederick Crane.[30] Some time later, Cushing was at Zuni Pueblo and heard one of these men, Waíhusiwa, retell this same Italian folktale, which Cushing then recorded. In *Zuñi Folk Tales*, therefore, Cushing included both the original Crane version of the tale and the retelling by Waíhusiwa "in order that the reader may not only see what transformation the original underwent in such a brief period, and how well it has been adapted to Zuñi environment and mode of thought, but also to give a glimpse of the Indian method of folk-tale making."[31]

Waíhusiwa's retelling of "The Cock and the Mouse" is, indeed, the genuine transformation that Cushing promises. The story that Cushing read to Waíhusiwa covers only one-and-a-half pages of text; Waíhusiwa's covers ten. More significantly, Waíhusiwa has turned the story, which concerns the Cock's efforts to repair his head from an injury he suffered at the hands of the Mouse, into a more complicated tale that demonstrates the necessity of offering payment to "medicine masters," of dutifully recognizing the divinity of the natural world, and of understanding that injuries can result from the wrongs that one unintentionally inflicts upon others. Not only has Waíhusiwa turned this tale of the etiology of the coxcomb into a didactic work that reflects a Zuni worldview, he has created a wholly different aesthetic object. In contrast to the dense prose of Crane's translation from the Italian, this Zuni version relies on a more elaborate narrative structure, complete with an initial altercation between the protagonists entirely absent from the original, as well as a rendering of the Cock's quest for a cure that forces the reader to ponder the relationship between healer and patient in a more serious way than did the version that the Zuni men heard from Cushing.

Cushing's prefatory remarks to this pair of texts invite the reader to make precisely such comparisons. By this point in the book, the reader has read over 400 pages of Cushing's translations—texts that presumably have taught readers a good deal about Zuni culture and prepared them to recognize these types of distinctions. Moreover, Cushing's introduction to "The Cock and the Mouse" does not mention the ethnographic data about the Zuni customs and history emphasized by the other tales of his collection. Instead, what Cushing calls our attention to is the way that this story has been carried across a cultural boundary so that it means something entirely new after "it has been adapted to Zuñi environment and mode of thought." In doing so, Cushing's "hybrid text" (Powell's term) recalls James Boon's comments on how the "accents" of hybridity "resoundingly disrupt projects in universalist abstraction" and prove "inevitable embarrassments to universals."[32] In other words, by showing how the same tale might be dramatically altered in its narrative accents, Cushing demonstrates that the aesthetic project of creating verbal art takes place through a culturally specific context at odds with the universalism articulated by Powell in the introduction to this very work. Cushing thus uses aesthetics to say something important about how culture should be studied—namely, that interpreting a verbal artifact within the context of a specific culture offers a more profound understanding of its significance than placing it into Powell's narrative of cultural evolution.

This example from Cushing's work does *not* show that the production of folkloric texts smoothly restored to their Native American subjects the agency that many recent critics believe was ignored by the social scientific study of culture at the turn of the century. Rather, "The Cock and the Mouse" demonstrates how the textualization of verbal expression created new possibilities for certain kinds of agency to be asserted. Texts could be judged by readers to be elegant, carefully crafted narratives—that is, to be aesthetic—and could be recognized to be conveying information about the customs and beliefs of a discrete group—that is, to be cultural. Equally important, these texts could be shaped by their authors to perform numerous functions, including the construction of a pre-national past, the confirmation of a universalist paradigm, or, as in the case of this story, the demonstration of how verbal art is created within social contexts. It is difficult to come away from reading the two versions of this tale without thinking the Zuni story at least equal, if not superior, to the Italian one, and this is not beside the point. The articulation of culture as defining the integrity and complexity of a people's existence was an attempt to argue for a non-hierarchical understanding of group-based identity. Cushing's juxtaposition of Crane's and Waíhusiwa's translations of the Italian story shows how the production of written texts could insist upon the necessity of cultural particularism. More broadly, "The Cock and the Mouse" demonstrates how the texts of translation could quietly carry an indigenous story from the realm of scientific curiosity into an engagement with theoretical arguments about the nature of cultural identity.

Oral Traditions, Indian Writers

The practice of producing written texts from oral traditions of vernacular expression created genres of publication that could be adopted by those Native Americans who aspired to write in English. One might even argue that the success of American Indian writers at the turn of the twentieth century (none of whom was successful in commercial terms) depended upon their ability to engage the vocabulary of culture. For instance, S. Alice Callahan's *Wynema: A Child of the Forest*, published in 1891, employed the idiom of the domestic novel without providing extensive descriptions of the traditional customs of the Muscogees, whom it depicted, focusing instead on the education and romance of its heroine. The novel, the first by a Native American woman, was neither widely reviewed nor read.[33] In contrast, Charles A. Eastman (1858–1939), Zitkala-Ša (1876–1938), and Francis La Flesche (1857–1932), who all produced work that addressed the desire of readers for ethnographic information about indigenous life, were able to publish with national magazines and presses. The three were even the subject of a 1902 review essay in *The Book Buyer*, "Recent Writings By American Indians," which warmly welcomed the new "opportunities to read a small amount of purely American literature in the writing of some of the educated American Indians."[34]

These writers had indeed been educated by Euro-American institutions. Eastman had received an undergraduate degree from Dartmouth and a medical degree from Boston University; Zitkala-Ša had attended boarding school and then Earlham College in Indiana; and La Flesche attended the Presbyterian boarding school near the Omaha reservation where he was raised, prior to his adult study of law in Washington.[35] Such educational experiences were crucial to these writers, particularly Zitkala-Ša and La Flesche. Moreover, the *Book Buyer* article explains that their formal schooling gave them a particular appeal to the reading public:

> It is interesting to observe that each of them has emphasized the finer aspects of the old order—which, for them, has changed forever—with a pride that cannot fail to be recognized by the casual reader, even where it is accompanied by the most courteous acknowledgment of the merits and advantages of civilization.[36]

The passage conveys an understanding of these writers as dwelling between the two models of culture described throughout this book: the evolutionary model of cultural development in which intelligent Indians would naturally recognize "the merits and advantages of civilization," and the model of cultural particularism in which manners of living could not be arranged in a pattern of narrative hierarchy. Such a judgment, rough though it may be, finds support in the literary and political activities of each of these three writers. All, though to varying degrees, engaged in advocacy efforts that had the underlying goal of assimilating Indians into the dominant U.S. culture. Eastman, for instance, participated in a project, spearheaded by realist author and critic Hamlin Garland, to rename Indians with more "American" names; Zitkala-Ša taught at Richard Henry Pratt's Carlisle Indian School; La Flesche played a critical role in the allotment of his own

Omaha reservation.[37] Yet the three also engaged in projects of writing that portrayed Native American life with an integrity and complexity that went beyond mere nostalgia for something that "has changed forever."

The turn-of-the-century popularity of folkloristic texts reproducing indigenous tales created one avenue by which such writers could address this task, and Charles Eastman took advantage of this opportunity on several occasions. His first book, *Indian Boyhood* (1902), is an autobiography but includes several stories he recalled hearing as a child. Eastman also published three book-length collections of tales, including two that he co-authored with his wife, Elaine Goodale Eastman. (The two met while he worked as a doctor at the Pine Ridge agency during the rise of the Ghost Dance and the aftermath of the Wounded Knee massacre.)[38] In many ways, Eastman's texts follow the typical formulations of this sub-genre of literature and ethnography. The stories in *Wigwam Evenings: Sioux Folk Tales Retold* (1909), for example, conclude with the bland, Aesop-like morals commonly appended to the published versions of Indian tales in translation, such as "Pride alone will not fill the stomach," "He who deceives others may himself be caught some day," and "Patience and quick wit are better than speed."[39] Less conventional is Eastman's initial book-length foray in this arena, the only one of these collections in which he appears as the sole author, *Red Hunters and the Animal People* (1904); this is a work that reviewers compared to naturalist Ernest Thompson Seton's *Wild Animals I Have Known* (1898), as well as to other collections of Native American stories presented for a general audience. Ethnographic descriptions of Indians and naturalist observations of animals were commonly linked throughout the nineteenth century,[40] and Eastman returns to this discursive connection from a new point of view, one that combines in this book "the common experiences and observations of the Red hunter" with "the fables, songs, and superstitious fancies of the Indian."[41]

Eastman notes in his forward to *Red Hunters* that he presents his stories about animals as the "Dakota or Sioux nation" might have told them "before 1870, when the buffalo and other large game still roamed the wilderness and the Red men lived the life I knew as a boy" (vii–viii). How Eastman here situates himself in relation to the tales that follow quietly signals what makes this collection unique to the period; he does not, like Boas or Mooney or countless other collectors of indigenous expression, purport to have actually *heard* these animal stories from other Indians. The stories that he had included in *Indian Boyhood* are ones he claimed to recall actually hearing from tribal elders while a boy. The stories of *Red Hunters*, in contrast, are based on Eastman's claimed ability to imagine how the Dakotas understand the world around them; the book results from his own firsthand observation of Dakota culture, yet it simultaneously produces new knowledge about that same culture through his imagination. Eastman's project therefore emphasizes culture as a series of acts of cognition rather than as something that can be easily collected and reproduced by those exterior to it. Eastman's foreword, in fact, explains the different kinds of knowledge about animals that an Indian hunter could have; the hunter could seek a superficial knowledge of an animal's "outward habits," if he were only interested in pursuing it as game, or he could devote himself to learning the "important messages" that "the spirits of the animals may communicate" (vi–vii). The deep knowledge that comes from the latter study, Eastman implies, is of a different register than the former kind.

Several stories in *Red Hunters* make clear that the pursuit of this knowledge, as portrayed by Eastman, shares the language of ethnography, for Eastman's narrators repeatedly describe animal behavior through the vocabulary of cultural observation. We hear about the taboos of the mountain lion, the "festival time" of buffalos, the different "tribes" of mice (respectively, 18, 100, 53). In this last instance, young Dakota boys who observe a ritualistic mouse dance learn a respect that seems more culturally than ecologically grounded. Says an elder to the boys, in the story, "These little folk have their own ways. They have their plays and dances, like any other nation" (55). The word with which Eastman ends this sentence is the same one the Lakotas used in their Ghost Dance songs, and the elder seems to be instructing the boy to regard the mice as having the same integrity as a "nation" or "people" (in Sioux dialects, one can use the same word, "oyate," for both) that the Ghost Dance songs demanded. In other words, training an ethnographic eye upon the natural world leads to a recognition of a kind of cultural pluralism. I call attention to Eastman's deployment of culturalist vocabulary not to call into question the accuracy of his portrayal of Dakota beliefs or manners of speaking about the natural world. Rather, I would note that *Red Hunters* contends that the Sioux share the realist interest in culture, that they, too, carefully investigate and observe the habits of others—in their case, "animal" others. For Eastman, therefore, this process of observation produces in the Sioux a level of respect much like that which James Mooney hoped to engender through his publications about Native peoples.

In this manner, the animals of *Red Hunters* function differently than, say, the animals that populate Joel Chandler Harris's *Uncle Remus*. While both collections make use of animals as entertaining characters—something that surely contributed to the appeal of folklore collections throughout the period—Eastman's text makes readers conscious of how animals are framed by the gaze of human scrutiny. As his title states, the book describes how the animal "people" are hunted by the Dakotas, in figurative as well as literal ways. Eastman ties careful and even sympathetic observation to the success of Dakota hunting in a way that sharpens the book's commentary about the ethnographic project in which he participated. To know and respect one's game may help one to learn its secrets, but it can also enable one to kill it. For this reason, *Red Hunters and Animal People* serves as a counterpart to Charles W. Chesnutt's publication of *The Conjure Woman*. Chesnutt and Eastman both use the literary interest in ethnographic information to provide a generic frame for their books, and in doing so, fashion stories that comment on the very process of collecting that very information. For Chesnutt, this technique meant creating exchanges between the white northerners and their African American informant, Uncle Julius, to call into question the value of the ethnographic impulse altogether. For Eastman, it meant describing how American Indians could be motivated by the same ethnographic impulse that inspired non-Indians, while still displaying an awareness of the problems raised by recording traditional forms of knowledge for a predominantly non-Indian audience.

Eastman's interest in using these tales of animals to raise questions of power extends beyond the dynamics of ethnographic inquiry to the political relationships between Native peoples and the government of the United States. The most overtly allegorical of the stories in *Red Hunters*, "On Wolf Mountain," opens with a family of wolves "driven away from their den on account of their depredations upon the only paleface in the Big Horn valley" (24). It then goes on to tell about how a "tribe" of wolves decides to make an orchestrated attack upon another white rancher threatening their hunting ground, an attack that will ultimately force them to remove farther westward. As if the basic plot, and the commonly drawn analogy between animals and indigenous peoples, were not enough for the reader to make the connection between the wolves and the nearby Dakota Indians, Eastman places obvious signposts throughout the story; a U.S. soldier, for example, tells the rancher, "We have got to rid the country of the Injuns and gray wolves before civilization will stick in this region!" (38)

What does this correspondence between these wolves and the nearby Dakota Indians mean, in light of my argument that Eastman's book incorporates a commentary on the process of ethnographic observation? Eastman seems to re-articulate the urgency of salvage ethnography; stories of Indians and wolves, and especially Indian stories about wolves, need to be recorded because they are in physical danger. At the same time, "On Wolf Mountain" offers two contradictory messages about the project of recording cultural information, including verbal texts. On the one hand, a story like this one seems to suggest the futility of ethnography: the white rancher will cling to his model of "civilization" regardless of what he learns about "Injuns and gray wolves." But the story, written from the point of view of the wolves, also offers a more optimistic conclusion, for it shows how producing ethnographic texts presents the writer an opportunity to show how the nineteenth century might appear, in the phrase used to introduce the *Narrative* of Frederick Douglass, were "the Lions [to] write history."[42] In *Red Hunters*, Eastman translates the language of ethnography to produce a culturalist text that refuses to separate the aesthetic properties of narrative from its political implications.

Zitkala-Ša's *Old Indian Legends* (1901) takes advantage of the same allegorical possibilities so important to Eastman's "On Wolf Mountain." Zitkala-Ša wrote this volume after her enormously popular autobiographical articles—later collected in her book *American Indian Stories* (1921)—appeared in the *Atlantic* and *Harper's Monthly*. The articles comprise a sort of work distinct from Eastman's *Indian Boyhood*, for in them Zitkala-Ša expends little effort in relaying ethnographic information about the Yankton Sioux reservation on which she was raised, and instead focuses almost exclusively on telling a story about the tortuously painful process of Americanization.[43] The essay "Recent Writings by American Indians" in *The Book Buyer* praises this work for the same reason that it has become widely reprinted in recent anthologies, the "poignant and utterly despairing note of revolt against what [Robert Louis] Stevenson calls 'the dingy ungentlemanly business of civilization.'"[44] That Zitkala-Ša represents herself as actively choosing, at least at first, to engage in this "dingy" business makes her writing about it all the more complicated.

As these autobiographical articles were winning Zitkala-Ša acclaim, including mention in a *Harper's Bazaar* column entitled "Persons Who Interest Us," the Boston publishing firm of Ginn and Company awarded her a contract for a book of traditional stories. Unlike the articles, this book would participate in the writing of culture that Zitkala-Ša was coming to increasingly believe a necessary project for American Indians trained in Euro-American institutions. A letter she wrote to Carlos Montezuma (a Yavapai Apache activist) while beginning work on the project is revealing:

As for my plans,—I do not mean to give up my literary work—but while
the old people last I was to get from them their treasured ideas of life. This
I can do by living among them. Thus I mean to divide my time between
teaching and getting story material.[45]

That Zitkala-Ša at first differentiates this project from her "literary work"
and then later refers to it as "getting story material" suggests that she understood how it would occupy a place between literature and ethnography,
while being embraced wholly by neither discipline.

On its surface, *Old Indian Legends* is more similar than Eastman's *Red
Hunters* to other collections of indigenous narratives, such as Cushing's
Zuñi Folk Tales, which appeared the same year. In her preface, Zitkala-Ša
emphasizes that her role has been as a mere conduit of these narratives: "I
have tried to transplant the native spirit of these tales—root and all—into
the English language, since America in the last few centuries has acquired
a second tongue."[46] Although Zitkala-Ša refers throughout this brief preface to the contemporary pressures upon Sioux culture from extensive
contact with Euro-American institutions, she also implies that the verbal
specimens she is replanting have a timeless quality. They are "relics of the
soil" that "belong as much to the blue-eyed little patriot as to the black-
haired aborigine" (v–vi).

But the nostalgic, universalist tone of Zitkala-Ša's preface belies the
complex ways in which the stories she presents recall the brutal history
that resulted from America acquiring its "second tongue." Consider, for
instance, "The Badger and the Bear," which describes the origin of Blood-
Clot Boy, a major figure in traditional Sioux narratives. In this rendition,
the prosperous Badger, a successful hunter, has been able to store an ample
supply of meat when a hungry bear enters his lodge. Bear asks for meat
from Badger and receives it. Day after day, Bear comes to beg meat, and he
becomes stronger and bolder each time. Eventually he forces the Badgers
out of their lodge, steals their weapons, and moves his own family. Without his arrows, Badger cannot support his family, and eventually he, in
turn, is forced to beg from Bear. Bear denies him. Finally, Badger manages
to steal a blood clot from a recently slain buffalo, and from this clot
emerges a hero—"the first human creature" (73)—who avenges Badger by
slaying Bear and his family.

As with Eastman's "On Wolf Mountain," the theme of dispossession and
the subsequent quest for justice readily calls to mind the historical relationship between American Indians and the European settlers. Zitkala-Ša

has even included a detail, which does not appear in other contemporary transcriptions of this story, to guide the reader further toward such an interpretation. Some versions of this story, such as the one included in Charles and Elaine Goodale Eastman's *Wigwam Evenings*, included a young bear cub who, unlike the other bears, sympathizes with Badger.[47] Zitkala-Ša's version places an additional emphasis upon this detail by describing this cub as having hair like "kinky wool," as being "laughed at by his older brothers," and as being unable to "change the differences between himself and his brothers" (69). Clearly, the sympathetic cub, in this retelling, evokes those African Americans who arrived in the Dakotas as slaves or soldiers.

Of course, to suggest that such symbolic correspondences exist does not necessarily make the story of "The Badger and the Bear" "about" the history of white-Sioux interaction in any transparent way. In fact, one could argue that this interpretive process could work in the other direction. Perhaps Zitkala-Ša shaped this story so that, being reminded of the injustice of white-Native relations, the non-Sioux reader would better place an unfamiliar indigenous story into a more familiar interpretive context. By establishing such correspondence through her selection and shaping of this tale, Zitkala-Ša used the textual genre as a mediation between traditional Sioux forms of knowledge and the necessities of tribal peoples in her present day. Her text made available, in other words, a level of interpretation that rendered Native American narratives into more than a "relic" of history. These stories might be, as her own title put it, "*Old* Indian Legends," but readers could read them as mute relics of a disappearing past only by disregarding a subtle, yet insistent, engagement with matters crucial to the status of Americans at the time of the work's publication.

The terms of this engagement shift slightly when the traditional Sioux narratives included in *Old Indian Legends* are juxtaposed with Zitkala-Ša's autobiographical writings published in the *Atlantic Monthly*. One of the most important themes of this autobiographical prose is the pain and suffering of being torn from one culture and assimilated into another— specifically, of being forced to conform to the standards of her boarding school and of then returning to her Sioux mother. In *Old Indian Legends*, Zitkala-Ša tells a story entitled "Iktomi and the Fawn," which tells how Iktomi, the mischief-maker, repeatedly desires to be something else. "How I wish that I were not I!" he exclaims (47). In the first two instances, when he wants to become a peacock and an arrow, Iktomi receives his wish, but he is returned to his original form when he proves unwilling to conform to the rules of conduct of those beings. (He tries to fly too high when he is a peacock and to move side-to-side when he is an arrow.) In the third instance, Iktomi desires to be like the fawn and to possess white spots on his face. A fawn tells Iktomi that it received its spots by being buried under a fire; Iktomi agrees to be so buried, and he burns up.

Iktomi's foolish desire, blind to the consequences of his action, comprises the driving force of this story, as well as others in which this trickster plays the leading role. Such urges parallel those of the headstrong child that Zitkala-Ša depicts in her autobiographical essay, "Indian Childhood," published the year before this story. In "Indian Childhood," Zitkala-Ša tells how she heard about the red apples of the East, and how she then so yearned to roam among the orchards, so wanted to taste the apples, that she ignored her mother's warnings about the suffering she would endure if she left home. "Iktomi and the Fawn"—as Zitkala-Ša tells it—demonstrates the same ambivalence to the process of assimilation as does her autobiographical work, but it does so with a comic edge that does not show up in "Indian Childhood." We can laugh at Iktomi even as we recognize the troubling nature of his belief that he can perfect his life by becoming something entirely new. In this sense, the traditional Iktomi story does not solve the problems raised by the autobiographical articles about Americanization, but rather rearticulates them in a more concise manner and with a distinct variation in tone. Zitkala-Ša's translation of "Iktomi and the Fawn" enables the reader to distance herself or himself from the assimilating subject, and therefore the emotive response to the story is perhaps more intricate than that which Zitkala-Ša's autobiographical writing allows. We sympathize with Iktomi; however, because the story frames his desires as absurd, our response is devoid of uncomplicated pity.

Like Eastman's *Red Hunters, Old Indian Legends* shows how the vocabulary of culture could produce a different kind of discussion about American Indian experience, one that uses the narrative materials of American Indian cultures and the texts that documented them as resources for understanding the contemporary moment. The translation of Indian oral narratives relied upon the premise that such texts could be both admired as well-crafted stories and scrutinized for anthropological data. By situating their work at this convergence, writers like Eastman and Zitkala-Ša could translate traditional expression to offer subtle reflections on the process of recording cultural knowledge and forging cultural identification. Neither, though, explored the disciplinary intersection of ethnography and literature in as sustained and careful manner as their contemporary, Francis La Flesche, who devoted his life both to the promise of Americanization and to the written documentation of American Indian cultures.

Writing from the "Middle": Francis La Flesche

The career of Francis La Flesche, an Omaha man who spent approximately half of his life living in the capital of the United States, epitomizes the nexus among ethnographic documentation, cultural dispossession, and literary production that shaped writing about American Indians in particular, and group-based difference in general, at the turn of the twentieth century. Born in the late 1850s, La Flesche was a contemporary of Franz Boas and, like Boas, went on to produce a significant body of ethnography that is still read today. Yet in many ways La Flesche's career as an anthropologist is the inverse of Boas's. La Flesche came to the discipline first as an informant and interpreter, and he was recognized to be a scientist in his own right only after years of labor. He did not receive anything like Boas's academic training, and was therefore never in any position to comment directly upon the more theoretical issues gripping the field, to assume leadership positions, or to train his own students. By the time that La Flesche gained an appointment with the Bureau of American Ethnology in 1910, Boas had already begun to move the center of the discipline away from government and museum-sponsored research to the university. Though they were nearly identical in age, La Flesche belonged to an earlier generation of American anthropology; Boas dominated the new one.

What La Flesche and Boas shared was a commitment to the concept of culture. Boas dedicated his career to separating the study of socially constructed culture from the study of biologically inherited race. During that same period, La Flesche pursued the documentation of American Indian cultures with equal dedication. The notion of culture as defining the distinct identity of a group is not only at the center of his ethnographies of the Omaha and Osage Indians, but also motivated his actions in the arenas of policy and social science that actually threatened the tribal autonomy of the Omahas, as we shall see. La Flesche, however, was hardly a passive recipient of the theories of his day. His slim, slightly fictionalized memoir, *The Middle Five* (1900), produced during his temporary shift from "science" to "letters," shows how he, like Charles Eastman and Zitkala-Ša, recognized the opportunities afforded by the overlap between ethnography and literature. Significantly, he used this intersection to do more than describe an American Indian culture. In *The Middle Five*, La Flesche reformulates the very idea of culture itself, in a manner that anticipates the questions that would later preoccupy Boas and his intellectual heirs.

La Flesche developed into an observer of culture during a time when his own family played an instrumental, though controversial, role in dramatically shaping the course of Omaha history. His mother was an Omaha woman, with the Omaha name Ta-in-ne and the Anglo name Elizabeth Esau. His father was Joseph La Flesche, a man of mixed (and disputed) Indian and French heritage, also known as Inshta'maza or Iron Eye, who became one of the principal chiefs of the Omahas after being adopted by his predecessor, Big Elk.[48] Joseph La Flesche later resigned this position after a dispute with the U.S. agent assigned to the Omahas, but he remained an influential voice of the "Citizen's Party," which favored embracing Anglo-American styles of living. Joseph La Flesche also founded what more traditional Omahas called "the village of the 'make-believe' white men," a settlement of log houses and agricultural fields near the Presbyterian mission boarding school that Francis would attend during the late 1860s. The La Flesche family entered a different political arena in 1879, when Francis's half-sister, Susette, or Bright Eyes, accompanied the Ponca leader Standing Bear on a speaking tour of the eastern United States to protest the forced removal of the Poncas to the Indian Territory. Susette La Flesche acted as Standing Bear's interpreter, and her success in captivating audiences became well known. A story soon circulated that, upon meeting her, Henry Wadsworth Longfellow looked into her eyes and called her by the name of his heroine in *The Song of Hiawatha.* "This is Minnehaha," he reportedly said.[49]

Francis La Flesche accompanied Susette on this tour as a chaperone, and his own skills as an interpreter enabled him to secure an appointment as a clerk in the Office of Indian Affairs. In 1881, La Flesche moved to Washington, D.C., where he would reside—with regular vacations back to Omaha land—until he retired in 1929. Soon after moving to the capital, he began to assist the self-trained anthropologist Alice C. Fletcher, and entered the complicated relationship that would eventually become the center of both their lives. They would be more than professional collaborators: The unmarried and previously childless Fletcher, a woman said to resemble Queen Victoria, informally adopted La Flesche as her son in 1891 by signing a document that declared him her son. The two shared a house in Washington (usually with a third person) for over thirty years. Fletcher was nearly twenty years La Flesche's senior, but their domestic arrangements made them subject to recurring gossip.[50]

When La Flesche started working with Fletcher in the early 1880s, the content of their efforts was as often policy as anthropology. Fletcher had come to Washington on behalf of those Omahas (including Joseph La Flesche) who desired that their reservation be allotted to them in severalty so that the tribal reservation would be divided into individually owned parcels. To Fletcher and the faction of Omahas she represented, individual land ownership was the only guarantee that the Omahas would be able to stay upon the land they occupied, and the only means of safe passage from traditional tribal life to the new American "civilization." Fletcher was successful in her lobbying efforts, and Congress approved the Omaha allotment in 1882, a precursor to the 1887 Dawes Act. Moreover, Fletcher herself was appointed to conduct the actual allotment, the process through which Omahas would select the tracts of land they would own, and she took Francis La Flesche with her to the reservation to act as her interpreter and clerk.[51]

La Flesche, therefore, actively participated in the reform efforts of the Friends of the Indian, described in the previous chapter. Through the division of the Omaha reservation, he hoped to give tribal members a new security as individual subjects of the United States. His actions as a cultural anthropologist present a similar contradiction. Even as La Flesche tirelessly attempted to present Omaha culture in all of its complexity upon the printed page, he helped to dismantle it by playing a key role in the removal of sacred objects to Harvard University's Peabody Museum of Natural History. La Flesche reasonably worried that without such intervention, the objects would be destroyed when their keepers passed away, but the historical evidence also reveals that he held himself superior to Indians who actually treated such objects with religious reverence. He scoffed, for instance, when rumors circulated that the death of his father resulted from a promise Joseph La Flesche had made to accept the divine punishment for allowing the Omaha Sacred Pole (Umon'hon'ti) to leave the tribe. "The people are yet in the shackles of superstition," La Flesche wrote to Harvard anthropologist Frederic Ward Putman, "and it will be hard to make them believe that my father's death was in no way the result of the taking away of the pole."[52] Two years later, La Flesche wrote to Putnam offering to exhume an Omaha skeleton for the Harvard museum collection.[53]

The complex position of a person who referred to the sacred as "shackles of superstition," a phrase reminiscent of Boas's "fetters of tradition," yet devoted his professional career to the description and understanding of the same shackles, inevitably shaped the ethnographic record that La Flesche and Fletcher accumulated in their writing about the Omahas.[54] The culmination of these efforts to document Omaha culture was *The Omaha Tribe*, a two-volume ethnography published by the Bureau of American Ethnology in 1911. Unlike the earlier *Study of Omaha Music* (1893), in which Fletcher appeared as the author "aided" by La Flesche, the two appear here as joint authors. Fletcher even once suggested in a letter that La Flesche did most of the writing so that the work would have "the true Omaha flavor."[55] While the actual process of composition is not certain, what is more important is the way in which *The Omaha Tribe* frequently offers detailed explanations of how the remarkable objects it describes came to be removed from their Omaha keepers. In doing so, the ethnography foregrounds La Flesche's dual position as both a member of the tribe and someone using a methodology of observation foreign to the Omahas. This dichotomy becomes most apparent when La Flesche inserts his "boy memory" of the Sacred Pole into the ethnography. This first-person narrative, set off from the main text by its smaller typeface, in fact consists of two memories, La Flesche's recollections about the Pole from his boyhood and his depiction of his role in persuading the final tribal keeper of the Pole to relinquish it to the Peabody Museum.[56] This story demonstrates how the concept of culture, which emphasized the need to study carefully the meaning of such tribal objects as scientific artifacts, played a role in La Flesche's negotiation of the divide between the life he knew as a boy and the life he lived as an adult.

Through this story, as well as through others explaining how the Omahas parted with both objects and customs, *The Omaha Tribe* dramatizes one of the corollaries to the Boasian culture concept that would later become commonly accepted: that a people can "lose" their culture through the encroachment of another, more dominant one. If the meanings ascribed to the Sacred Pole are part of what make Omahas distinct from other groups, then removing it will lessen the force of this distinction. Furthermore, although Fletcher and La Flesche could hardly be said to have belonged to the Boasian school, *The Omaha Tribe* consistently shares Boas's emphasis on how the complexity of relationships among often seemingly disparate elements of culture forms an integral whole. As Christopher Herbert has argued, a basic principle of the culture concept as applied by Boasian ethnographers such as Ruth Benedict (in *Patterns of Culture* [1934]) is that the observable particulars of a group share hidden, nearly imperceptible ties that give each culture its unique essence.[57] Fletcher and La Flesche posit this holistic interpretation of culture when they emphasize how the tribal organization of the Omaha symbolizes a union of masculine and feminine parts, when they suggest that the Sacred Pole was created to fulfill the Omaha need for a symbol of tribal unity, and when they argue that the Omaha "Sacred Legend" proves "remarkably true" to what Benedict might have called the "pattern" of Omaha culture: "religious, thoughtful, and practical rather than imaginative and emotional."[58]

The stress that Fletcher and La Flesche put on Omaha tribal life as an integrated whole is crucial to the narrative arc of their ethnography— to how the work portrays time and sequences of change. Like Boas himself, Fletcher and La Flesche emphasize synchronic description; they attempt to present the complexity of traditional Omaha life at a moment just before it was drastically altered by the Omahas' efforts to assimilate Euro-American manners of living. The idea of culture as a complex whole helps Fletcher and La Flesche to explain both the scale of these changes and the necessity of preserving what came before them. Because Omaha life was so seam-lessly integrated, once one element of it (hunting) changed, the entire culture began to unravel; traditional customs became neglected, which in turn weakened the power of "ancient beliefs," and "as a result the Omaha became less strong to resist the inroads of new and adverse influences which came with his closer contact with the white race."[59] In other words, although Fletcher and La Flesche describe a series of changes in Omaha culture (the same changes that occurred between La Flesche's "boy mem-ory" of encountering the Sacred Pole and his adult one of removing it to a museum), they imply that Omaha culture will cease to exist after these changes are complete. For that reason, the "Recent History" of Omahas living in frame houses and attending the mission school is included only in an appendix, rather than in the main body of the work, for the true cul-ture of the tribe can be investigated only by describing the moment that precedes this history.

This emphasis on synchronic description typically offered American anthropologists in the early twentieth century an alternative to the stagist narratives of social Darwinism. However, in their portrayal of the "Recent History" of the Omahas, Fletcher and La Flesche also employed the model of culture-as-progress that motivated their political activities in the 1880s. Even though the bulk of the two volumes was dedicated to detail-ing the complexity of Omaha culture in a way that would not insert that culture into a hierarchical scheme of human progress, the ethnography ended with a congratulatory tone as it furnished evidence that the Omahas had abandoned their tribal customs and were "maintaining themselves under the new conditions imposed on them by the white race."[60] In other words, while *The Omaha Tribe* was dominated by the particularism that we now think of as central to the anthropological concept of culture, in order to describe what had happened to the Omaha Indians, it fell back upon the familiar narrative of cultural evolution (savagery to barbarism to civilization).

The jointly authored *Omaha Tribe* was not the first time that La Flesche

had faced the question of how to reconcile these two ways of understanding culture—culture as timeless description and culture as progressive
narrative. This same dilemma reverberates throughout *The Middle Five*,
La Flesche's earlier memoir in which he recounts his experiences as a
student in the Presbyterian mission school on the Omaha reservation. In
The Middle Five, La Flesche steps outside of social science, not to abandon
questions of culture, but rather to address them in an alternative discursive
forum. La Flesche wrote this autobiographical work at a moment when
he had good reason to reflect upon the events that had made him into a
professional observer of cultural difference. This was the moment, after all,
that he and Fletcher had agreed that he would alter his "avocation" so as
to communicate his knowledge of Native American cultures to a larger
audience. Equally relevant, at this time both La Flesche and Fletcher began
to feel a new ambivalence about the program of allotment and assimilation
that they had implemented among the Omahas.[61] That La Flesche chose to
write the first book-length work of his new career about a crucial site of
his own assimilation seems appropriate under such circumstances.

The *Middle Five*, released in 1900 by the trade publisher Small, Maynard,
and Company, has a notably different narrative scope than similar books
about education and assimilation.[62] Unlike Eastman's *Indian Boyhood*
(1902), La Flesche's account of his childhood does not focus on traditional
Native life, nor does it tell a complete story of his transformation from
one way of living to another. Works like Zitkala-Ša's autobiographical
essays (published in the *Atlantic Monthly* in 1901) and Eastman's *From
Deep Woods to Civilization* (1916) evoke the trajectory of the uplift narrative exemplified by Booker T. Washington's *Up From Slavery* (1901), even
when they work to foil its premise of a hierarchical cultural ladder, as
Zitkala-Ša's essays surely do. *The Middle Five* begins with La Flesche (called
"Frank" in the memoir) entering the mission school, and ends with him
still there. While significant changes do occur—Frank learns how to function at the school, develops new friendships, and, finally, loses one friend
to disease—La Flesche does not delineate the progressive sequence of a
Bildungsroman. Like the later *Omaha Tribe*, *The Middle Five* is governed by
the synchronic description characteristic of cultural particularism rather
than the diachronic narration of cultural evolution. La Flesche uses this
synchronic frame to depict the features of his cultural moment, a moment
in which the young Frank spends the majority of his time at the mission
school but still travels regularly to the village of his relatives, just as La
Flesche would later travel each summer from Washington to visit the
Omaha lands of his family.

The title of La Flesche's memoir refers to a "gang" that young Frank forms with four other boys. While Frank and his friends use the word "middle" to refer to their age relative to other boys at the school, La Flesche's book reports from the middle of mission-school life in other ways as well. Like many other culturalist works produced during the late nineteenth and early twentieth centuries, *The Middle Five* emphasizes the figure of an informant—a cultural go-between—who can narrate experiences from a point of view not usually accessible to the reader, but who is willing and able to communicate to a world outside the group in question. Harris's Uncle Remus and Chesnutt's Uncle Julius exemplify this device; as aging storytellers they appear to be of the world they describe yet slightly apart from it. In the case of La Flesche's work, the act of reportage is performed by a first-person narrator who reports from the perspective of young Frank. Even though this narrator speaks in the past tense and with a more polished diction than we might expect of a boy of Frank's age, the main text is free from overt intrusions and commentary about these adolescent experiences from a distanced, adult point-of-view. Only the preface gives us the voice of the older author looking back at his boyhood. As a result, there is little that is reflective in *The Middle Five;* the work does not address explicitly the question of how, with the passage of time, La Flesche might have come to regard his boyhood experiences in a different light.

La Flesche writes in his preface to *The Middle Five* that misconceptions about "Indian life and character" stem from ignorance of "the Indian's language, his mode of thought, his beliefs, his ideals, and his native institutions"—in short, from ignorance of the elements of culture that ethnography typically sought to capture. However, La Flesche continues, he has chosen to "write the story of my school-fellows rather than that of my other boy friends who knew only aboriginal life" so that the volume can perform the pedagogic function of educating the non-Native reader about the "true nature and character of the Indian boy." The school uniform did not change him or his classmates, the author states, but "it may help these little Indians to be judged, as are other boys, by what they say and what they do."[63] Such a purpose implies that a distinct cultural identity goes beyond any of its tangible elements, that group-based difference persists beyond the students' simple exchanges of dress and language. Such an interpretation of the preface is congruent with the cultural particularism necessary not just to ethnography, but also to the local-color and dialect fiction of American literary realism. At the same time, La Flesche is engaged in an invocation of "The Universal Boy," to whom he dedicates the book. The boy's "true nature and character" transcends local circumstances, he suggests; it is similar regardless of group affiliation.

La Flesche's appeal to the universality of cross-cultural boyhood character leads to another body of literary texts that flourished during the late-nineteenth century: boy books. Literary historians usually trace the genesis of the postbellum tradition of "boy books" or "bad-boy books" to Thomas Bailey Aldrich's *The Story of a Bad Boy* (1869), and include among its constituents well-known and lesser-known works of American literary realism, such as Mark Twain's *Adventures of Tom Sawyer* (1876) and *Adventures of Huckleberry Finn* (1885), Edward Eggleston's *The Hoosier School-Boy* (1883), William Dean Howells's *A Boy's Town* (1890), and Stephen Crane's *Whilmoville Stories* (1899).[64] These texts—sometimes autobiographical, sometimes not—valorize boyhood in narratives written primarily, if not exclusively, for adults. They are generically characterized not only by their nostalgic tone, but also by their insistence that boyhood is properly a time of innocuous mischief, freedom, and (limited) rebellion against authority. "I call my story the story of a bad boy, partly to distinguish myself from those faultless young gentlemen who generally figure in narratives of this kind," Aldrich states on the first page of his book.[65] *The Story of a Bad Boy* appeared in more than forty editions in the thirty years following its publication, and its popularity attests to the degree that its central premise, that a boyhood ought to include a certain freedom at the expense of personal safety, resonated in an age of increasing anxiety about the production of masculinity.[66]

To its original audience, La Flesche's *The Middle Five* would have been instantly recognizable as belonging to this tradition of boy books, through its portrayal of childhood pranks and camaraderie. At least one review, in fact, compared the book to Aldrich's *Story of a Bad Boy*. "Although the two books differ widely in detail," the anonymous review contended, "they are alike in the simplicity and truthfulness with which they reveal The Boy."[67] Like Aldrich's protagonist or Twain's Tom Sawyer, "Frank" aligns himself with a gang of boys that plans mischievous schemes and provides for its members' physical defense against rival gangs at school. Early in the memoir, La Flesche describes fighting as central to the entrance of a boy into the world of the mission school. Cut off from their tribal order and tradition, the male students must fashion a new identity in the mission school by displaying a willingness to both inflict and endure bodily suffering. "At the school we were all thrown together and left to form our own associates," La Flesche writes. "The sons of chiefs and of prominent men went with the sons of the common people, regardless of social standing and character. The only distinction made was against cowardice; ... I had to show that I was not afraid to stand up and fight" (11–12).

This passage portrays fighting among the boys as a key step in their removal from one culture and assimilation into another. Yet it might also be possible to understand these fisticuffs in another way. La Flesche and Fletcher would later write, in *The Omaha Tribe*, about fighting as integral to Omaha tribal identity. Early in the monograph, they state that the Omaha word "uki'te" has "a double import: As a verb, it means 'to fight'; as a noun, it signifies 'tribe'"; therefore, there is a direct tie between the practice of physically fighting and the Omahas' sense of themselves as a distinct people. Fletcher and La Flesche are quick to add a caveat, though. "The term *uki'te* is never applied to quarrels among members of the tribe in which fists and missiles are used; the words *niun'*, *nage'*, *ki'na* are used to designate such contentions from which the winner receives no renown."[68] In other words, while some kinds of fighting are culturally sanctioned, others are not.

In *The Middle Five*, La Flesche describes the protagonists' actions and leaves the reader to decide upon their propriety. Given what La Flesche would later write about the Omahas' valuation of physical fighting, one manner of reading those episodes where violence figures prominently is to ask how they might be judged from this Omaha system of belief. The passage (quoted above) in which fisticuffs enable the boys to establish an order replacing the rules and boundaries of village life defies, according to La Flesche's later ethnography, the Omaha standard.[69] While La Flesche does not write that these boyhood brawls were condoned by the missionaries who ran the school, readers acquainted with the "boy book" tradition would have recognized them as familiar, even normative, occurrences in an "American" childhood—and therefore, paradoxically, a necessary prelude to the passage from Omaha "barbarism" to U.S. "civilization."[70]

This first account of fighting at the mission, in which Frank realizes he must earn respect at the school by physically defending himself, represents an obvious moment in the conflict produced by the transition from one way of living to another, but the boyhood fighting in *The Middle Five* is not always so easily interpreted. The mission boys engage, for instance, in a "terrific battle" (110) with a group of Ponca boys wearing buffalo robes and scalp-locks. Upon first seeing these boys approach the mission, the schoolchildren laugh at their appearance (107); the Poncas, in turn, sit near the window of the classroom so that they can mimic the actions of the teacher and students (108). When the Poncas steal the sleds of the Omaha boys, the fight begins:

The Ponkas made a determined resistance. I cannot very well relate what
happened around me; for I was engaged in a lively bout with an impish-
looking little chap for whom I had taken a sudden unreasonable spite....
I noticed that he was more afraid of my brogans than of my fists; taking
advantage of this, I pretended to lift my foot for a fierce kick; he hopped
backwards, and, in so doing, bent his body toward me. Quick as a flash,
I grasped his two braids, pulled his head down, and brought my right
knee up against it with tremendous force, and he went sprawling in the
snow. (110)

The text offers at least three ways of understanding this violence. La
Flesche's calling the Ponca boy "an impish-looking chap" gives the scene
an air of comedy and places it as a harmless, though perhaps foolish, boyhood scrap. The contrast between Frank's brogans and the braids of the
Ponca boy characterize the episode as an example of conflict between
assimilationist and traditional ways of living. And the emphasis on tribal
affiliation raises the possibility that this action is the sort of honorable
tribal self-defense that the Omahas have in mind in using the same word
to mean both "tribe" and "to fight." A bit later, La Flesche provides another
reminder that some kinds of conflict are subject to Omaha disapproval;
Frank's father scolds him for neglecting to help a destitute Winnebago
man being teased by a crowd of Omahas in the village. But the significance
of the Omaha-Ponca "battle" remains uncertain, an indeterminacy that
signals the obliqueness of cultural identity itself during a period when the
pressures of assimilation were so powerful and so complex.

Through its depiction of fighting, *The Middle Five* engages questions
about the meaning of culture, and portrays the world of the mission
school as the site of transition, a characterization reinforced throughout
the text. The narrative follows Frank as he regularly visits his family, with
whom he participates in activities more traditionally Omaha than are
those of the mission. Equally important, the Omaha boys do not abandon
their language or forget what they have learned prior to entering the
school. In one scene, a newly arrived student tells the Omaha story of First
Man and First Woman, while another boy interrupts with the Genesis
account of Adam and Eve (58–64). Later, the "Middle Five" joins another
gang in an invocation of the tribal "word of command," by which the
boys meet at night, in secret, to appoint two runners to sneak to the village
after a bag of pemmican for the boys to eat (113–18). These episodes remind
the reader that this back-and-forth shuttling between tribal and mission
manners of living is far from easy, and also ensure that the memoir does
not offer a smooth narrative of "progress" from one culture to another. *The*

Middle Five asks what constitutes culture, what keeps cultures distinct, and what the consequences are when members of a tribal culture absorb the practices of a non-tribal one.

To think of La Flesche as writing from outside (and not *against*) the standard assimilationist paradigm may help make sense of one scene in *The Middle Five* in which he indirectly addresses the roots of his own career as an ethnographer. When visitors, most likely associated with the governing Presbyterian Board of Foreign Missions, come to the school, one inquires of the students, "Have your people music, do they sing?" After a bit of further prompting, the students respond with a demonstration:

> There was some hesitancy, but suddenly a loud clear voice close to me
> broke into a Victory song; before a bar was sung another voice took up
> the song from the beginning, as is the custom among the Indians, then the
> whole school fell in, and we made the room ring. We understood the song,
> and knew the emotion of which it was the expression. We felt, as we sang,
> the patriotic thrill of a victorious people who had vanquished their
> enemies; but the men shook their heads, and one of them said, "That's
> savage, that's savage! They must be taught music." (100)

The passage is a forceful reminder of the chauvinism that motivated the missionary movement and the reform efforts of Friends of the Indian. This obviously well-meaning and sympathetic observer, after asking for the rare (for him) pleasure of hearing an Indian song, considers Omaha singing patently inferior. He does not think it, in fact, "music" at all. Therefore, these children already skilled, at least by this account, in "savage" music must learn the songs sung by middle-class whites throughout the United States.

There is no bitterness in the narrator's tone as he recounts this episode and what results from it. La Flesche reports that he and his classmates enjoyed the singing lessons that followed, and recounts that the limitations of his own singing voice became the subject of good-natured mirth (101–2). His laconic narration of the episode and its consequences could even allow someone in sympathy with the assimilationist program of Indian reform to feel reassured that this "savage" outburst has been contained by the mechanisms of "civilization." But the gap between the emotional force of the victory song and the response it engenders in its white auditor prevents a more careful reader from losing sight of what is at stake here. As much as the young La Flesche might have wanted to believe that what the mission represented would not alter the culture that created the victory song, the adult La Flesche through this scene shares his realization that the relationship between the world of the mission and the world of the Omaha village is fraught with possibilities for misunderstanding. What proves dangerous, the text insists, is not the desire of the missionaries to teach the Omaha children to sing in a Western style, but the failure of the missionaries to recognize the integrity of the culture that the Omaha victory song represents.

In *The Omaha Tribe*, La Flesche and Fletcher explain more precisely what a victory song signifies. Sung after the return of a war party, they write, the music of such songs was "vivacious, and the words were frequently boasting or taunting in character." Such songs did not stress individual prowess or exploits; rather, they emphasized the common welfare and accomplishments of the tribe.[71] In other words, the ethnography ties the victory song to the kind of honorable fighting denoted by the Omaha word for "tribe." The Omaha schoolchildren, however, have not returned from war. Why, then, would they sing the song at this moment—the only time the mission authorities have actively encouraged them to speak in their native language? What have they won? Perhaps the singing of the song is a self-referential act; the victory to which the song refers could very well be the enunciation of the song itself by the Omaha children in this missionary classroom. That the students still know and are still prepared to sing a song that elicits such a "patriotic thrill" in the face of the pressures upon them to embrace a different set of allegiances constitutes a form of tribal self-defense. Such a victory may not be what their Omaha parents and grandparents once had in mind when singing the song, but this shift is much to the point of what the students' performance celebrates. They have managed to continue Omaha verbal expressions while learning others that would replace them, even though such continuance has required redefining the cultural meaning that such expressions acquire in a new context.

That La Flesche's text articulates this point in an episode in which song figures so centrally can hardly be accidental. Music played a key role in his career as a social scientist. Much of his early work with Fletcher revolved around the recording and analysis of traditional Omaha songs, and these efforts in ethnomusicology, including *A Study of Omaha Music*, were widely recognized as innovative and necessary contributions to anthropology.[72] Once, Fletcher even admitted, in a letter, that La Flesche had the idea to transcribe Omaha songs before she did.[73] La Flesche's efforts to preserve in print verbal expressions like the victory song connect him with the salvage imperative so influential to both social science and literature during this period. Salvage ethnographers from the late nineteenth and early twentieth centuries have since been accused of creating flat, lifeless texts, as well as of caring more for recording vernacular expressions than for engaging the people who created them. *The Middle Five*, however, suggests that La Flesche understood ethnography in quite different terms. Frank's singing of the victory song presages the devotion that the adult La Flesche would have to the documentation of culture, and dramatizes how traditional songs, stories, games, and even ceremonies could continue to be part of how Omahas understood themselves and experienced the world, even as they engaged the challenges of living in a world altered by the Dawes Act and other pro-assimilation policies of Indian reform.

Ethnography, the writing of culture, plays a necessary part in this process for someone like La Flesche, for it offers a medium through which he and other Indians could explain the symbolic meaning possessed by seemingly trivial practices. The ethnographic explanation of the victory song in the singing scene in *The Middle Five* is not in the memoir itself. This absence, in fact, dramatizes the need for that information—a point that La Flesche demonstrates further with another instance of song near the end of the book. Instead of a moment of climactic unity, though, this later episode is mundane: Frank and his friends are playing "Oo-hae'ba-shon-shon"—which La Flesche translates into "tortuous path" and describes as a version of "follow my leader"—and singing a short "Children's Song" that accompanies the game (144). Here La Flesche actually produces, as he does not in his description of the students singing the victory song, two bars of music and the lyrics, both set off from the main text under its title. He has given the reader, in other words, a full-fledged ethnographic speci-men, complete with information about the boys from whom he heard it (probably not for the first time) and a description of the game. This infor-mation is exactly what one expects of a good ethnographer, and it is nearly identical to what he and Fletcher provide in *The Omaha Tribe*, with one crucial exception. In *The Omaha Tribe*, the discussion of this game and song occurs within the broader description of traditional tribal life; for example, the music faces a photo of Omaha boys standing in front of a tepee.[74] In *The Middle Five*, in contrast, the boys play the game while returning to their village during the weekend. If the culture concept em-phasizes the unseen relationships among the constituent parts of a single culture, then this contextual shift calls our attention to the way the game functions differently for the schoolchildren than for those playing it in the village. To the schoolchildren, the game is more than a remnant of a holis-tic tribal culture that has been relegated to the past, as it is for La Flesche-the-ethnographer; the boys are neither nostalgic nor wistful when they play the game. To the contrary, it has become part of the complex, occasionally

unconscious efforts of these boys to imagine themselves as Omahas nonetheless wholly engaged with the challenges and pressures placed upon them
by the mission school.

It is tempting to interpret La Flesche's portrayal of the Omaha schoolchildren as making the case for their being capable of something postmodern—of inhabiting a border zone that creates new possibilities for
cultural montage in a manner similar to, for example, what Renato Rosaldo
identifies in Gloria Anzaldúa's *Borderlands/La Frontera.* "In making herself
into a complex persona," Rosaldo writes, "Anzaldúa incorporates Mexican,
Indian, and Anglo elements at the same time that she discards the homo-
phobia and patriarchy of Chicano culture. In rejecting the classic 'authenticity' of cultural purity, she seeks out the many-stranded possibilities
of the borderlands."[75] Likewise, La Flesche's boys incorporate elements of
Omaha culture into their Presbyterian mission routines, as well as language and lessons from the mission into their village life, and so manage
to survive the jarring experience of forced assimilation. But the diction
and tone of *The Middle Five* do not support the active agency of picking
and choosing, of careful selection, that Rosaldo attributes to Anzaldúa.
For La Flesche, culture shapes his characters (including the younger self
that acts as the narrator), not the reverse. To make this point is not to
say that La Flesche renders the Omaha boys passive; to the contrary, it is
to argue that, for an ethnographer like him, agency is circumscribed by
culture. To use Michel de Certeau's phrase, the Omaha elders and the mission teachers both instruct the boys in "ways of operating"—of dressing,
of singing, of storytelling—and *The Middle Five* emphasizes the formative
power of these ways upon the boys, instead of the boys' opportunity to
choose among them.[76] At the level of narrative style, the text reinforces
the constraint of culture by rarely pulling back from the perspective of
young Frank. La Flesche forces his reader to occupy the point of view of a
boy who must constantly make decisions taking into consideration both
his Omaha education and his mission one, yet who does not necessarily
understand all of the options he might have to act differently.

In this manner, *The Middle Five* confronts a fundamental problem that
the anthropology of La Flesche's time was largely incapable of resolving:
how the integrity of a culture could persist while going through periods
of dramatic change. La Flesche is not ultimately writing a story of inno-
cents caught between two cultures. Rather, he shows how the boys of the
mission school struggle to integrate their experiences and to imagine a
way of understanding the world that comprises both Omaha tradition and
the mission lifeways so unfamiliar to their parents. In doing so, they must

reject the version of modernity put forward by the project of American-ization, in which "modern" Indians could participate in tribal practices only as nostalgic indulgences, and somehow reformulate modernity as a configuration of Omaha meanings and actions that exist simultaneous to the manners of living taught at the mission. The narrative structure of *The Middle Five* insists upon the simultaneity necessary to reimagining moder-nity in this way—of dispensing with the temporal division between tradi-tional "culture" and modern "civilization." Equally important, the printed text of the children's song near the conclusion of *The Middle Five* reminds us that, for La Flesche, ethnography will play a role in this process. As a memoir, the text shows us how La Flesche came to regard the documen-tation of culture as a tool that could be employed by tribal peoples in their continuing efforts to imagine themselves *as* tribal peoples while confronting the challenges of often chaotic change, even if social scientific literature regularly disregarded that very chaos in order to produce a more orderly tradition.[77] The form of the memoir, in other words, both illumi-nates the limits of documenting culture and articulates its purpose.

On at least one occasion in *The Middle Five*, La Flesche presents an episode in which he overtly allegorizes the method of observation com-mon to ethnography and literary realism. Frequently, the narrator tells us, the boys would borrow the "spy-glass" of the school superintendent and climb to the belfry of the mission building. From there they could survey their surroundings, including the fields tended by the Omahas, the steam-boats on the Missouri River, and the nearby grave of Big Elk, the chief who adopted Joseph La Flesche and who was therefore a member of Frank's clan (10).[78] On one occasion, the boys use the glass to watch the procession of the Omaha hunt, such an exciting sight that Frank and a friend decide to run away and join it, only to be returned to the mission by Frank's father (84–92). The spyglass—a symbol that Zora Neale Hurston would also employ to signify anthropological observation—works here as the means by which Frank negotiates and strengthens the relationship between the mission and the tribal custom of the hunt. While the spyglass makes it possible for him to occupy a more secure ground of cultural identity, it does not open up a space of complete agency; rather, he is compelled by the tools that he sees with, the place that he occupies, and the finite number of things the glass lets him see, even though such a view encom-passes more than he could observe with the naked eye. Equally important, the choice that Frank makes to join the hunt is met with the greater force of his father's desire that he return to the mission school. The young La Flesche, like his mature counterpart, may attempt to engage in the process of making a cultural identity, but he will in turn be made by the culture in which he lives.

A few years after the period covered by *The Middle Five*, La Flesche did participate in the Omaha buffalo hunt; in fact, he once stated that he did so three times before the hunt was abandoned in 1876 (due to diminished herds).[79] On at least one occasion he even served as runner, scouting out the buffalo on foot and, according to his obituary, covering one hundred miles in about eighteen hours.[80] Perhaps the most useful way of thinking about *The Middle Five* is as an attempt by La Flesche to describe the experiential underpinnings of a concept of cultural identity that would explain how he could attend the mission school, enter fully into the tribally significant buffalo hunt, and then proceed to a professional career in which he wrote about the Omahas from a distance.

La Flesche takes on this problem by combining the genre of the boy book, with its framework for discussing the limited freedom of childhood, with the ethnographic description in which he was already well-versed. While this generic overlap forms the foundation of *The Middle Five*, the reading public proved less interested in his project of accounting for cultural change than La Flesche surely hoped. The first editor to read the manuscript remarked that La Flesche should instead produce something that focused on "the other *wilder* existence"—in other words, tepees instead of missions. Although La Flesche did eventually acquire a publisher for the memoir, his subsequent literary efforts followed this early editor's advice. He began, but never completed, a set of stories about Omaha traditional life (including one that seems based on his own experiences on the buffalo hunt), stories similar to Eastman's *Indian Boyhood* or to La Flesche's own ethnographic representations of the Omahas in *The Omaha Tribe*. During this period, he also seems to have attempted a novel on assimilation—about a man who is born to Indian parents, adopted by whites, and then elects to return to the Indian tribe of his origin—yet, again, he did not complete the book.[81] Such starts and finishes suggest that La Flesche must have found a more comfortable home in the discipline of cultural anthropology, to which he returned with indubitable success, and indicate the difficulty of addressing those issues that seem to matter most in the meditations upon culture implicit in *The Middle Five*.

Throughout his career as a writer, La Flesche employed the idea of culture to describe how the men and women who understood themselves to be Omaha might continue in that communal understanding. For the Omahas to constitute a culture did not have to mean that they removed themselves entirely from the other cultures with which they came into contact. Indeed, in *The Middle Five* La Flesche demonstrates that ideas of cultural identity and cultural difference only become recognizable through cross-cultural interaction. Throughout the memoir he incorporates verbal expressions—the Omaha origin story, the victory song, the song that accompanied the boys' game—that the Omaha boys understood differently than their white counterparts might have. The distinctions that comprise culture emanate from the ways such expressions acquire differing meanings. As an ethnographer, La Flesche dedicated himself to seemingly contradictory purposes, describing cultures as distinct, complex entities, while attempting to render such entities transparent to those viewing them from the outside.

The paradoxical nature of this project may help to explain the incongruities of La Flesche's actions throughout his life. As a young man, he fostered the removal of sacred Omaha objects and the division of the Omaha reservation. In the late 1910s, however, he defended the use of peyote by the Native American Church as reflecting the cultural values of those Indians who participated—a stance that aligned him with fellow ethnographer James Mooney but against Charles Eastman and Zitkala-Ša.[82] When placed against a reading of *The Middle Five*, such actions suggest someone coming to grips with the importance of cultural identity and developing a new sense of how culture might respond to change without losing its ontological status *as* culture.

I must be careful, however, to explain what La Flesche did and did not claim on behalf of culture. Noticeably absent from *The Middle Five*, and from the works I have discussed by Eastman and Zitkala-Ša, are the economic issues and vocabulary that dominated turn-of-the-century debates about the "Indian Question." Cultural identity does not seem to have been directly related to a distinct, self-sufficient tribal economy for La Flesche, nor does he argue that the Omahas should continue to possess political sovereignty. Even if he did regret the role that he played in allotment (something that we can only guess at now), La Flesche does not articulate the necessity of self-determination in the way that many Native American intellectuals have done since the middle of the twentieth century. [83]

Instead, La Flesche argued for cultural integrity, and in doing so he very likely contributed to the sense that Omahas continue to have of themselves as a distinct people, a sense that neither he nor Alice Fletcher nor many other of his contemporary anthropologists probably believed would survive into the twenty-first century. That the Omahas do continue to imagine themselves as a culture is perhaps best exemplified by the recent return to them of many of the objects, including the Sacred Pole, that La Flesche arranged to move to Harvard's Peabody Museum. Such repatriations of objects are predicated upon the premise that they have particular value and meaning to certain groups, and that those meanings take precedence over the interests of others. The conviction with which Omaha tribal leaders have asserted the power of such objects to make the Omahas "one people, one unit" demonstrates that the notion of culture that La Flesche and his contemporaries struggled with continues to matter—even to those working to undo the actions of that same generation of anthropologists.[84]

The convergence of the genres of ethnography and literature that La Flesche enacts in *The Middle Five* continues to matter, as well. Literary texts throughout the twentieth century became conveyors of ethnographic information that invited audiences to regard culturally distinct practices, beliefs, and expressions as aesthetically compelling. The vocabulary of culture, in other words, has come routinely to inform the manner in which aesthetic writing about group-based difference in the United States is produced and received. However, *The Middle Five* also shows how texts drawing upon both literary and ethnographic traditions could be used to reformulate the notion of culture central to each of these forms of writing in the late nineteenth century. The complete legacy of this confluence to twentieth-century literature would require another book (if not two) but in the concluding chapter I will try to show how one author writing in Boas's wake, Zora Neale Hurston, made the possibilities and problems of culture central to her career.

6

Beyond Boas:
The Realism of Zora Neale Hurston

In his preface to a 1993 collection of criticism on Zora Neale Hurston, Henry Louis Gates Jr., commented on how suddenly Hurston had emerged as a canonical figure in American literary history and how widespread the interest in her writing had become. "Last year at Yale alone," he stated in a parenthetical aside, "seventeen courses taught *Their Eyes Were Watching God!*"[1] This speaks to the extent of the canonization of Hurston, a canonization that is still secure. Equally significant, this observation reminds us how, at the moment that multiculturalism became the governing rubric of college curricula, writers like Hurston came to figure prominently not only in disciplines of literary studies, but in the reading of literature by other disciplines, as well as in interdisciplinary endeavors. (It is hard to imagine that every one of the seventeen courses Gates mentions was offered by the English department.)

The recuperation of Hurston's works in the late twentieth century and the popularity of her works across disciplines indexes the continuing importance of the convergence of literature and ethnography that I have been tracing in regard to the period of American literary realism.[2] In the twentieth century, the cross-disciplinary endeavor of documenting culture through literary and scientific texts not only continued, but flourished. In the 1910s, for instance, modernist poets in the United States, including Carl Sandburg, Amy Lowell, and Vachel Lindsay, would further extend the attention to the aesthetic qualities of cultural documents by taking Native American verbal works collected by professional ethnographers and interpreting them in books like *Path on the Rainbow* (1918), edited by George Cronyn, and in literary magazines such as *Poetry: A Magazine of Verse*, which produced a special "Aboriginal" issue in 1917.[3] Yet prose narrative ultimately proved more significant than poetry in the production of culturalist texts situated at the convergence I have described, for issues of narrative are bound up with the most difficult questions that such texts attempt to address.

Hurston's corpus plays a complicated role in this trajectory of twentieth-century writing. As a result of her training in the methods and theory of the Boas school and her acumen as a writer of fictional narrative, her work in social science and in literature affords the opportunity to consider how the textual forms that gained popularity in the late nineteenth century changed after the advent of literary modernism, both in their formal properties and in their engagement with questions of group-based difference. The resurgence of interest in Hurston's work during the last twenty-five years, meanwhile, compels us to consider how current practices of reading literature regard the documentation of culture. It is with this double frame in mind—Hurston as a writer of the 1930s *and* as a literary icon of the 1990s—that I turn to her work and step out of the chronological period that has occupied me throughout this book. My hope is not to provide a complete discussion of Hurston's writing in either social science or literature, but to contend that the continued convergence between these two realms poses a challenge to literary studies that must be addressed.

This challenge can be met through an engagement with Hurston's manipulation of the traditions of cultural realism in American writing. Like Chesnutt and La Flesche, Hurston employs the idiom of ethnography in her fiction to make configurations of group-based difference at once seem "real" to the reader and seem the product of social construction. In this way, the textualization of culture becomes both authentic and distinct from biological determinism. However, Hurston's texts also undermine our confidence in the reliability of culture as an accurate way of understanding human identity. Her ethnography and her novels show culture to be more than a conceptual tool for understanding how groups participate in distinct patterns of living; rather, her work shows the violence that ways of living can enforce upon those who make up a group. If Hurston's writing and its reception shows the prevalence of culture as an appealing and even tactical way of understanding difference, it also shows the danger of attributing to culture the normative power of the real.

The Chemise of Culture

Critical arguments about the writing career of Zora Neale Hurston (1891–1960) frequently pivot around interpretation of her relationship to the Boasian anthropology she encountered in her studies at Barnard College and Columbia University—and especially to Franz Boas himself. For some, such as Houston A. Baker Jr., the relationship between Hurston and the discipline of anthropology was antagonistic; she subverted its dull and dreary conventions, bristled at the condescending supervision of "Papa Franz," and used the scienticity of ethnography as a cover for the creative energies that she released more fully in her novels.[4] In contrast, Hazel V. Carby has argued that Hurston shared too much with the Boasian enterprise, that her commitment to anthropology—which Carby believes was a dangerous search for a romanticized, nostalgic version of the "folk"— confined the scope and achievement of her fiction.[5] Instead of pursuing either of these arguments, I wish to ask what a talented writer fully immersed in the Harlem Renaissance of the 1920s and 1930s might have found compelling about the social scientific documentation of culture. Hurston herself described her complex relationship to anthropology in the often-quoted first paragraph of her introduction to *Mules and Men*, an ethnographic account of African American life in the rural South:

> When I pitched headforemost into the world I landed in the crib of negroism. From the earliest rocking of my cradle, I had known about the capers Brer Rabbit is apt to cut and what the Squinch Owl says from the house top. But it was fitting me like a tight chemise. I couldn't see it for wearing it. It was only when I was off in college, away from my native surroundings, that I could see myself like somebody else and stand off and look at my garment. Then I had to have the spy-glass of Anthropology.[6]

Hurston's story of moving from the "crib of negroism" to the "spy-glass of Anthropology" is a story about knowledge, culture, and even storytelling itself. To have "known" of Brer Rabbit and Squinch Owl as she did in her early childhood, she suggests, is not the only way of knowing them. Rather, the writing of what follows in the "Folk Tales" section of *Mules and Men* required a different knowledge at which she arrived only through distance ("away from my native surroundings") and training ("the spy-glass of Anthropology"). Like Francis La Flesche, she has found both in the practice of professional ethnography. It is as a scholar from the metropole that she revisits the rural region of her youth, traveling, like the tourists of local color fiction, to a remote region in search of "material."

Hurston emphasizes just how difficult it has been for her to achieve this professional distance through the metaphor of the "tight chemise"— a close-fitting, sexualized garment—a metaphor that suggests how vulnerable the speaker of this passage imagines herself in executing this project. For Hurston to view the chemise of culture, and to share that view with her audience, requires a strip-tease. In this image, Hurston captures her commitment to the Boasian division between race and culture, as well as the impossibility of deflecting a racially motivated gaze from her own black body as she takes on the office of ethnographer. She follows the realist tradition of portraying culture as a distinct, tangible entity that can be, finally, separated from the physical bodies that bear it, just as verbal artifacts can be rendered tangible through texts. But in Hurston's case, this process may invite the audience to stare at her as much as at the chemise she has struggled to remove.[7]

Hurston was among the very few ethnographers instructed in the theory and methods of the Boas school who used that training to study the culture in which she was raised (a practice now labeled "autoethnography").[8] The structure of the ethnographic project presumed a distance between the observer and the culture being documented that necessarily created difficulty for those undertaking such an autoethnographic project. The cultural boundary that typically divided the anthropologist from his or her subject was considered crucial to the practice of anthropology as an objective science. For the generation of cultural anthropologists who trained Hurston, this encounter with otherness constituted an antidote to cultural chauvinism by offering Westerners the chance to see that cultural practices were the result of accidental historical accretions and not the result of either biological superiority or divine plan. In *Coming of Age in Samoa*, published in 1928 while Hurston was at Barnard, Margaret Mead characterized the anthropological necessity of bridging the cultural divide in more pointedly Eurocentric terms: "[I]f we step outside the stream of Indo-European culture," Mead writes, "the appreciation which we can accord *our civilization* is even more enhanced" (emphasis added).[9]

The separation that Mead takes for granted was at odds with one of Hurston's presumed assets as an ethnographer. Her familiarity with the "crib of negroism" enabled her, as Boas wrote in his foreword to *Mules and Men*, "to penetrate through that affected demeanor by which the Negro excludes the White observer effectively from participating in his inner

life" (3). The scientific distance required for the "spy-glass of Anthropology" was both a necessity and an impossibility for Hurston. As Karen
Jacobs states in her assessment of Hurston's use of cultural anthropology,
"Boasian theory . . . provides a fully realized conceptual basis from which
to revalue African-American expressive forms, but it requires a problem-
atically objectifying distance from its selected objects of study to do so."[10]
Like La Flesche, Hurston would respect this distance and employ it as a
means of framing the vernacular expression vital to her work, but would
also collapse it to narrate the experiences of someone speaking that same
vernacular.

　　Hurston's position returns us to questions of determinism and the place
of the individual in culture. For even though Boasian culture underscored
the necessity of documenting the group-based expression and systems of
meaning that Hurston found so valuable in the African American community of her youth, it did not explain how an individual member of that
group, like Hurston, could somehow stand outside that system. Hurston
went farther than any of her contemporary Boasians in addressing this
question; indeed, the relationship of the individual to culture shapes the
narrative structure of both her first book-length work of ethnography,
Mules and Men (1935), and her two earliest published novels, *Jonah's Gourd
Vine* (1934) and *Their Eyes Were Watching God* (1937). In her consideration
of how a culture makes and shapes an individual, Hurston participated
in a larger dialogue within Boasian anthropology, in which the strength
and nature of culture were being reexamined. In Boas's early writing,
including texts such as *The Mind of Primitive Man* (1911), the force of the
culture concept revolved around its negation of racial determinism. Culture was regularly invoked (often without even using the word "culture")
to demonstrate why behavioral phenomena were the result of social, rather
than biological, forces. By the time that Hurston began her studies at
Barnard in 1925, this division between race and culture had become a
settled point within the discipline, and the burden of the Boasians, at least
when speaking to other social scientists, had shifted. Anthropology now
needed to explain how culture operated as "a thing *sui generis* which can
be explained only in terms of itself," as one Boasian put it in 1918.[11] This
task had already sparked two well-known statements of Boasian anthropology: Alfred L. Kroeber's "The Superorganic" (1917) and Edward Sapir's
"Culture, Genuine and Spurious" (1924).

　　Each of these articles, Kroeber's and Sapir's, speaks of culture as a
more coherent force than Boas ever did—and each addresses the relationship between the individual and the group, in an attempt to theorize

culture. For Kroeber, biology and the study of the organic can account for the production of individual genius or character, which is thus outside the province of social science. Conversely, the "social or cultural," the subject of anthropology and other social sciences, "is in its essence non-individual."[12] By the end of "The Superorganic," Kroeber attributes to the cultural a metaphysical quality that "transcends" the organic; he describes culture as a "social substance—or unsubstantial fabric, if one prefers that phrase" that dwarfs the individual in importance.[13] In "Cultures, Genuine and Spurious," Sapir attempts to make greater room for the significance of the individual, but the article also characterizes culture as an entity greater than the sum of the individuals who comprise it. In fact, it is the relationship of the individual to the culture that makes some cultures more successful, more "genuine," than others. "A genuine culture," he writes, "must be looked upon as a sturdy plant growth, each remotest leaf and twig of which is organically fed by the sap at the core."[14] Sapir's metaphor describes what he believes most crucial to culture, a harmonious equilibrium between each individual (the "remotest leaf and twig") and the cultural whole ("the sap at the core").

Ruth Benedict's *Patterns of Culture* (1934)—the best-known single-volume work produced by any anthropologist of the Boas school, with the exception of Mead's *Coming of Age in Samoa*—extended the efforts of Kroeber and Sapir to describe cultures as existing in coherent wholes. *Patterns* offers an important reference point for the fiction and ethnography that Hurston published during the same period. Although Benedict's book did not appear until 1934, Hurston would have almost certainly been familiar with its argument long before, since Benedict had, as early as 1928, delivered papers and published articles subsequently incorporated in the book.[15] Moreover, as Mark Helbling has pointed out, the relationship between Benedict and Hurston was more extensive than accounts of Hurston's anthropological training typically mention. Benedict taught Hurston at Barnard, and the two corresponded during Hurston's fieldwork and into the 1940s. Hurston even wrote to Boas that she hoped Benedict would "sort of" edit *Mules and Men*.[16]

In *Patterns of Culture*, Benedict puts forward what came to be known as the "culture-and-personality" thesis, the argument that cultures frequently, although not always, cohere around a dominant theme, such as a personality type or a psychological configuration.[17] While not every member of a culture will display this quality, the culture as a whole exhibits this "pattern" through its institutions, stories, and prohibitions. Like Kroeber and Sapir, Benedict therefore emphasizes that cultures "are more than the sum of their traits"—that they are integrated into a whole.[18] Notably, Benedict remarks that the "integration of cultures ... is the same process by which a *style in art* comes into being and persists" (emphasis added).[19] And like an aesthetic style, a cultural pattern will favor those individuals most disposed to its features. Benedict goes even farther, in fact, than Kroeber or Sapir in suggesting the powerlessness of an individual in the face of cultural forces. "The life-history of the individual," she writes in the first chapter, "is first and foremost an accommodation to the patterns and standards traditionally handed down in his community."[20]

The same year that Benedict's book was published, Hurston's article "Characteristics of Negro Expression" appeared in Nancy Cunard's *Negro* anthology. "Characteristics" was not Hurston's first ethnographic work to appear in print, but it differed from both her earlier articles (such as those in *The Journal of American Folk-Lore*) and her later books (*Mules and Men* and *Tell My Horse*) in its effort to synthesize ethnographic data and reach conclusions about African American lifeways much as Benedict did for the Zuni, Kwakiutl, and Dobu cultures described in *Patterns*. The short first paragraph of Hurston's article reads as though she were deliberately employing Benedict's methodology to see the culture of "the Negro" as organized around a single theme:

> The Negro's universal mimicry is not so much a thing in itself as an evidence of something that permeates his entire self. And that thing is drama.[21]

The desire for the dramatic, Hurston continues, forms the pattern of the African American culture. It explains the use of metaphor in African American speech, the ways in which African Americans decorate their homes, and the cadences of their religious services.[22]

Benedict's characterization of culture as being like a "style in art" is closely tied to what Hurston is describing as the "Characteristics of Negro Expression." In her article, Hurston claims that what typifies African American culture is a certain style of expression, not what is actually said. The Biblical apostle Peter, John D. Rockefeller, and Henry Ford can all figure in African American cultural expression, Hurston argues, because of the style through which African Americans delineate them as dramatic figures. Similarly, it does not matter that some African Americans follow the religious beliefs first imparted to them by white Christians; what matters is that African Americans turn their services into "excellent prose poetry.

Both prayers and sermons are tooled and polished until they become true works of art" (834). Mimicry is both prevalent and aesthetically accomplished, according to Hurston, but does not make African American culture less integrated or pure. Instead, mimicry demonstrates the love of drama that Hurston believes at the center of this cultural pattern.

The logic of Hurston's characterization of African American culture is nearly reducible to a tautology; being a Negro, she seems to write, consists of acting things out in a Negro way. Were Hurston to stop there, she would seem to deploy the essentialism typical of biological definitions of racism, for African American culture would simply be those things that, by virtue of their birth, African Americans know how to do. Yet Hurston attempts to rearticulate Benedict's equation between culture and artistic style in a way that evades such essentialism. For if a certain desire for, and method of, dramatization stands at the center of Negro culture, then it would be theoretically possible for people who are not biologically Negro to actually engage in Negro behavior, as well as for people of Negro ancestry to act in ways not characteristic of the culture. Hurston, in fact, charts out both of these possibilities. The performance of Mae West on the stage offers her an example of the former phenomenon; West "had much more of the flavor of the turpentine quarters than she did of the white bawd," Hurston writes (844). On the other hand, the Fisk Jubilee Singers furnish Hurston with an instance of a "trick style of delivery" not actually consistent with the style of Negro culture (845). In each instance, Hurston describes cultural identity not as something that one *has* by virtue of group affiliation, but something one *does*.[23]

In "Characteristics of Negro Expression," Hurston puts forth an understanding of culture that explains several hallmarks of her longer fiction and ethnography from the same period. First, Hurston brings us to a subtly different relationship between the individual and culture than that described by Kroeber, Sapir, and Benedict. Like Benedict, Hurston sees African Americans dramatically enacting the psychological qualities central to their cultural configuration. At the same time, Hurston stresses the individual act of that drama as Benedict does not. As I shall show with both *Mules and Men* and *Jonah's Gourd Vine*, this accent upon individual creativity allows Hurston to describe culture as a realm of tension as well as of harmony, where cultural forms not only reflect, but also produce, the medium of conflict between the individual and the group. As with the other theoreticians of culture from the Boas school, Hurston is keenly interested in how culture determines the behavior and actions of an individual, but she focuses on the dilemma posed by Boas in "An Eskimo

Winter": what does it mean for an individual to be at odds with the culture in which he or she lives?

Hurston's 1934 article on Negro vernacular expression highlights a second formal principle of her writing crucial to her career. According to Hurston, representations of African American culture—by blackface comedians, Broadway shows, the Jubilee Singers—frequently fail to reproduce the characteristic style of Negro dramatics. Her own task as a writer therefore continues the tradition prominent in the realist period; she must convince her audience of her claims to reproduce culture accurately. In the case of this article, she does so with a strategy that would have been familiar to readers of nineteenth-century literary realism; she designates alternative depictions of African Americans as unfaithful to the reality of experience. She also displays her proficiency in the idiom of ethnography by including the tangible verbal evidence central to that discipline, such as a vocabulary list and recorded folktales. But, while Hurston incorporates such markers of authentic difference, the theatrical language so important to "Characteristics of Negro Expression" points to the necessity of developing narrative forms to adequately represent how culture is staged and performed. In her formulation, cultural expression is not something to be simply collected; rather, it can only be interpreted and evaluated within the context of a larger drama. Hurston drew on both social science and literature to create the modes of writing suitable for this project of showing how distinct cultural meanings are articulated and negotiated through speech and action. Equally important, the convergence of fiction and ethnography enabled her to demonstrate that the very processes of observing and documenting culture play a central role in how a culture is lived.

Tell Me Your Lies: *Mules and Men*

Hurston's simultaneous relationship to the Harlem Renaissance and to Boasian anthropology furnished her with a unique set of discursive tools. We have seen how the emerging emphasis upon cultural particularism led American literary realists and ethnographers to shift their attention from diachronic narrative associated with evolution to synchronic description— a shift considered by critics to favor "analysis" over "storytelling." Writing in a later period, Hurston reinvigorated the tension between chronological narration and static description, because her work managed to bridge the two while simultaneously avoiding a return to the stagist model of social evolution. To rewrite the title of Lukács's essay, Hurston wanted to narrate *and* describe.[24] She wished both to hold the "chemise" of culture at arm's length so that she could report its qualities in detail—and also to tell the story of what happens to someone who chafes at wearing such a tight-fitting garment.

Hurston had already emerged as a member of the Harlem Renaissance's junior set when she enrolled in Barnard College in the fall of 1925, nine months after her arrival in New York City. During her first semester, in fact, her story "Spunk" would be published in Alain Locke's seminal anthology, *The New Negro*. As the sole African American student at the college, Hurston became "Barnard's sacred black cow," as she later described in her autobiography, *Dust Tracks on a Road;* "If you had not had lunch with me, you had not shot from taw."[25] While at Barnard, Hurston's success in her anthropology courses translated into lasting ties with members of the Boas school including Benedict, Gladys Reichard, Melville Herskovits, and Boas himself. Her early fiction may offer some clue as to what about the discipline interested her. Consider the first sentence of "Black Death," a story that Hurston wrote prior to her matriculation at Barnard, "The Negroes in Eatonville know a number of things that the hustling, bustling white man never dreams of."[26] The intrigue of Hurston's story, as she would describe it, is a cultural secret, the practice of "hoodoo," a subject that played a central role in her career as a social scientist. "Black Death" does possess a plot in the literary sense (Hurston tells the story of how a jilted lover gets revenge through hoodoo), but the way the story engages its audience bears similarity to ethnographic works such as James Mooney's *Ghost-Dance Religion*. In fact, Hurston later incorporated this story into her social science; a nearly identical version appears in her article "Hoodoo in America," published in 1931 in *The Journal of American Folk-Lore.*[27] Both Mooney in *The Ghost-Dance Religion* and Hurston in "Black Death" purport to tell how and why particular groups perform certain practices presumably alien to those reading the anthropological work; moreover, both works focus on systems of religious belief that many of their readers would consider bogus and self-destructive. Hurston's literary efforts were not simply derivative of social science, nor should one reduce her literature to anthropology, but at this particular moment, the literary circle in which she developed shared a specific temperament with anthropological inquiry. Each treated the culture of the racially marked "other"—whether that of Eatonville or the Lakota territory—as an exotic place into which only the most skilled observers could venture and return with trustworthy descriptions.

Hurston's best-known research during her time at Barnard in the 1920s took place under the supervision of Melville Herskovits, a former Boas student making his way up the academic ranks.[28] At that time, Herskovits's role in Boasian anthropology was to work toward overturning long-held notions about the physical inferiority of African Americans, through the same kind of methodical, rigorous, quantitative research that Boas had employed in his growth studies of immigrant children. For Herskovits, who sent Hurston with a set of calipers to Harlem, his new student must have been a real boon. Langston Hughes wrote of the project, "Almost nobody else could stop the average Harlemite on Lenox Avenue and measure his head with a strange-looking, anthropological device and not get bawled out for the attempt, except Zora, who used to stop anyone whose head looked interesting, and measure it."[29]

Herskovits wrote in a 1927 letter that Hurston was "more White than Negro in her ancestry" but that her "manner of speech, her expressions,— in short, her motor behavior" were "what would be termed typically Negro."[30] The underlying distinction of Herskovits's description was basic to the Boasian vision: Hurston possessed one set of biological (racial) properties, and another set of cultural ones. Herskovits's characterization also reminds us of the difficult position that Hurston was forced to accept as an African American student of anthropology. While she was standing on Harlem streetcorners observing passersby, Herskovits was observing *her* as an example of that same populace. She was, in other words, both a subject and an object of her discipline, and, as Boas's foreword to *Mules and Men* suggests, her teachers expected her to capitalize upon this duality.

Neither Boas nor Benedict nor Herskovits had attempted autoethnography, however, and their inability to anticipate the difficulties of executing such a project may help to explain why Hurston was initially ill-prepared for the challenges of her ethnographic research. Her first fieldwork, conducted in 1927 under the auspices of Carter G. Woodson's Association for the Study of Negro Life and History, produced no substantial results whatsoever. Hurston had hoped to collect folklore in her native town of Eatonville, but was unequal to the task.[31] As she put it in *Dust Tracks on a Road*, "O, I got a few little items. But compared with what I did later, not enough to make a flea a waltzing jacket."[32] Even worse was the result of a separate trip that Hurston made to Alabama (but did not discuss in her autobiography). There, she interviewed Cudjo Lewis, an eighty-year-old survivor of the *Clotide*, the ship believed at the time to have been the last to bring slaves from Africa to the United States, in 1859. Hurston's article, "Cudjo's Own Story of the Last African Slaver" appeared in the *Journal of Negro History*, but her account was nearly entirely plagiarized from the 1914 volume *Historic Sketches of the Old South*, a book that Hurston never mentions in her footnotes.[33]

Boas had arranged for these professional excursions into the field, but the methodology of cultural anthropology presumed a relationship between the anthropologist and her object that, at first, proved difficult for Hurston to master. When she did have a productive field trip—the trip of 1928, conducted with the money of her patron, Charlotte Osgood Mason—Hurston had trouble putting her results into written form.[34] She wrote to Mason that, upon looking at the first draft of what would become *Mules and Men*, Knopf editor Harry Block insisted that Hurston "had not a book but *notes* for a book," and that the work needed to be crafted "into a geographical and chronological narrative."[35]

Mules and Men is a combination of the "chronological narrative" that Block desired and the detailed cultural description that characterized Boasian ethnography. At one level, the resulting volume reads as much like the adventure narrative of Frank Hamilton Cushing's "My Adventures in Zuñi," from the early 1880s, as like the standard works of the Boas school. As Cushing did in his articles, Hurston stages the drama of ethnographic fieldwork so that her own persona stands at the center of the show.[36] With its goal of scientific objectivity, the American cultural anthropology of this period did not encourage ethnographers to describe their own actions at length. James Mooney's *Ghost-Dance Religion*, though it predates the Boasians, offers an example of how this professional distance figured in ethnographic writing. Mooney describes his meeting with Wovoka to establish the authority of his account of the messiah and his teachings, but the author rarely refers to his own presence in the field in other chapters. Hurston, on the other hand, foreshadows the turn of the postmodern anthropology of the late twentieth century by emphasizing her role in the drama of ethnographic documentation, from the first chapter of *Mules and Men*, when she describes her arrival at the Eatonville store porch:[37]

> "Ah come to collect some old stories and tales and Ah know y'all know a plenty of 'em...."
> "What you mean, Zora, them big old lies we tell when we're jus' sittin' around here on the store porch doin' nothin'?" asked B. Mosely.
> "Yeah, those same ones about Old Massa, and colored folks in heaven, and—oh, y'all know the kind I mean."
> "Aw shucks," exclaimed George Thomas doubtfully. "Zora, don't you come here and tell de biggest lie first thing...." (13–14)

This dialogue was part of what Hurston described in a letter to Boas as "the between-story conversation," material she implied (perhaps disingenuously) she only included to make the book more palatable to commercial publishers.[38] In particular, this scene establishes Hurston's peculiar role as someone who is familiar to the community yet remains a outsider. *Mules and Men* takes a more pointed jab at the salvage imperative of her chosen profession when the narrator suggests that the folktales must be collected before they are forgotten. "No danger of that," comes the reply from the porch. "That's all some people are good for—set 'round and lie and murder groceries" (14).

Through this device—"between-story conversation" framing the actual folktales and hoodoo rituals that constitute the ethnographic data of *Mules and Men*—Hurston is able to relate her own story—her experience of traveling first to Florida and then to New Orleans and learning enough to write the text itself. The narrative frame of Hurston-as-ethnographer recalls the characters that Charles Chesnutt (and others) used to frame texts of vernacular expression. Like the white carpetbaggers of *The Conjure Woman*, Hurston's textual persona must be instructed in *Mules and Men* about cultural practices, traditions, and histories that she does not know. The depiction of the ethnographer in the text does more than to confer upon the book narrative continuity; it enables *Mules and Men* to address the dynamics of the ethnographic process itself.[39]

Yet the presence of Hurston as a character is neither consistent nor constant, particularly in the "Folk Tales" section—the longer of the two sections, dealing with Hurston's native Florida.[40] Upon her arrival in Eatonville, the narrator sounds almost like a parody of the naive, uninitiated anthropologist, telling her informants that she needs to write the folk tales down "before everybody forgets them" and asking questions to which Hurston herself probably knew the answers ("Say, what is this toe party business?" [20]).[41] Later, Hurston's narrator has the savvy to do some lying of her own, passing herself off as a fugitive bootlegger to gain the confidence of people around her. Moreover, Hurston's narrative instability extends beyond such obvious strategic dissembling to more subtle discrepancies within the text. In some scenes, Hurston makes us aware of her presence among her informants; we see her asking questions and worrying about overcoming the envy elicited by her "$12.74 dress from Macy's" (66). At other times, Hurston's narrator slips into the verbal backdrop and nearly disappears altogether; we read long episodes and even whole chapters (chapters 5 and 7) in which we rarely hear her speak. In *Mules and Men*, Hurston is an unreliable narrator in the most literal sense. The reader never can be sure when she will show up, or how.

The ethnographic canvas of *Mules and Men* may be stretched across the narrative frame of Hurston's return and immersion, but this frame has been less solidly constructed in some places than in others. This narrative instability registers the difficult balance that Hurston attempts between telling her own story about the difficulties and pleasures of ethnography and describing the vernacular modes of expression that she had come to collect. Hurston's ethnographer persona is least present in those scenes where her informants are most useful to her *as* an ethnographer: during the fishing trip, for example, when her companions tell story after story involving the major figures of their folkloric traditions. An ethnographer might be too busy recording these tales to insert herself into such a conversation, and Hurston's narrative disappearance during these scenes suggests a gold standard of ethnography—a moment when the scientist renders herself invisible and simply records the words that surround her. Here, ethnographic description supersedes the narrative that holds the book together.

At such moments, Hurston stresses the dramatic qualities of the narrative performances of her informants. The speakers in the book refer to these tales as "lies"—a term that emphasizes not only the fact that they are imaginative works, but that they are created, embellished, and rearticulated in contexts (so-called "lying contests") in which imaginative power is regarded highly and rewarded by their culture. In a letter written to Hurston during her initial fieldwork in 1927, Boas had asked her "particu larly to pay attention, not so much to the content, but rather to the form of diction, movements, and so on" of the vernacular material she collected.[42] Hurston's *Mules and Men* goes beyond Boas's simple instruction to record the "manner of rendition." The volume provides a context for understanding the tales, songs, and hoodoo rituals included, such that readers recognize her informants as speaking agents often capable of using vernacular expression in ways that require careful attention to comprehend their multiple levels of meaning.[43] As other Boasian anthropologists had, Hurston was struggling to document culture in a way that incorporated her informants as active narrators instead of merely as passive repositories of information.[44]

What is at stake in trying to bring together these two kinds of narrative—Hurston's story about her own ethnography and the stories that her informants call "lies"—becomes more clear when the residents of Eatonville and Polk County begin to tell "lies" that directly confront the power relations affecting their lives. One Polk County tale (which Hurston would use again in *Their Eyes Were Watching God*), for example, explains why blacks (and especially black women) work harder than whites (76–77).[45] In this tale, "Ole Missa" tells "Ole Massa" to pick up the bundle full of hard work, "Ole Massa" tells the black man to get the bundle, and the black man, finally, passes on the order to his wife. "Dat's de reason de sister in black works harder than anybody else in de world," the lie concludes. But this story does not end the matter. Another informant interjects immediately, "Aw, now, dat ain't de reason niggers is working so hard," and he begins to tell *his* tale to explain the same phenomenon (77). In this second lie, the primordial black man and the primordial white man race to two bundles "that God let down 'bout five miles down de road." The black man wins the race and chooses the larger bundle, which, unfortunately, contains "a pick and shovel and a hoe and a plow and a chop-axe." The white man's smaller bundle contains a pen and ink, so "ever since then de nigger been out in de hot sun, usin' his tools and de white man been sittin' up figgerin.'"

These two etiologies of a racialized division of labor offer conflicting messages about African Americans' own complicity in this history. In the first story, the whites actively oppress the black figures, although the black male, too, participates in this pattern by handing the bundle off to the black female. One can interpret the second tale in two ways, either as a story about the black man's overeager foolishness or about the vagaries of chance. Either way, this second lie relieves the primordial white man of responsibility for the resulting injustice. Neither story, moreover, describes any possibility for reversing this unequal distribution of hard labor. Rather, they suggest that such inequities have been created as part of the permanent social landscape. These narratives describe the world as it is, not as it should be.

The context provided by Hurston encourages readers to engage these tales much less pessimistically than they might otherwise. Read as discrete texts, they portray these rural African Americans as resigned to a certain power structure. Read together, and within the context of the book, they open up other interpretive possibilities. Hurston hears these stories during a competitive "lying" session, staged for her benefit, among several men who are trying to avoid their white foreman and the performance of actual labor as long as possible. The tellers have been, in fact, debating whether to present themselves as laborers to the foreman or to continue hiding. In this setting, the stories can be understood as hyperbolic fictions that earn laughter through a collective self-congratulation for the temporary reprieve granted their tellers. These stories explain how difficult it is for blacks to hide from physical labor, and also remind the auditors of the authority the foreman still has over them. Finally, the contradictory stances of the two tales toward the same social phenomenon show that the relation of race to labor in this community is hardly a settled issue. Listening to the competitive nature of this storytelling forces us, as readers, to consider how conscious an artistic endeavor lying is for Hurston's informants. In turn, we must rethink whether these storytellers have passively accepted the social order or whether their lying sessions might be a strategy for bringing the community together to thrash out strategies for responding to the system of power in which it is enmeshed.[46]

Hurston's documentation of African American culture in *Mules and Men* alters the model of culture itself deployed in works like Benedict's *Patterns*. Benedict stresses the wholeness and integration of each culture that makes it possible to deduce its psychological pattern. Margaret Mead's *Coming of Age in Samoa* works with the same premise: "Each primitive people has selected *one* set of human gifts, *one* set of human values, and fashioned for themselves *an* art, *a* social organization, *a* religion, which is their unique contribution to the history of the human spirit" (emphasis added).[47] Just as in "Characteristics of Negro Expression," Hurston's *Mules and Men* describes a creative desire to dramatize as the central feature of rural African American folkways, but this same feature forces the reader to recognize the culture as a common terrain in which a variety of interests and actors compete. The fierce, even dangerous, battles over gender and sexuality in *Mules and Men* that have been the subject of frequent critical commentary, for instance, again invite the reader to consider the competitive artistry of Hurston's informants rather than the existence of a unified cultural scheme.[48] Instead of utilizing the "spy-glass of Anthropology" to give us a distanced, contained view of African American culture, Hurston uses it to magnify the threads to the point that we can see where the fabric is torn and frayed.

The incorporation of such conflict in *Mules and Men* marks an important shift from the earlier culturalist texts we have encountered. In each of those texts, the most obvious tensions resulted from the contact between a group-centered way of life characteristic of a remote location, and the representatives of metropolitan "civilization." This pattern could account for the relationship between Louisiana Rogers and the Ferrols, between Uncle Julius and the carpetbaggers, between the young La Flesche and the missionaries, and even between the Lakota Ghost Dance singers and the U.S. Army. However, in *Mules and Men*, dissonance not only exists within culture, it is fundamental to the way that group-based identity is constituted. Moreover, as the examples cited demonstrate, Hurston's text often makes it possible for the reader to understand how these conflicts were situated within larger relationships of racial and economic power.

What has made Hurston's work so compelling to readers of the last twenty-five years has been, in part, the balance that *Mules and Men* exemplifies. Here, Hurston casts culture as a site of previously underappreciated creativity, as the process through which social meanings are made, especially through language, but she also portrays culture as a raucous arena, a distillation of the everyday ways in which certain patterns of behavior are enforced. Her book registers the potential for violence as the conflicts inherent to group-based culture threaten to engulf the individual—and suggests that this threat extends to the individual ethnographer as well. Hurston shows throughout the "Folk Tales" section, which takes place in the region of her upbringing, that her relationship to the culture about which she is writing has been complicated by both her departure to the north and the circumstances under which she has returned. Reminiscent of Boas's "An Eskimo Winter," the final image of the Central Florida section of *Mules and Men* is Hurston's flight from the Polk County "jook," a roadhouse where she has been violently threatened by a rival of her friend, Big Sweet. No matter how much appreciation she hopes to have imparted to her reader for the rich verbal tapestry of her native region, she reminds us in the end that she has left it behind. "I was in the car in a second," she writes, "and in the car too quick" (175). The danger that drives Hurston from Florida epitomizes the precariousness of her position as both an observer of and a participant in the culture in question.

If the moments when Hurston is absent from the page signify her success as an ethnographer, this melodramatic turn in the narrative frame epitomizes the difficulty of her project. Hurston uses the drama of the ethnographic inquiry to narrate her own growth as an observer of culture and someone capable of leaving "the crib of negroism" behind. On the other hand, no matter how carefully and with what complexity Hurston may describe the creative traditions of her informants, they remain unchanged objects of her scientific inquiry. In other words, the narrative change of Hurston's individual story stands in contrast to the synchronic portrait of a cultural group that she has rendered through the discipline of ethnography. Her flight from central Florida may therefore also be interpreted as the decision she has made to leave, at least temporarily, ethnography behind to attend to that same culture of rural African American life through the "spy-glass" of fiction.

The Predicament of Cultural Realism

The novels that Hurston published during the mid-1930s extended her struggles to resolve the impasses of Boasian anthropology: to portray culture as a coherent object without ignoring the possibility of cultural change, and to appreciate the complexity and power of culture while still accounting for the fate of the individual at odds with it. Fiction did not, finally, free Hurston's writing about culture from these dilemmas. Rather, fiction became a medium in which she could sharpen her formulation of these problems by removing the figure of the literal social scientist and replacing her with characters who raised even more difficult problems of cultural mobility and observation. What Hurston did not abandon was the insistence of ethnography that cultural authenticity—the expression of group-based identities—could be represented accurately on the page. The resurgence of interest in Hurston's work during the late twentieth century may in fact stem from the complicated way she both anticipated the desires of her readers for the permanence of such authenticity and critiqued that same unreflective valorization. Fiction allowed her to stage more fully than ethnography the creativity of those performances that make rural African American cultures distinct, as well as to show how culture endows every-day actions with a texture of meaning too often neglected. Fiction, though, also enabled Hurston to show how the very stability of culture makes it a nearly tyrannical force for those unwilling to live within its parameters.

Jonah's Gourd Vine (1934) appeared a full year before the publication of *Mules and Men*, but in certain ways the novel followed the ethnography: Hurston began writing *Jonah's Gourd Vine* in 1933, nearly four years after she had completed the fieldwork for *Mules and Men*, and she had finished at least one draft of *Mules and Men* before attempting the novel.[49] Loosely based on the biography of Hurston's father, *Jonah's Gourd Vine* tells the story of John Buddy Pearson, who leaves his Alabama sharecropping family to live and work across the "Big Creek" in the town of Notasulga, on the plantation of Alf Pearson. After a brief foray into a railroad work camp, John returns to Notasulga and marries Lucy Potts, whose mother opposes her involvement with this "big yaller boy from cross de Creek."[50] Despite his initial devotion to Lucy, John later resumes his philandering, and for much of the novel he rises and falls in the reader's estimation, vowing to reform one moment and failing to the next. The couple eventu-ally settles in Eatonville, where John becomes a property owner and suc-cessful preacher but comes to neglect his wife again. In the final chapters, he leaves the pulpit and Eatonville to search for a new life—and finds it, even though his accidental death is preceded by one final failure of virtue.

While John Pearson takes on more shape and depth as a character after his arrival in Eatonville, in the first part of the book he often reproduces the role that Hurston played as a narrative presence in *Mules and Men*. In the opening chapters, when John moves across the "Big Creek," he is a sus-pected cultural outsider through whom the reader observes the practices of the community that he has entered. He sees dances, hears songs, and plays games representative of the kind of cultural practices that ethnographers, including Hurston, collected:

> Furious music of the little drum whose body was still in Africa, but whose soul sung around a fire in Alabama. Flourish. Break.
>   Ole cow died in Tennessee
>   Send her jawbone back to me
>   Jawbone walk, Jawbone talk
>   Jawbone eat wid uh knife and fork
>   Ain't ah right?
>   CHORUS: Yeah!
>   Ain't I right? Yeah!
> Hollow-hand clapping for the bass notes. Heel and toe stomping for the little one. Ibo tune corrupted with Nango. Congo gods talking in Alabama. (29)

Hurston provides precisely the information—the African origin of the drum, the type of clapping and stomping, the reproduction of the exact words of the song—that a social scientist would expect from an account of such a dance. Here and elsewhere in the novel, she uses the conventions of ethnography to establish her authority to accurately represent the cultural milieu as well as to produce concrete information about rural African American culture. At such moments the narrative positions the reader in the same role as John, as an outsider who comes to understand the culture by learning about the nature of its practices and their meanings. Hurston reaffirms the ethnographic function of *Jonah's Gourd Vine* by including a glossary of vernacular phrases similar to the one that accompanied *Mules and Men*.

Just as Hurston's position in *Mules and Men* was more complicated than that of the usual social scientist, John Pearson is more than simply a cultural observer. The Pearson farm is the site of John's birth (as Eatonville was of Hurston's) and the place where he meets his grandmother, who points out to him the tree under which his "nable string is buried" (19). On the one hand, John is so unfamiliar with town and plantation life that he is the butt of more than one joke; on the other, he can already claim a place in this community. What Hurston seems to have learned from anthropology is a narrative balancing act in which participant-observers quickly shift from being outsiders who can only observe, to being active, integral participants—and back again. The day after John learns about wearing shoes, the railroad, and the location of his navel string, he is able to capture the center spotlight in the evening revelry by telling traditional tales:

"And Brer Rabbit and Brer Fox and Raw-Head-and-Bloody-Bones walked the earth like natural men" (25). At moments like these, John, with his exaggerated physical proportions, his ability to succeed in new settings, and his sexual magnetism (Alf Pearson calls him a "walking orgasm"), seems less a literary character than a traditional folklore hero like "High John de Conquer," the culture-hero who plays a role in many of the stories that Hurston collected.[51] At the same time, he is an *anthropologist's* hero, a figure representing a type of professional wish-fulfillment. John Pearson carries southern, African American traditions with him but, because he must learn and relearn what these traditions entail, he remains enough of an outsider to appreciate their value. In the language of *Mules and Men*, he is able both to wear the "tight chemise" and to make it available to the "spy-glass" of cultural anthropology.

John Pearson's picaresque wanderings, first in Alabama and later in Central Florida, correspond both to the travels of a folkloristic protagonist and to the path of the ethnographer herself, who travels from community to community attempting to insinuate herself with the notable personalities and to master the particular idiosyncrasies of each locale to reproduce them through the methods of social science. Repeatedly, John demonstrates his ability to enter new cultural settings, understand what makes them distinct, and master them. This pattern, in which John Pearson first observes and then bears the same cultural phenomena, may reveal the extent to which Hurston was occupied with the structure of cultural anthropology. However, it ultimately threatens that structure. If one cannot find the line between cultural observation and performance, then the authority of the ethnographer to document culture by a distanced methodology cannot remain stable. In fact, the ease with which John Pearson adopts and adapts to new cultures makes us wonder whether the differences between them, put forward by Hurston in the vocabulary of ethnography, are meaningful.

John Pearson eventually tries to stop wandering, in Eatonville, the setting for portions of both *Mules and Men* and *Their Eyes*. In Eatonville, John becomes well-regarded as a leading citizen, an owner of property and a highly regarded preacher. In fact, Hurston reprints a sermon collected during her fieldwork as one of Pearson's (145–51).[52] His moral failings continue, though, and he gradually becomes a domineering, arrogant man who neglects his family and his pulpit. While the novel explains that his mistress has sought hoodoo charms to cause John's dissatisfaction with his life, it also suggests his unhappiness has more elusive and intangible causes. The metaphor of the vine named in the title—a metaphor that echoes Sapir's depiction of culture as a plant in "Culture, Genuine and Spurious"—explains John's dilemma. The soil in which John stands nourishes and cultivates his prodigious growth as a character, yet that same growth threatens the life that surrounds him, just as creeping vines can spread so quickly that they endanger the health of neighboring plants. Even though he embodies the verbal creativity and aesthetic power of African American folk life, he does not live in a harmonious relationship with the culture from which he has obtained that repertoire. When the characters of the novel refer to John as "Jonah's gourd vine," they do so because they believe he must be cut down (123).

Jonah's Gourd Vine realizes the possibilities of a cultural realism that translates ethnography into the narrative world of the novel, but it also demonstrates the shortcomings of this project. For if John Pearson represents the ethnographer's fantasy of a person able to circulate through different cultures and absorb their practices—of an ideal ethnographer—he also represents an ethnographer's nightmare as an informant; he is a person who seems practically unaffected by culture. John Pearson is able to assume the speech of the plantation, the work camp, and the pulpit with equal mastery and aplomb. He tells tales of "Brer Rabbit," sings work-camp songs, *and* preaches a vernacular Christianity with equal effectiveness. For cultural patterns to be significant, they must have some predicative value for the individuals who belong to a group. John seems able to choose any pattern he likes, to conform momentarily to any that he comes across, and, most important, to be able to leave the pattern behind when he so decides. He walks away from his Eatonville property, his central role at the plantation, and his work-camp success. Ethnographers were supposed to be able to make such exits, but their objects of inquiry were not. As a result, the novel confounds any deterministic relation we might posit between culture and the individual.

Culturalist texts assert their authority to represent authentic cultural phenomena with accuracy. Hurston does this throughout *Jonah's Gourd Vine* in a way that renders cultural difference legible to her readers. But even as she shows how group-based identities are made through verbal performances—the songs, stories, and sermons that John Pearson masters—her novel shows how an extraordinary individual can raise questions about the very meaning of those performances. In giving us a character who both masters culture and resists its constricting force, Hurston provides an alternative to the cultural determinism fashioned by her fellow Boasians. At the same time, she does not resolve the Boasian dilemmas of accounting for cultural change or of reconciling the individual to culture. Instead, she uses the episodic form of this novel to return us to precisely those questions. Narrative structure enables readers to understand why characters do what they do, to uncover a logic to their behavior, but John's rising and falling remains a mystery. The novel fails, or refuses, to translate the group-centered concept of cultural identity in a way that would explain the extraordinary individual at its core.

Hurston's most widely read work, *Their Eyes Were Watching God* (1937), places this tension between group-oriented culture and the portrayal of individual development at its narrative center. Like John Pearson, Janie in *Their Eyes Were Watching God* proves willing to travel to new culture areas, to enthusiastically participate, and to observe.[53] *Their Eyes* is salted with the same kind of ethnographic information present in *Jonah's Gourd Vine*; there are "lying" sessions on the Eatonville porch, work songs in "the muck," and "Saws," the Bahamian dancers who populated Hurston's first article for *The Journal of American Folk-Lore*, "Dance Songs and Tales from the Bahamas."[54] But Janie's movement more closely resembles the movement of Hurston herself in the first part of *Mules and Men*. Both cross cultural boundaries by leaving Eatonville for work camps farther south, Hurston to Polk County and Janie to the Everglades, and both expose themselves to danger by doing so. [55]

Equally important, Janie differs from John Pearson in her ability to *learn* from the various cultures in which she observes and participates. *Their Eyes* is a novel that charts Janie's development in a way that *Jonah's Gourd Vine* deliberately eschews. When her first husband, Logan Killicks, scolds Janie, "she gave Logan's speech a hard thought and placed it beside other things she had seen and heard," and then decides to leave him.[56] And as her next husband, Joe Starks, begins to fight with her, Janie "pressed her teeth together and learned to hush" until his death, after which she deserts everything that he had built and bought.[57] In both the post-bellum sharecropping society of Janie's grandmother and Logan Killicks and the new bourgeois world of Eatonville, Janie is at odds with her cultural setting. While Hurston does suggest that the structures of these societies oppress any woman who lives in them, Janie experiences their coercive power most keenly.

Their Eyes takes up the dilemma posed by Boas's short story, "An Eskimo Winter." There, Boas closed his fictional account of the Eskimos by describing the departure of No-tongue, who leaves the cultural setting of the story for a more satisfying life. Boas is unable to reach a compromise between the dissatisfied individual and the culture that dissatisfies, but the narrative frame of *Their Eyes Were Watching God* gestures toward such a reconciliation. In the first chapter, Janie returns to Eatonville, the town she once scorned, where she will recount her story—including the Everglades hurricane and the death of Tea Cake, her third husband. Unlike *Mules and Men*, in which Hurston portrays the protagonist returning enthusiastically to Eatonville and its store-porch storytellers, the beginning of *Their Eyes* shows Janie deliberately passing the porch by. Her removal from the porch as she tells her story to Pheoby marks a divide between Janie and the community to which she has returned.

At best, Janie and the porch-dwellers of Eatonville have reached an unspoken agreement to keep their distance. Janie's conflicts with the representatives of society, meanwhile, have rendered those in the community who oppose her unsympathetic characters. Janie may articulate the possibilities of cultural mobility, but Hurston portrays the habitués of the Eatonville porch (as Hazel V. Carby has pointed out) as limited, narrow, and static.[58] Moreover, the working-class culture of the "muck" that Janie has chosen does not completely accept *her*. That African American community stands all too ready in the courtroom to convict Janie of murdering Tea Cake. Janie first celebrates the diversity of cultural experience that she encounters, only to learn two difficult lessons: culture is not something that one can ever completely escape, and to be at odds with it can have dire consequences.

The narrowmindedness of the people who surround Janie makes her heroism possible. As in Hurston's earlier *Jonah's Gourd Vine*—and as in much of scientific ethnography—ethnographers and their readers can learn and change, but the majority of people, unable to recognize their culture "for wearing it" (as Hurston says in *Mules and Men*), do not. Hurston desires to celebrate the folkways of rural communities while portraying them as in conflict with their most gifted individuals. This depiction of rural blacks as at once entertaining and narrowminded fueled criticisms of *Their Eyes* by Richard Wright and Alain Locke, who felt that, in spite of Janie's struggles to emancipate herself from the boundaries of gender, Hurston's characters were too narrowly confined to what Wright called "that safe and narrow orbit in which America likes to see the Negro live."[59]

Even though Wright considers Hurston's characters to be within a "safe and narrow orbit," Hurston's novels of cultural realism, especially *Their Eyes*, resist a tautological narrative structure that consigns characters to act out the roles assigned by their cultural setting. While some characters do behave in this manner, others move on to develop in unpredictable ways. Nothing in the birth or upbringing of either John Pearson or Janie determines their narrative development as characters. If the concept of culture attempts to explain and recognize the often overwhelming influence of group difference, Hurston's cultural realism affirms the possibility for the individual to resist that influence through cross-cultural experience of the kind that John Pearson, Janie, and Hurston herself have undergone. No wonder Hurston's most powerful novel of individual success ends with its protagonist entreating her reader, not with a program for social or cultural reform, but with a message that reads almost like a credo of ethnographic fieldwork: "It's uh known fact," Janie says, "you got tuh *go* there tuh *know* there."[60]

Janie insists on firsthand experience within a novel that attempts to represent that same experience textually. One of the major conceits of *Their Eyes* is that Janie is able to relate her story fully because of the presence of a compassionate listener, Pheoby. Yet Janie is not the narrator of the novel; her storytelling voice is replaced by a third-person narrator except in the opening and closing of the book. Indeed, one of the most consistently praised features of the book since it again became widely known, in the 1970s, has been this third-person narration that incorporates a mastery of a remarkable rural vernacular, a free indirect discourse that represents both the interior voices of individual characters, particularly Janie, and the "collective black community's speech and thoughts."[61] In this shift away from Janie's own oral telling, Hurston creates not only a connection between the character of Janie and the narrator of *Their Eyes*, but also a congruence between Janie's friend Pheoby and the reader. The power of the novel rests on this set of substitutions. The experience of cultural immersion and observation has been transformed from the subjective consciousness of Janie to a third-person narrator who combines the vernacular diction of oral traditions with authorial distance—functions usually divided between informant and observer in earlier instances of cultural realism. The reader meanwhile hears about both Janie's life and the cultures of rural African Americans, positioned not as a total outsider made to feel like a cultural voyeur, but rather as an understanding listener whose sympathies are presumed. While the novel still lays claim to ethnographic accuracy and still foregrounds the act of cultural observation, it has transformed the narrative mode of ethnography into a novelistic form that encourages readers to enter into the lives of its subjects.

With *Their Eyes Were Watching God*, Hurston completes the replacement of ethnographic modes of narration and representation with literary ones. The problems of an ethnography based on the Boasian model of culture, however, still remain unresolved by the novel. If culture produces the verbal texture that makes this book a compelling aesthetic work for most readers, it also produces an imposition of conformity visible in the racism that follows the hurricane, the resentment against Janie's unorthodox lifestyle in both Eatonville and the "muck," and even her grandmother's desire to see her married to a property owner at a young age. By failing to resolve the standoff between Janie and the Eatonville front porch at the close of the novel, Hurston returns us to the inability of the vocabulary of culture to describe meaningful, substantive cultural change.

My sense is that this very problem has facilitated the resurgent popularity of this novel, and of Hurston's writing more generally, in the late twentieth century. I do not wish to discount the crucial context of black feminism, as illustrated by Alice Walker's role in recovering Hurston as a forgotten literary ancestor, but the limits and quandaries of culture that I have been describing throughout this book may also have had some part in the popularity of Hurston. Like the late nineteenth century, the late twentieth century was a period in which Americans became increasingly aware of both social diversity and an increasing homogenization of everyday life. Books like *Their Eyes Were Watching God* posit culture as a mediating realm, a way of investing value into the quotidian and into routine verbal expression, as well as a way of deriving pleasure from the recognition of difference as based in socially made culture rather than biologically inherited race. The problems of such a manner of reading, of course, were foreshadowed by the earlier works of cultural realism discussed here: the danger of conjoining the search for cultural distinction to the articulation of an essence of a racial genealogy, the risk of isolating culture from the political and economic forces that shape it, and the jeopardy of falling into a nostalgia for a simpler past removed from our present complexity and frozen in time.

In *Their Eyes Were Watching God*, Hurston has crafted a novel that actually allows the careful reader to become aware of these dilemmas. The variety of cultural milieux through which Janie travels reminds us that behavior is not simply the product of biology; the disempowerment of black laborers and the presence of the courts play pivotal roles in the novel; and the ostracization suffered by Janie in her quest for sexual freedom prevents us from becoming uncritical of the rural cultures in which she lives. In other words, the novel makes it possible for readers to take a critical stance toward the same notion of culture that produces their aesthetic pleasure. Hurston's new popularity coincided with the interest of the academy in what James Clifford called "the predicament of culture," and this synchronicity may be more than accidental. Like Clifford's book by that title, Hurston reveals the difficulties of a concept that neither she nor her readers can abandon.

Others have argued that the proper response to the dilemmas raised by Hurston's novel—and by the tradition of culturalist writing examined here—is to dismiss the ethnographic model of culture once and for all as a way of imagining group affiliation. The canonization of Hurston in the late twentieth century, as well as the interest in her work from disciplines other than literary studies, demonstrates for me the impossibility of doing so. Regardless of how accurately Hurston's books depict the lives of rural African Americans, both the extent and the manner in which they are read attest to the way in which culture continues to matter as a manner of imagining lived experience. One could make the same observation of many figures whose literary reputations flourished under late-twentieth-century multiculturalism, including those, such as Maxine Hong Kingston and Sherman Alexie, who have created controversy through their supposed inaccuracies or political harmfulness, the same charges leveled at Hurston in the 1930s.[62] These writers have been subject to such criticism because culturalist works of literature are presumed to share with ethnography the goal of producing a mimetically accurate portrayal of a distinct group to a wide audience.

Such debates arising from the convergence of social science and literature generate more heat than light for the works at their center. They suggest to me that the solution to the predicaments of cultural realism may not be to abandon the model of culture I have been describing, but to realize the implications of yoking this ethnographic culture concept to realism. For over one hundred years (at least), our vocabulary for discussing the presence of cultural difference in written texts has presumed a mimetic referentiality, a relationship to truth that can be apprehended through methodical observation. The burden of this mimetic accuracy weighs more heavily on those literary texts that attempt to represent groups outside of the dominant culture than on those that do not. While the presumption of authenticity enables such texts to flourish outside more traditional literary studies in the academy, the example of Paul Laurence Dunbar being encouraged to write dialect poetry instead of verse in standard English, or of Francis La Flesche being directed to write of a "wilder existence" than he does in *The Middle Five*, should remind us of the price that such a standard exacts.

Realism, of course, has long been recognized by literary criticism to be a series of devices employed in texts to produce the sensation of reality. Realism requires authors both to engage in the "social construction of realism" (to use the title of Amy Kaplan's book) and to anticipate an audience "reading for realism" (to use the title of Nancy Glazener's) in their depictions of the world. We have seen how writers of literary and ethno-graphic texts in the late-nineteenth-century United States participated in this process in order to articulate and engage a cultural model of group identity, the same model more explicitly described by Boasian anthro-pology in the early part of the twentieth century. To say that culturalist writing is grounded in the conventions of a fictional realism is not simply to dismiss culture as a fiction. Rather, it requires that instead of presuming that culturalist texts perform a kind of mimetic reportage, we take the imaginative work that they perform seriously *as* imaginative work that may also have tangible material consequences—from the production and consumption of literary texts as commodities, to the economic value of everyday objects invested with cultural meaning, to the claims of sover-eignty by tribal peoples. Our primary attention must shift from cultural difference as a subject of *representation* to culture as a subject of *imagi-nation*. If it does not, then we run the risk of losing sight of how these texts emphasize group-based identity as a social construction, of ignoring their indebtedness and contribution to the larger constructivist intellectual his-tory so important to the twentieth and now the twenty-first century. To make such a mistake is to repeat the error made so often in the twentieth century of rearticulating biological essentialism under another name.

We need to take care with the kinds of work that we ask culturalist texts to do within the academy. Part of this care requires that we situate these texts in the institutions and intellectual frameworks that influenced their production; part of this care requires that we take their creators seriously as intellectuals; and, perhaps most significantly, part of this care requires that we finally forego the search for cultural authenticity without scorning those who in the past have attempted its documentation. Such restrictions would force us to consider the ways culturalist texts have been, and con-tinue to be, regarded aesthetically, and would limit the ability of such texts to serve as the synecdochic repository of the experience of a culture. They would ask us to attend to the global forces that have shaped cultural pro-duction, at the same time that we localize the imagination of group-based identity within particular moments of production and reception. These limitations, though, do not necessitate separating culturalist texts either from the political and economic concerns of the time of their own pro-duction, or of the moment in which we read them. Instead, we should be challenged to recognize the specific ways that the political and economic figure in the articulation of group-based difference, without reducing the imagination of culture to the political or economic. In the late nineteenth century, literary realists and ethnographers alike presumed that written texts could help men and women come to a new knowledge about the differences that divide humanity, with the purpose of producing a more just social order. Put so baldly, such a purpose sounds hopelessly naive. However, I (perhaps equally naively) believe this goal motivates most of us who currently labor in humanistic and social scientific inquiry. The textual nuances and narrative maneuvers of cultural writing—writing that imagines group-based identities *as* cultural—can not only instruct us in the history of this collective endeavor, but also help us to formulate the new directions and strategies that it demands.

Notes

Where more than one edition or printing of a work is listed under Works Cited, the page numbers given in these notes refer to the most recent.

Introduction

1. Barbara Duden, "Rereading Boas: A Woman Historian's Response to Carl N. Degler," in Carl N. Degler, *Culture Versus Biology in the Thought of Franz Boas and Alfred L. Kroeber*, 24.

2. Adam Kuper, *Culture: The Anthropologists' Account*, 23–46. Two other well-known accounts of the genealogy of "culture" are Alfred L. Kroeber and Clyde Kluckhohn, *Culture: A Critical Review of Concepts and Definitions*, and Raymond Williams, *Keywords: A Vocabulary of Culture and Society*, 87–93. Robert J.C. Young's chapter on "Culture and the History of Difference" in *Colonial Desire: Hybridity in Theory, Culture and Race*, 29–54, has also been useful to me, particularly in its account of Herder.

3. For a sophisticated discussion of the complex relationship between Boasian anthropology and nineteenth-century German science, see the articles collected in George Stocking Jr., ed., *Volksgeist as Method and Ethic: Essays on Boasian Ethnography and the German Anthropological Tradition*.

4. Alfred L. Kroeber, *The Nature of Culture*, 6.

5. Matthew Frye Jacobson, *Barbarian Virtues: The United States Encounters Foreign Peoples at Home and Abroad*, 108–9.

6. Charles Dudley Warner, *A Little Journey in the World*, 1.

7. Hamlin Garland, *Crumbling Idols: Twelve Essays on Art Dealing Chiefly with Literature, Painting, and the Drama*, ed. Jane Johnson, 49.

8. William Dean Howells, "Mr. Charles W. Chesnutt's Stories," 700.

9. Laura Wexler, *Tender Violence: Domestic Visions in an Age of U.S. Imperialism*, 102–5.

10. Marc Manganaro, ed., *Modernist Anthropology: From Fieldwork to Text* [see especially Manganaro's "Textual Play, Power, and Cultural Critique: An Orientation to Modernist Anthropology," 3–47]; Walter Benn Michaels, *Our America: Nativism, Modernism, and Pluralism;* and Susan Hegeman, *Patterns for America: Modernism and the Concept of Culture.* Hegeman, for instance, makes a coherent and persuasive case for thinking of Boasian culture as modernist in nature by interpreting culture as a *spatial* model, an interpretation based upon close reading of the ethnography of the 1930s. By way of contrast, I am interested here in the *temporal* dimensions of the culture concept, something that I think earlier ethnographic and literary works make apparent.

11. Raymond Williams, *The Country and the City.*

12. William Dean Howells, *A Hazard of New Fortunes,* 161.

13. Walter Benn Michaels, "Political Science Fictions," 649–64, esp. 651.

14. Scott Michaelsen, *The Limits of Multiculturalism: Interrogating the Origins of American Anthropology,* 7–8.

15. On American literary realism, I refer to Nancy Glazener, *Reading for Realism: The History of a U.S. Literary Institution;* Amy Kaplan, *The Social Construction of American Realism;* Kenneth W. Warren, *Black and White Strangers: Race and American Literary Realism;* Michael Davitt Bell, *The Problem of American Realism: Studies in the Cultural History of a Literary Idea;* and, on the history of American anthropology, I refer to Curtis M. Hinsley, *The Smithsonian and the American Indian: Making a Moral Anthropology in Victorian America;* Regna Darnell, *And Along Came Boas: Continuity and Revolution in Americanist Anthropology;* George W. Stocking Jr., *Race, Culture, and Evolution: Essays in the History of Anthropology.*

16. James Clifford, *The Predicament of Culture: Twentieth-Century Ethnography, Literature, and Art,* 10.

1. Culture, Race, and Narrative

1. Douglas Cole's *Franz Boas: The Early Years, 1858–1906* provides a biographical account of the first half of Boas's life. Although not a complete account of Boas's life, it is the first full-scale attempt to write his biography using the collection of personal writing in the Boas papers at the American Philosophical Society in Philadelphia, an archive I have consulted for Boas's professional papers. Cole's volume supplements two more modest biographies: Melville J. Herskovits, *Franz Boas: The Science of Man in the Making,* and Marshall Hyatt, *Franz Boas, Social Activist: The Dynamics of Ethnicity.*

2. On Mason's career and intellectual background, see Hinsley, *The Smithsonian and the American Indian,* 84–91.

3. Franz Boas, "The Occurrence of Similar Inventions in Areas Widely Apart," 485, 486. For a complete account of the Boas-Mason controversy, see Ira Jacknis, "Franz Boas and Exhibits: On the Limitations of the Museum Method of Anthropology" in *Objects and Others: Essays on Museums and Material Culture,* ed. George W. Stocking Jr., 75–111.

4. William Dean Howells, "Editor's Study," 987.

5. Boas, "The Occurrence of Similar Inventions in Areas Widely Apart," 486.

6. Richard Handler, "Boasian Anthropology and the Critique of American Culture," 253.

7. "Environmentalist," 37–42.

8. Darnell, *And Along Came Boas,* 175.

9. Adam Kuper, for instance, tells this story in *The Invention of Primitive Society: Transformations of an Illusion,* 151. Reportedly, Boas's final words were, "I have a new theory about race …" (Margaret Mead, *An Anthropologist at Work: Writings of Ruth Benedict,* 355).

10. The Bureau of American Ethnology was originally named the Bureau of Ethnology, but I use the former name throughout this book. Neither of these first two professors of anthropology—Frederic Ward Putnam at Harvard and Daniel G. Brinton at the University of Pennsylvania—actually had the term "anthropology" in their titles. Putnam was appointed as a professor of "American archaeology and ethnology", Brinton as a professor of "ethnology

and archaeology." During the late 1880s and early 1890s, "anthropology" gradually replaced "ethnology" as the most general label of the field. (Regna Darnell, *Daniel Garrison Brinton: The "Fearless Critic" of Philadelphia*, 33–34; Joan Mark, *Four Anthropologists*, 31–32.)

11. On the professionalization of social science, see generally Dorothy Ross, *The Origins of American Social Science*, esp. 62.

12. Boas, "The Occurrence of Similar Inventions in Areas Widely Apart," 485.

13. E. B. Tylor, *Primitive Culture*, 2 vols., 1: 1.

14. Matthew Arnold, *Culture and Anarchy*, ed. Samuel Lipman, 33.

15. One of the earliest and clearest distillations of this comparison of which I know occurs in the introduction to Raymond Williams's *Culture and Society, 1870–1950*, xvi.

16. Stocking, "Matthew Arnold, E. B. Tylor and the Uses of Invention," in *Race, Culture, and Evolution*, 69–90. Stocking notes, on page 90, that both Arnold and Tylor were influenced by the German tradition of using "culture" to describe the history of humanity.

17. Lewis Henry Morgan, *Ancient Society*.

18. Boas, "The Occurrence of Similar Inventions in Areas Widely Apart," 485.

19. Jacknis, "Franz Boas and Exhibits," 97–103. Hinsley points out that Mason later adopted this approach as well, though this change was not the result of Boas's direct influence (*The Smithsonian and the American Indian*, 100).

20. Franz Boas, "Museums of Ethnology and Their Classification," 589.

21. Stocking, *Race, Culture, and Evolution*, 203–4.

22. In fact, late in his career Boas warned that "the study of human cultures should not lead to a relativistic attitude toward ethical standards. The standards within the group are the same everywhere, however much they may differ in form" ("An Anthropologist's Credo," 202).

23. Marvin Harris, *The Rise of Anthropological Theory*, 316 (emphasis in original).

24. Boas received an appointment as an Assistant Curator of Ethnology and Somatology at the American Museum of Natural History in New York in 1896, and he resigned it in 1905 (Jacknis, "Franz Boas and Exhibits," 76–77). He spells out his feelings about the limitations of museum exhibition in "Some Principles of Museum Administration," 921–33.

25. In his study of turn-of-the-century museums, Steven Conn traces this turn away from object-based learning to text-based interpretation in anthropology. Conn writes, "With Boas leading the way, anthropologists lost faith both in the power of objects to convey meaning about different cultures and in the frameworks into which those objects had been placed" (*Museums and American Intellectual Life, 1876–1926*, 111).

26. Darnell, *And Along Came Boas*, 246–60, esp. 253.

27. Charles L. Briggs and Richard Bauman, "'The Foundation of All Future Researches': Franz Boas, George Hunt, Native American Texts, and the Construction of Modernity," 499.

28. John Wesley Powell, *Report on the Methods of Surveying the Public Domain to the Secretary of the Interior at the Request of the National Academy of Sciences*, 15–16.

29. Quoted in Cole, *Franz Boas*, 205.

30. T. Jackson Lears, *No Place of Grace: Antimodernism and the Transformation of American Culture, 1880–1920*.

31. Ira Jacknis, "The Ethnographic Object and the Object of Ethnography in the Early Career of Franz Boas," in *Volksgeist as Method and Ethic*, ed. George W. Stocking Jr., 197.

32. Franz Boas, *Chinook Texts*, Smithsonian Institution, Bureau of American Ethnology Bulletin 20, 6.

33. Briggs and Bauman, "'The Foundation of All Future Researches,'" 512.

34. Krupat writes that Boas's "work as a whole either perversely insists upon conditions for scienticity that are in no way attainable, or asserts positions that so thoroughly contradict one another as abusively to cancel each other out, moving beyond the oxymoronic to the catachrestic, and thus subverting the conditions of possibility for any scientific hypothesis whatsoever" (*Ethnocriticism: Ethnography, History, Literature*, 88–89). Krupat's reading of Boas has informed mine significantly throughout this chapter.

35. Discussions of aesthetic contemplation and especially "disinterestedness" invariably refer to Immanuel Kant's *Critique of Judgment*, first published in 1790. I have also found Gérard Genette's more recent *The Aesthetic Relation*, trans. G. M. Goshgarian, to offer a usefully succinct, if polemical, account of twentieth-century attempts to define the aesthetic.

36. Howells, *A Hazard of New Fortunes*, 265.

37. Lears, *No Place of Grace*, 20.

38. See, for example, the following articles by Boas: "What is Race?" 89–91; "The Problem of the American Negro," 284–95; review of *The Rising Tide of Color against White World-Supremacy* by Lathrop Stoddard in *The Nation*, 656; and review of *The Passing of the Great Race* by Madison Grant in *The New Republic*, 305–7. In "Anthropology as *Kulturkampf*: Science and Politics in the Career of Franz Boas," George W. Stocking Jr., provides an overview of Boas's involvement in political matters (*The Ethnographer's Magic and Other Essays in the History of Anthropology*, 92–113).

39. Michaels, *Our America*, esp. 121–39.

40. George W. Stocking Jr.'s "The Turn-of-the-Century Concept of Race" gives a concise account (10) of how physical and cultural inheritance were linked to one another during this period. See also Stocking's essay on "Lamarckianism in American Social Science, 1890–1915" in *Race, Culture, and Evolution*, 234–69.

41. Thomas Jefferson, *Notes on the State of Virginia* in *Writings*, ed. Merrill D. Peterson, 264–65.

42. Jefferson, *Notes on the State of Virginia*, 270.

43. The nineteenth-century history of science providing empirical evidence for racial oppression has been the subject of intense scholarly scrutiny. Among the most useful analyses are George Fredrickson, *The Black Image in the White Mind*; Robert E. Bieder, *Science Encounters the Indian, 1820–1880*; and Audrey Smedley, *Race in North America: Origin and Evolution of a Worldview*.

44. These remarks appear in a monograph that Agassiz contributed to Josiah Nott and George R. Gliddon's widely popular *Types of Mankind*, lxxiv.

45. Carl N. Degler, *In Search of Human Nature: Biology and Culture in American Social Science*, 15–16, and Nancy Stepan, *The Idea of Race in Science*, 54–55.

46. Richard Hofstadter, *Social Darwinism in American Thought, 1860–1915*, describes the "Darwinian collectivism of the nationalist or racist variety" (175); Robert C. Bannister, *Social Darwinism*, discusses more egalitarian invocations of Darwinism.

47. W. E. B. Du Bois, "The Conservation of Races" in *Writings*, ed. Nathan Huggins, 818.

48. However, Mia Bay has pointed out that "the racial essentialism that marked Du Bois's 1897 address already may have been on its way out among the new generation of educated black men who attended the American Negro Academy's first meeting." Bay observes that Du Bois's address received a "mixed response" and that other speakers at the meeting voiced ideas more congruent with the environmentalism that Boas advocated. In fact, Bay shows that African American intellectuals were, later, in the forefront of embracing the Boasian culture concept (*The White Image in the Black Mind: African-American Ideas about White People, 1830–1925*, 195, 196–97).

49. Du Bois, *Dusk of Dawn* in *Writings*, ed. Nathan Huggins, 640.

50. Lee D. Baker, *From Savage to Negro: Anthropology and the Construction of Race, 1896–1954*, 107–25.

51. For instance, in *Rethinking Race: Franz Boas and His Contemporaries*, Vernon J. Williams argues that the "schism between the values of cultural determinism and the values of racial determinism, a direct product of his methodological rigor, was the major weakness in [Boas's] philosophical position on race" (10). Williams is certainly correct that Boas's empiricism can prove frustrating, particularly in Boas's discussion of race and brain weight in the first edition of *The Mind of Primitive Man* (1911). There, Boas first makes two key points on this issue: that there is no evidence linking brain weight to intelligence, and that most

people of different races have brains that weigh within the same range. However, he also notes that some whites have brains that weigh more than those usually found in African Americans: "If we were to assume a direct relation between the size of brain and ability—which, as we have seen before, is not admissible—we might, at most anticipate a lack of men of high genius, but should not expect any great lack of faculty among the great mass of negroes living among the whites, and enjoying the advantages of the leadership of the best men of that race" (35).

I concur with Williams here that "methodological rigor" hampered Boas as a progressive thinker and a public activist, but I also consider it worth speculating as to his motives for making such statements. At the time, Boas was hoping to conduct further anthropometric studies on the African American population of the United States. My sense is that he expected that such research would provide the empirical evidence to shelve matters such as brain weight permanently; until then, perhaps he believed that statements such as the one above would be provocative enough to help him procure the necessary funding. See *The Mind of Primitive Man*, 274–75; and "Changing the Racial Attitudes of White Americans" in *A Franz Boas Reader: The Shaping of American Anthropology, 1883–1911*, ed. George W. Stocking Jr., 316–18.

52. On Lodge, see John Higham, *Strangers in the Land: Patterns of American Nativism 1860–1925*, 2nd ed., 141–42.

53. Ibid., 189.

54. Boas, *Changes in Bodily Form of Descendants of Immigrants*, U.S. Senate Document no. 208. Boas also used this same title for discussions of the study that appeared in *American Anthropologist* in 1912 and 1940, as well as for the edited version that appears in his retrospective collection of articles, *Race, Language, and Culture*, 60–75.

55. Boas entertains a number of specific hypotheses for his findings, only to dismiss them all (*Changes in Bodily Form of Descendants of Immigrants*, 64–76).

56. "The American Type," 3. Some other articles reporting on Boas's findings are: "What America Is Doing for the Children of Immigrants: Prof. Boas Gives Startling Results of Inquiry," 3; "Say Aliens Soon Get American Physique," 18; and Burton J. Hendrick, "The Skulls of Our Immigrants," 36–50.

57. For biographical information, see Darnell, *Daniel Garrison Brinton*, 1–40.

58. Daniel G. Brinton, "The Aims of Anthropology," 61. Subsequent references to this article appear parenthetically within the text.

59. Johannes Fabian, *Time and the Other: How Anthropology Makes Its Object*, 31.

60. Lee D. Baker has pointed out that when the written version of "The Aims of Anthropology" appeared in 1896, it did so only months before the U.S. Supreme Court announced its infamous *Plessy v. Ferguson* decision. The parallels are striking; both Brinton and the Court strive to label racially-marked groups as somehow "separate but equal" (*From Savage to Negro*, 35–36).

61. "Narrative" is a term used in so many ways that it has nearly lost its critical usefulness. In this book, I use "narrative" to refer to the linking together of events over the course of time in a way that creates some logical order. Through this "chrono-logic," narrative usually suggests some principle of causation or at least some contingent, discernible relationship. The following works have been especially important to my understanding of temporality in narrative: Peter Brooks, *Reading for the Plot*; Seymour Chatman, *Coming to Terms: The Rhetoric of Narrative in Fiction and Film*; and the first volume of Paul Ricoeur, *Time and Narrative*, 3 vols., trans. Kathleen McLaughlin and David Pellauer, particularly its introductory section on "The Circle of Narrative and Temporality" (1: 5–87)

62. Daniel G. Brinton, *Races and Peoples: Lectures on the Science of Ethnography*, 287; also quoted in Baker, *From Savage to Negro*, 36.

63. According to Darnell, at least some members of the audience understood Boas's address to be a direct refutation of Brinton (*Daniel Garrison Brinton*, 70).

64. Boas included "The Limitations of Comparative Anthropology" in his collection, *Race, Language, and Culture*, 270–80. Subsequent references to this edition of the article appear parenthetically within the text.

65. In *Time and the Other*, Fabian states that Boasian culturalism "did not solve the problem of universal human Time." Instead, culturalism "ignored it at best, and denied its significance at worst" (21). What I am suggesting here is that the Boasian turn from deep, universal time was more strategic than Fabian allows, even though I agree with the core of his analysis.

66. Boas, *Chinook Texts*, 6.

67. Briggs and Bauman, "'The Foundation of All Future Researches,'" 494. I am indebted to Bauman and Briggs for their scrupulous efforts to show how Boas "systematically detextualized material concerning the ethnographic encounter" (484–85) in his Kwakiutl (or Kwakwaka'wakw) ethnography.

68. Georg Lukács, "Narrate or Describe?" in *Writer and Critic and Other Essays*, ed. and trans. Arthur Kahn, 133, 116.

69. [Charles Cultee], "Coyote Establishes Fishing Taboos," in Nina Baym, gen. ed., *The Norton Anthology of American Literature*, 5th ed., 2 vols., I: 140–46. Arnold Krupat, the editor of this entry in the anthology, has drawn upon both the Boas recording of Cultee and a more recent reinterpretation of this story to produce a composite text.

70. Lukács, "Narrate or Describe?" 130.

71. See Harris's Table of Contents for the arrangement of this volume: Joel Chandler Harris, *Uncle Remus: His Songs and Sayings*, 49–51.

72. Richard H. Brodhead, *Cultures of Letters, Scenes of Reading and Writing in Nineteenth-Century America*, 121. Brodhead also notes the proliferation of titles containing the word "old" (120–21).

73. Boas's skepticism about a global history of culture is confused by the labeling of his method as "historical." However, historicism for Boas represented careful attention to individual, local facts for their own sake as opposed to their role in universal laws of development. As Douglas Cole puts it, "Boas's historicism.... discarded any teleological ingredient. Histories were so different and complex that no single aim or plan could be envisaged" (*Franz Boas*, 126). See also Boas's "The Study of Geography" (1887; reprinted in *Race, Language, and Culture*, 639–47), as well as Krupat's *Ethnocriticism* (91–93) for a discussion of this essay.

74. Boas's student Robert H. Lowie ultimately provided the complete critique of cultural evolution in his *Culture and Ethnology* (1918) and *Primitive Society* (1920) (Degler, *In Search of Human Nature*, 100–2; Darnell, *And Along Came Boas*, 285–87). See also Adam Kuper's chapter on "The Boasians and the Critique of Evolution," which gives a concise account of how Boas and his students attacked the theories and evidence of evolutionists like Lewis Henry Morgan throughout the first two decades of the twentieth century (*The Invention of Primitive Society*, 125–51).

75. Berthold Laufer, review of *Culture and Ethnology* by Robert H. Lowie, 90. In this review, Laufer illustrates the degree to which cultural evolution had been discredited by Lowie, for he calls it "the most inane, sterile, and pernicious theory ever conceived in the history of science" (90).

76. Boas, *The Mind of Primitive Man*, 197.

77. Ibid., 208–9.

78. Ibid., 241.

79. Boas uses the word "integrated" to describe culture, in the 1932 "Aims of Anthropological Research" (in *Race, Language, and Culture*, 256). My contention that, prior to the 1920s, Boas describes culture as a system that generates meaning disagrees with the recent genealogy of the culture concept by Adam Kuper, who believes Boas took his cue on this point from the work of his students, Edward Sapir, Ruth Benedict, and Margaret Mead (*Culture: The Anthropologists' Account*, 61–62). Kuper argues that Boas's emphasis on the complex historical

forces that create culture preclude it from being tightly integrated. I concur that for Boas culture was not as coherent a whole as it was for many of his students, but nonetheless I believe *The Mind of Primitive Man* stresses that culturally specific meanings are created through the interaction of its constituent elements.

80. For example, see William H. Sewall Jr., "Geertz, Cultural Systems, and History: From Synchrony to Transformation," 35–55, in which Sewall uses Clifford Geertz's writing to address many of the same issues that I am discussing through the figure of Franz Boas.

81. In my reading, one of the most powerful of such critiques is made by Scott Michaelsen in *The Limits of Multiculturalism*. Even though Michaelsen and I are in some ways writing at cross-purposes—Michaelsen revisits the history of anthropology to argue for the necessity of abandoning culture, while I revisit it to attend to its possibilities—I have found his book enormously useful in helping to explain the contours of the Boasian culture concept.

82. Christopher Herbert, *Culture and Anomie: Ethnographic Imagination in the Nineteenth Century*, 8.

83. Werner Sollors, "A Critique of Pure Pluralism," *Reconstructing American Literary History*, ed. Sacvan Bercovitch, 160.

84. Horace M. Kallen, "Democracy versus the Melting-Pot: A Study of American Nationality," in *Theories of Ethnicity: A Classical Reader* ed. Werner Sollors, 78. Kallen's essay was originally published in *The Nation*.

85. Boas, *Chinook Texts*, 6.

86. Kuper, *Culture: The Anthropologists' Account*, 14.

87. The most informative examination of Boas's Jewishness takes place in Leonard B. Glick, "Types Distinct from Our Own: Franz Boas on Jewish Identity and Assimilation," 545–65. Gelya Frank extends Glick's depiction of Boas and incorporates it into a broader discussion in "Jews, Multiculturalism, and Boasian Anthropology," 731–45. In 1954, Stanley Edgar Hyman actually made Jewish identity the linchpin of his comparison of Boas to Freud in a short but fascinating review article, "Freud and Boas: Secular Rabbis?" 264–67.

88. In "An Anthropologist's Credo," for example, he mentions that his parents had "broken through the shackles of [religious] dogma" (201), thus sparing him. However, he does not name *which* dogma. Perhaps this would have been obvious to readers of *The Nation* in 1938, but I still find the omission significant. Glick writes, "It seems probable that Boas never identified himself in his public writings as Jewish, but he had much to say on the subject of his own identity and on the situation of Jews as a social category" ("Types Distinct from Our Own," 554).

89. Julia E. Liss, "German Culture and German Science in the *Bildung* of Franz Boas," in *Volksgeist as Method and Ethic*, ed. Stocking, 167–69. See also Cole, *Franz Boas*, 57–60.

90. Frank, "Jews, Multiculturalism, and Boasian Anthropology," 734; Glick, "Types Distinct from Our Own," 552–54.

91. Liss, "German Culture and German Science in the *Bildung* of Franz Boas," 181–82.

92. Glick, "Types Distinct from Our Own," 545; Boas, *Mind of Primitive Man*, 254.

93. Burton J. Hendrick, "The Skulls of Our Immigrants," 40–41.

94. Using Glick's discussion of Boas's Jewishness, Arnold Krupat has described Boas as fashioning a "cosmopolitan" identity. Cosmopolitanism, for Krupat, is a global ethical humanism that allows one to escape the confining traditions of one's cultural background while simultaneously maintaining some connection to it (*The Turn to the Native: Studies in Criticism and Culture*, 102–4).

95. Originally printed in *The Nation* in December 1919, "Scientists as Spies" appears in *A Franz Boas Reader*, ed. Stocking, 336–37.

96. By 1938, when he wrote his "Credo," Boas was ready to make this statement stronger: "[M]y whole outlook upon social life is determined by the question: how can we recognize the shackles that tradition has laid upon us? For when we recognize them, we are also able to break them" ("An Anthropologist's Credo," 202).

97. Desley Deacon's *Elsie Clews Parsons: Inventing Modern Life* offers a thorough and compelling account of Parsons's life, but Deacon was able to uncover only a few details about *American Indian Life* and Boas's contribution to it (236–38).

98. Kroeber to Parsons, 25 Dec. 1920 or 1921, Elsie Clews Parsons Papers.

99. Kroeber to Parsons, 2 Aug. 1920, Parsons Papers.

100. See Stocking's chapter, "From Physics to Ethnology," in *Race, Culture and Evolution*, 133–60.

101. The recent publication of *Franz Boas among the Inuit of Baffin Island, 1883–1884: Journals and Letters*, ed. Ludger Müller-Wille, trans. William Barr, provides a compilation of primary sources related to this journey. I have also relied upon the selections of letters and diaries in Ronald P. Rohner, ed., *The Ethnography of Franz Boas;* and Cole covers this expedition in *Franz Boas*, 63–82.

102. Douglas Cole, "'The Value of a Person Lies in His *Herzensbildung*': Franz Boas' Baffin Island Letter-Diary, 1883–1884," in George W. Stocking Jr., ed., *Observers Observed: Essays on Ethnographic Fieldwork*, 33. Boas wrote this five-hundred-page "letter-diary" to his future wife, Marie Krackowizer, over a fifteen-month period. Cole's published translation of this letter-diary represents only a small portion of the complete document. For an alternate translation, see *Franz Boas among the Inuit*, ed. Müller-Wille, 159.

103. As Shari M. Huhndorf has recently pointed out, Boas's treatment of actual, living Eskimos did not always match up with the intellectual ideals articulated in his writing. In particular, while still on the staff of the American Museum of Natural History, Boas presided over the study of six living Eskimos brought to New York by the explorer Robert Peary in 1897. (Boas had requested that a single Eskimo be brought to New York for a year.) Four of the Eskimos soon died. Boas arranged for a fake funeral to be staged for the benefit of one of the survivors, a boy named Minik, and the Museum quietly retained the remains of Minik's father for scientific study. In later years, Minik attempted to obtain his father's bones, but was denied. Minik subsequently voiced fierce criticism of both Peary and Boas. See Huhndorf, *Going Native: Indians in the American Cultural Imagination*, 79–82, 123–27, for a discussion of Minik's opposition to professional anthropology; see Kenn Harper, *Give Me My Father's Body: The Life of Minik, the New York Eskimo*, for a full account of Minik's story.

104. Nelson Antrim Crawford, "The Indian As He Is," 637.

105. Elsie Clews Parsons, ed., *American Indian Life*, 3. Subsequent references to this edition are made parenthetically within the text.

106. In his introduction to the book, Kroeber lamented, "Only at one point have we broken down completely: that of humor. One might conclude from this volume that humor was a factor absent from Indian life" (*American Indian Life*, 15).

107. Boas printed this song in 1894 and attributed it to a man named Utitaq ("Eskimo Tales and Songs," 49–50.)

108. See H. A. Andrews, et al., "Bibliography of Franz Boas," 67–109.

109. Franz Boas, *Anthropology and Modern Life*, 13.

2. American Literary Realism and the Documentation of Difference

1. George Washington Cable, "Creole Slave Songs," 807–28; Alice C. Fletcher, "Indian Songs," 421–32.

2. See George Washington Cable, *The Negro Question: A Selection of Writings on Civil Rights in the South*, ed. Arlin Turner.

3. See, for instance, Fletcher's "On Indian Education and Self-Support," 312–15, and "Land and Education for the Indian," 6.

4. Earl F. Briden provides a short account of Kemble's career as an illustrator of African Americans in "Kemble's 'Specialty' and the Pictoral Countertext of *Huckleberry Finn*," in Mark Twain, *Adventures of Huckleberry Finn*, eds. Gerald Graff and James Phelan, 383–406.

5. While he does not address Cable specifically, Henry B. Wonham makes this point in "'An Art to Be Cultivated': Ethnic Caricature and American Literary Realism," 185–219.

6. William Dean Howells, "The Man of Letters as a Man of Business," in *Literature and Life: Studies*, 6–7; this essay was originally published in *Scribner's* in 1893.

7. Howells, "Man of Letters as a Man of Business," 6–7, 34–35.

8. William Dean Howells, *The Rise of Silas Lapham*, ed. Walter J. Meserve, vol. 12, *A Selected Edition of William Dean Howells*, 197.

9. Ibid., 241.

10. A highly useful distillation of this interpretation of realism occurs in Walter Benn Michaels, *The Gold Standard and the Logic of Naturalism*, 36–40. Another brief account of Howellsian realism that has especially influenced mine is Wai Chee Dimock, "The Economy of Pain: The Case of Howells," 99–119.

11. Warren, *Black and White Strangers*, 82.

12. The most sustained and convincing account of how sentimentality, even when engaged in antiracist causes, privileged whiteness is in Laura Wexler's *Tender Violence: Domestic Visions in an Age of U.S. Imperialism*. Equally valuable to my understanding of the sentimental in nineteenth-century fiction have been the articles collected in Shirley Samuels, ed., *The Culture of Sentiment: Race, Gender, and Sentimentality in Nineteenth-Century America*.

13. Harriet Beecher Stowe, *Uncle Tom's Cabin*, ed. Elizabeth Ammons, 385.

14. William Dean Howells, *Selected Literary Criticism*, eds. Ulrich Halfmann, Donald Pizer, and Ronald Gottesman, 3 vols. (vols. 13, 21, 30) of *A Selected Edition of W. D. Howells*, 2: 14. Michael Davitt Bell describes the "anti-literary" bias in *The Problem of American Realism*, 17–38.

15. Frank Norris, "Zola as a Romantic Writer" (1896), in Donald Pizer, ed., *Documents of American Realism and Naturalism*, 168.

16. Howells, "The Man of Letters as a Man of Business," 29.

17. Howells, *Selected Literary Criticism*, 1: 275–76.

18. Quoted in Hamlin Garland, *A Son of the Middle Border*, 282. Garland describes here how he began this article, which appeared as a three-part series in *The American Magazine*, but the sentences he gives in the autobiography do not actually appear in the published version. See Hamlin Garland, "Boy Life on the Prairie," 299–303, 571–77, and 684–90.

19. Nancy Glazener, *Reading for Realism*, 49.

20. See Brodhead's chapter, "The Reading of Regions," in *Cultures of Letters*, 107–41; and, generally, Gavin Jones, *Strange Talk: The Politics of Dialect Literature in Gilded Age America*.

21. Thomas Bailey Aldrich, "Unguarded Gates," 57.

22. Higham, *Strangers in the Land*, 97–105; Aldrich, "Unguarded Gates," 57.

23. William Dean Howells, *Selected Literary Criticism*, 2: 62.

24. George Pellew, "Ten Years of American Literature," 29–31, 30. On the similarity to the salvage imperative in American regionalism, see Brodhead, *Cultures of Letters*, 119–21.

25. Garland, *Crumbling Idols*, 21.

26. See, for example, James Herbert Morse, "The Native Element in Fiction," 362–75. Morse's article appeared following the publication of Burnett's *Through One Administration* (1883), her most sustained attempt to produce a realist novel. In her monograph, Phyllis Bixler details Burnett's efforts to write for the highbrow audience of magazines such as the *Atlantic, Century*, and *Harper's* (*Frances Hodgson Burnett*, 19–49).

27. Glazener's argument that realism "might be more accurately identified as a reading formation than a body of texts or textual features" has led me to pay attention to critical debates surrounding realism with, I hope, a care that matches hers (*Reading for Realism*, 14). In part, my argument in this chapter is that the same institutions that taught late-nineteenth-century readers to read for realism also taught them to read for culture.

28. Frances Hodgson Burnett, *Louisiana*, 7. Further references to this edition are made parenthetically within the text.

29. Otis T. Mason, "The Natural History of Folk-Lore," 99–100; quoted in Regina Bendix, *In Search of Authenticity: The Formation of Folklore Studies*, 127.

30. Charles Egbert Craddock [Mary Noailles Murfree], "The Dancin' Party at Harrison's Cove," 576–86. Brodhead points out that the book in which this short story appeared, *In the Tennessee Mountains* (1884), went through seventeen printings in its first two years of publication (*Cultures of Letters*, 118).

31. Boas, "The Occurrence of Similar Inventions in Areas Widely Apart," 485, 486.

32. "The Free Parliament," 158.

33. Richard Watson Gilder, "Certain Tendencies in Current Literature" (1887) in Pizer, ed., *Documents of American Realism and Naturalism*, 106.

34. Henry James, "William Dean Howells," 394.

35. Maurice Thompson, "The Analysts Analyzed," 20.

36. William Roscoe Thayer, "The New Story-Tellers and the Doom of Realism" (1894) in Pizer, ed., *Documents of American Realism and Naturalism*, 161, 165–66.

37. Georg Lukács, "Narrate or Describe?" 140.

38. Gilder, "Certain Tendencies in Current Literature," 105.

39. Pellew, "Ten Years of American Literature," 29.

40. Ibid., 29.

41. Thayer, "The New Story-Tellers and the Doom of Realism," 164.

42. Clarence Darrow, "Realism in Literature and Art" (1893) in Pizer, ed., *Documents of American Realism and Naturalism*, 140.

43. In particular, see "The Sociable at Dudley's," in Hamlin Garland, *Prairie Folks*, 225–54. Another story, "Some Village Cronies" (167–83), centers on the story-swapping denizens of a country store reminiscent of the one that Zora Neale Hurston would later describe in *Their Eyes Were Watching God*.

44. Kaplan, *The Social Construction of American Realism*, 20.

45. James Lane Allen, "Realism and Romance" (1886), in Pizer, ed., *Documents of American Realism and Naturalism*, 102.

46. Nancy Bentley, *The Ethnography of Manners: Hawthorne, James, Wharton*, 14.

47. June Howard, "Unraveling Regions, Unsettling Periods: Sarah Orne Jewett and American Literary History," *American Literature* 68 (1996): 367.

48. Hjalmar Hjorth Boyesen, *Literary and Social Silhouettes*, 73–74.

49. Mark Twain, "What Paul Bourget Thinks of Us," in *Collected Tales, Sketches, Speeches, and Essays*, 2 vols, ed. Louis Budd, 2: 167–68.

50. Jones, *Strange Talk*, 34.

51. Garland, *Crumbling Idols*, 31.

52. Kaplan, *The Social Construction of American Realism*, 11.

53. For a more complete and nuanced reading of *Hazard of New Fortunes*, see Kaplan, *The Social Construction of American Realism*, 44–64.

54. Howells, *The Rise of Silas Lapham*, 139, 215, 88. Further references to this novel are made parenthetically in the text.

55. This analysis owes something to Pierre Bourdieu's description of how cultural choices are used to legitimate the existence of social divisions; see Bourdieu's introduction to *Distinction*, trans. Richard Nice, 1–7.

56. Hamilton Wright Mabie, "A Typical Novel" (1885), in Pizer, ed., *Documents of American Realism and Naturalism*, 62.

57. For example, George Pellew writes in "The New Battle of the Books" (1888), "The romanticist thinks the realist is like an ignorant man who tries to give an idea of a complicated machine by a photograph of it, taken indifferently from any side" (in Pizer, ed., *Documents of Realism and Naturalism*, 120–21).

58. Sandra A. Zagarell's reading of *Country* suggests to me that the world of Dunnet Landing is another version of the locked room that Burnett describes in *Louisiana*, "entirely

local, congruent with its particular geography and none other" ("*Country's* Portrayal of Community and the Exclusion of Difference," in June Howard, ed., *New Essays on* The Country of the Pointed Firs, 44).

59. William Dean Howells, "Henry James's Modernity," in *Selected Literary Criticism*, 2: 151.

60. Fletcher, "Indian Songs," 431.

61. Cable, "Creole Slave Songs," 813.

3. Between Race and Culture

1. Charles W. Chesnutt, *The Journals of Charles W. Chesnutt*, ed. Richard H. Brodhead, 140.

2. William Dean Howells, *Selected Literary Criticism*, 2: 62.

3. William Dean Howells, "Mr. Charles W. Chesnutt's Stories," 700.

4. Reviews of Chesnutt's fiction, for example, frequently addressed the political implications of his books, while the reviews of Garland's rural fiction did not. Compare the reviews of *Prairie Folks* in James Nagel, ed., *Critical Essays on Hamlin Garland*, 52–54, to the reviews of Chesnutt's *The Wife of His Youth and Other Stories of the Color Line*, such as Hamilton Wright Mabie, "Two New Novelists," 440–41; and Howells, "Mr. Charles W. Chesnutt's Stories," 699–701.

5. Gavin Jones, *Strange Talk*, 39.

6. Howells, *Selected Literary Criticism*, 2: 221–22.

7. George Washington Cable, "A Protest Against Dialect," *Critic* n.s. 4 (1884): 52–53.

8. Mark Twain, *The Adventures of Huckleberry Finn*, 27.

9. Jones writes in *Strange Talk*: "The 'Explanatory' is not so much a comment on the techniques of *Huck Finn* as a burlesque of the assumptions upon which dialect writing had depended since the early 1870s" (3).

10. Harris, *Uncle Remus*, 39–40.

11. See Hemenway's "Note to the Text," in Harris, *Uncle Remus*, 36.

12. Harris, *Uncle Remus*, 59.

13. For a more complete account of the plantation tradition, see Lucinda H. Mackethan, "Plantation Fiction, 1865–1900," and Merrill Macguire Skaggs, "Varieties of Local Color," in Louis D. Rubin Jr., gen. ed., *The History of Southern Literature*, 209–18 and 219–27.

14. Thomas Nelson Page, *In Ole Virginia, or Marse Chan and Other Stories*, 1.

15. A Southern Matron, "'Marse Chan' Again," 114.

16. Page, *In Ole Virginia*, n.p. The complete dedication reads: "To My People / This Fragmentary Record of Their Life Is Dedicated."

17. Paul Laurence Dunbar, "We Wear the Mask," in *The Collected Poetry of Paul Laurence Dunbar*, ed. Joanne Braxton, 71.

Henry Louis Gates Jr., has offered the most explicit argument that the "use of dialect in Afro-American poetry itself was a form of masking," and that the tradition of the African mask must be understood to interpret Dunbar's work ("Dis and Dat: Dialect and the Descent," in *Afro-American Literature: The Reconstruction of Instruction*, eds. Dexter Fisher and Robert B. Stepto, 94). The purpose of recent Dunbar criticism has almost exclusively been to question whether and to what extent the dialect obscures Dunbar's true poetic voice, including subversive tendencies. For instance, Houston Baker has suggested that "Dunbar's [poetic] speaker plays the masking game without an awareness of its status as a game" (*Modernism and the Harlem Renaissance*, 39–40); Marcellus Blount has contended that Dunbar's "An Ante-Bellum Sermon" "straddles the boundary between literary convention and African-American vernacular culture" ("The Preacherly Text: African American Poetry and Vernacular Performance," 586); John Keeling has complained that "critics have misrecognized the 'mask' that is never removed in [Dunbar's] poems" ("Paul Dunbar and the Mask of Dialect," 27); and Gavin Jones has written that throughout "his work, Dunbar highlights the conventionality of written dialect by representing very different voices in close proximity" (*Strange Talk*, 196).

18. The three poems were: "A Negro Love Song," April 1895; "Curtain," May 1895; "The Dilettante," July 1895 (Virginia C. Cunningham, *Paul Laurence Dunbar and His Song*, 119). On Dunbar's early career, which included a reading at the "Colored America Day" of the 1893 Columbian Exposition in Chicago, see Cunningham, 54–144, and Felton O. Best, *Crossing the Color Line: A Biography of Paul Laurence Dunbar, 1872–1906*, 33–62.

19. Charles Chesnutt to S. Alice Halderman, 1 Feb. 1896, in *"To Be an Author": Letters of Charles W. Chesnutt, 1889–1905*, eds. Joseph R. McElrath Jr., and Robert C. Leitz III, 89. Chesnutt writes, "There is a young colored man formerly of Dayton, Ohio, by the name of Paul Dunbar, who has written poems in the James Whitcomb Riley style, which have been widely copied in the newspapers and have brought him into considerable notice."

20. Howells's relationship with Dunbar went beyond this single review. The most complete account of which I know is James B. Stronks, "Paul Laurence Dunbar and William Dean Howells," 95–108.

21. William Dean Howells, "Life and Letters," 630. As this review consists of a single page (of approximately 3,500 words), all quotations from it refer to this citation.

22. William Dean Howells, introduction to Paul Laurence Dunbar, *Lyrics of Lowly Life*, xiii.

23. Blount, "The Preacherly Text," 586.

24. Myron Simon notes that a fifth of the dialect poems printed in Dunbar's *Complete Poems* "are in white dialect, i.e., dialect that Dunbar plainly distinguished from the poems in Negro dialect" ("Dunbar and Dialect Poetry," in *A Singer in the Dawn: Reinterpretations of Paul Laurence Dunbar*, ed. Jay Martin, 125). In her biography, Cunningham describes an incident in which a *New York Sun* newspaper reporter reacted unfavorably when Dunbar recited a poem in Irish dialect at a reading (*Paul Laurence Dunbar and His Song*, 154).

25. Howells, "Life and Letters," 630.

26. See Paul Laurence Dunbar, *Majors and Minors*, 87.

27. H. T. Peck, "An Afro-American Poet," 568. For two other reviews that laud Dunbar's lyric poetry while holding the "literary" verses in less esteem, see the unsigned reviews in *Outlook* (55 [2 Jan. 1897], 95–96) and *Critic* (n.s. 27 [1897]: 20).

28. Page, *In Ole Virginia*, 1–37, 143–65.

29. Howells, *Selected Literary Criticism*, 2: 49.

30. "A Note Not Heard Before," 286.

31. Dunbar, "A Banjo Song," in *The Collected Poetry of Paul Laurence Dunbar*, ed. Braxton, 21.

32. Addison Gayle Jr., "Literature as Catharsis: The Novels of Paul Laurence Dunbar," in *Singer in the Dawn*, ed. Martin, 144. Grace Isabel Colbron's review of *The Uncalled* was typical in this regard. Colbron asserted that Dunbar's "knowledge of his subject is intimate and secure, but it is the knowledge of an outsider"—and concluded the review by calling for Dunbar to return to his own "specialisation" ("Across the Colour Line," 338–41). As if to punctuate the point, *Bookman* published a poem of Dunbar's written in dialect, "Christmas Is A-Comin," beneath the review. In contrast, just a month before, *Bookman* had published a review praising *Folks from Dixie* as the "first expression in national prose fiction of the inner life of the American negro" (George Preston, "Folks from Dixie," 348).

33. Paul Laurence Dunbar, "At Shaft 11," in *Folks from Dixie*, 205–31.

34. Stories about plantation life comprise about two-thirds of Dunbar's *In Old Plantation Days*, and in only one, "The Easter Wedding" (226–35), does Dunbar dwell at all on the suffering that slaves endured under that system. Even there, however, the master of the two married slaves about to be separated at auction is portrayed as a sympathetic character tortured by the fate of the newlyweds.

35. "Unpublished Letters of Paul Laurence Dunbar to a Friend," 73.

36. Paul Laurence Dunbar to Alice Ruth Moore, 17 April 1895, reprinted in Jay Martin

and Gossie H. Hudson, eds., *The Paul Laurence Dunbar Reader*, 428. Alice Moore's reply of 7 May 1895 to Dunbar is equally revealing. "You ask my opinion about Negro dialect in literature. Well, I frankly believe in everyone following his bent. If it be so that one has a special aptitude for dialect work, why it is only right that dialect should be made a specialty. But if one should be like me—absolutely devoid of the ability to manage dialect—I don't see the necessity of cramming and forcing oneself into that plane because one is a Negro or a Southerner." Quoted in Eugene Wesley Metcalf Jr., "The Letters of Paul and Alice Dunbar: A Private History," 37–38.

37. Harriet Beecher Stowe, *Oldtown Folks*, ed. Dorothy Berkson, 3–4. Myron Simon makes this connection between Stowe and Dunbar as interpreters of local color scenes ("Dunbar and Dialect Poetry," 127).

38. The first paragraph of "A Family Feud" reads, "I wish I could tell you the story as I heard it from the lips of the old black woman as she sat bobbing her turbaned head to and fro with the motion of her creaky little rocking-chair, and droning the tale forth in the mellow voice of her race. So much of the charm of the story was in that voice, which even the cares of age had not hardened" (Dunbar, *Folks from Dixie*, 137).

39. Chesnutt, *The Journals of Charles W. Chesnutt*, ed. Brodhead, 121. I am also indebted to Brodhead's discussion of Chesnutt in *Cultures of Letters*, esp. 190–95, for my analysis of this journal entry.

40. Chesnutt, *The Journals of Charles W. Chesnutt*, 124–25.

41. Kenneth M. Price, "Charles Chesnutt, the *Atlantic Monthly*, and the Intersection of African-American Fiction and Elite Culture," in *Periodical Literature in Nineteenth-Century America*, eds. Price and Susan Belasco Smith, 259–60.

42. The quotation is from David N. Livingstone, *Nathaniel Southgate Shaler and the Culture of American Science*, 40. Shaler's contributions to the *Atlantic* included "The Negro Problem" (1884), "Racial Prejudices" (1886), and "Science and the African Problem" (1890). Lee D. Baker gives a brief account of Shaler's ideas and their place in late-nineteenth-century American thought in *From Savage to Negro*, 45–48.

43. Chesnutt, *"To Be an Author,"* 44.

44. Richard H. Brodhead, introduction to Charles W. Chesnutt, *The Conjure Woman and Other Tales*, ed. Brodhead, 15–16. Further references to this edition of *The Conjure Woman* are made parenthetically within the text.

45. Chesnutt, *"To Be an Author,"* 105.

46. Brodhead writes in *Cultures of Letters:* "Chesnutt's conjure tales are in one sense remarkable for their massive conventionality . . . Chesnutt stays so close to generic conventions that they inevitably become revealed, though without comment or over parody, as conventions." (196).

47. Robert Hemenway, "The Functions of Folklore in Charles Chesnutt's *The Conjure Woman*," 296.

48. Craig Werner, "The Framing of Charles W. Chesnutt: Practical Deconstruction in the Afro-American Tradition," in *Southern Literature and Literary Theory*, ed. Jefferson Humphries, 351.

49. Charles W. Chesnutt, "Post-Bellum—Pre-Harlem" (1931), in Chesnutt, *Essays and Speeches*, eds. Joseph R. McElrath Jr., Robert C. Leitz III, and Jesse S. Crisler, 544; Werner, "The Framing of Charles W. Chesnutt," 357.

50. In 1901, Chesnutt published "Superstitions and Folk-Lore of the South," an article in which he suggested that he shared John's skepticism about conjure. "Relics of ancestral barbarism are found among all peoples," he writes, "but advanced civilization has at least shaken off the more obvious absurdities" (in Chesnutt, *Essays and Speeches*, 156). This article has led some critics to debate whether Chesnutt identified as much with John as with Julius. See, for example, Werner Sollors, "The Goopher in Charles Chesnutt's Conjure Tales: Superstition, Ethnicity, and Modern Metamorphoses," 119–20.

51. Hemenway, "The Functions of Folklore in Charles Chesnutt's *The Conjure Woman*," 301. Hemenway asserts that "Julius believes all his conjure stories are true" (297), something that John calls into question.

52. Chesnutt, *The Conjure Woman and Other Tales*, 185. "Tobe's Tribulations" has been restored to this new edition of the book.

53. Ben Slote, "Listening to 'The Goophered Grapevine' and Hearing Raisins Sing," 689.

54. Charles W. Chesnutt, *The Marrow of Tradition*. Further references to this edition of the novel are made parenthetically within the text.

Chesnutt mentions *Uncle Tom's Cabin* several times in his letters written during and after the composition of *The Marrow of Tradition*. See Chesnutt, *"To Be an Author,"* 156, 160, 162.

The major novel that I have left out of this account of Chesnutt's career is his first, *The House Behind the Cedars* (1900). I have done so because I hope to chart a broad trajectory rather than a detailed description. However, biological race plays a similarly important role in the narrative structure of *House* as in *Marrow*.

55. "Charles W. Chesnutt's Own View of His New Story, *The Marrow of Tradition*," (1901), in Chesnutt, *Essays and Speeches*, 169.

56. Werner Sollors, *Neither Black nor White Yet Both*, 92–93 and 446–47n.

57. Robert Stepto has argued that Chesnutt's conjure tales offer a coherent story about the development of John into a "reliable listener" to Julius's performances, but he also points out that the stories that portray this growth were omitted from the published volume of *The Conjure Woman* ("'The Simple But Intensely Human Inner Life of Slavery': Storytelling, Fiction and the Revision of History in Charles W. Chesnutt's 'Uncle Julius Stories,'" in *History and Tradition in Afro-American Culture*, ed. Günter H. Lenz, 48, 50.)

58. Eric J. Sundquist, *To Wake the Nations: Race in the Making of American Literature*, 287.

59. Gavin Jones traces back the marginal place of Dunbar within the canon of African American writing to James Weldon Johnson's preface to *The Book of American Negro Poetry* (1922). There, according to Jones, "Johnson implies that Dunbar inevitably conformed to the minstrel and plantation traditions that defined white depictions of black speech." Moreover, Jones argues that Gayl Jones, Houston Baker Jr., and Henry Louis Gates Jr., have "echoed Johnson's evaluation of Dunbar" (*Strange Talk*, 183).

60. James Weldon Johnson, *Along This Way*, 161.

61. Measuring the literary reputations of Dunbar and Chesnutt against each other during the period of their original publication is difficult. My reading has suggested that Dunbar was often hailed as the leading African American writer of poetry, and Chesnutt as his equal in prose. In "The Negro in Literature and Art" (1913), for example, W. E. B. Du Bois capped his account of the 1890s by asserting that "Chesnutt's six novels and Dunbar's inimitable works spoke to the whole nation" (in *Writings*, 865). On the other hand, there can be no doubt that Chesnutt is currently a source of widespread interest in American literary studies, and that Dunbar is not. Compare, for instance, the publication of volumes of Chesnutt's letters, journals, essays, and previously unpublished novels during the 1990s with the dearth of such republication of Dunbar's work.

62. Chapter 1 briefly discussed Boas's efforts to use anthropometric measurements to demonstrate that physical races were unstable. For a sample of Boas's work in this area, see his "The Half-Blood Indian" (1894) and "Changes in Bodily Form of Descendants of Immigrants" (1910–1913), in his *Race, Language and Culture*, 138–48 and 60–75. George Stocking Jr., gives a more complete account of these efforts in his chapter, "The Critique of Racial Formalism," in *Race, Culture, and Evolution*, 161–94.

63. Chesnutt, "The Future American: A Complete Race-Amalgamation Likely to Occur," (1900) in Chesnutt, *Essays and Speeches*, 131–36; Franz Boas, "The Problem of the American Negro," 384–95.

4. Searching for the "Real" Indian

1. James Clifford, "On Ethnographic Allegory," in *Writing Culture: The Poetics and Politics of Ethnography*, eds. Clifford and George E. Marcus, 115.

2. Ibid., 112.

3. Vizenor discusses "survivance" throughout the essays that comprise his *Manifest Manners: Postindian Warriors of Survivance*.

4. Hinsley, *The Smithsonian and the American Indian*, 147.

5. Mark, *Four Anthropologists*, 103–5. Following current practice, I have removed the diacritic from the name "Zuni" except when quoting Cushing's use of it.

6. Frank Hamilton Cushing, "My Adventures in Zuñi," in *Zuñi: Selected Writings of Frank Hamilton Cushing*, ed. Jesse Green, 78. Further references to this edition appear parenthetically within the text. ("My Adventures" originally appeared in three parts in *Century*: 25 (1882): 191–207 and 500–54, and 26 (1883): 28–47.

7. Brad Evans, "Cushing's Zuni Sketchbooks: Literature, Anthropology, and American Notions of Culture," 717–45.

8. On Indian performances in Barnum's American Museum, see Paul Gilmore, "The Indian in the Museum: Henry David Thoreau, Okah Tubbee, and Authentic Manhood," 25–63. On the Wild West shows, see L. G. Moses, *Wild West Shows and the Images of American Indians, 1883–1933*.

9. Quoted in Curtis M. Hinsley, "Zunis and Brahmins: Cultural Ambivalence in the Gilded Age," in *Romantic Motives: Essays on Anthropological Sensibility*, ed. George W. Stocking Jr., 181. Hinsley's article offers the most detailed account of which I know of this tour and the way popular magazines represented it.

10. Evans orients this tension differently by contending that articles such as Cushing's, when published in magazines like the *Century*, employed "notions of Arnoldian and ethnographic cultures [to] create a new hybridized entity" ("Cushing's Zuni Sketchbooks," 737). While I agree with Evans's argument that Cushing shuttles between competing definitions of culture, I believe the evolutionary concept of culture as the process by which the group improves is more relevant to the production and dissemination of his work than is the Arnoldian idea of individual development.

11. Mark, *Four Anthropologists*, 111–13.

12. Frank Hamilton Cushing, *Zuñi Breadstuff*, 220. This book compiles a series of articles that Cushing published in *The Millstone* between January 1884 and August 1885.

13. "The theory of cultural evolution, as it turns out," Leah Dilworth has noted, "dovetails nicely with the notion of assimilation; it made the process of civilization seem inevitable and natural" (*Imagining Indians in the Southwest: Persistent Visions of a Primitive Past*, 27).

14. Among the most helpful works in the general history of the Indian reform movements of this period are Frederick Hoxie, *A Final Promise: The Campaign to Assimilate the Indians, 1880–1920*; Francis Paul Prucha, *The Great Father: The U.S. Government and the Indians*, 2 vols.; D. S. Otis, *The Dawes Act and the Allotment of Indian Lands*; and Prucha's edited collection, *Americanizing the American Indians: Writings by the "Friends of the Indian" 1880–1900*.

15. "Address of President Merrill E. Gates," *Proceedings of the Fourteenth Annual Meeting of the Lake Mohonk Conference of Friends of the Indian, 1896*, ed. Isabel C. Barrows, 9.

16. Morgan, *Ancient Society*, n.p.

17. Ibid., 10–11.

18. Hoxie, *A Final Promise*, 17. For more on the impact of Morgan's *Ancient Society* upon Powell, see Hinsley, *The Smithsonian and the American Indian*, 149.

19. Gail Bederman, *Manliness and Civilization: A Cultural History of Gender and Race in the United States, 1880–1917*.

20. Francis A. Walker, "Immigration and Degradation," 643, 644. For a detailed discussion of the rhetoric surrounding Americanization of immigrants, see Priscilla Wald, *Constituting Americans: Cultural Anxiety and Narrative Form*, esp. 243–60.

21. This attitude toward Native Americans actually preceded the creation of the reservation system. From at least "Jefferson forward," Arnold Krupat writes, "America will stand as one of the world's foremost laboratories for anthropological science, a science Americans proceed to establish on the basis of a first-hand study of the Indian" (*Ethnocriticism*, 63).

22. *The Fifteenth Annual Report of the Board of Indian Commissioners*, 69.

23. U.S. Bureau of the Census, *Statistical Abstract of the United States: 1991*, 111th edition, 9.

24. U.S. Bureau of the Census, *Negro Population in the United States, 1790–1915*, 25.

25. Herbert Welsh summed up this piece of the reformers' logic in 1886: "It is clear that the Indian's alienation is mainly attributable to the persistent policy of isolation, and to our perpetuation of the tribal cohesion, by dealing with the nation and not the individual" (*The Helplessness of the Indians Before the Law with an Outline of Proposed Legislation*, 5). Otis's chapter, "Aims and Motives of the Allotment Movement" (*The Dawes Act and the Allotment of Indian Lands*, 8–32), is of particular interest on the possibility of railroad influence. See also Hoxie, *A Final Promise*, 45–50.

26. Prucha's *American Indian Treaties: The History of a Political Anomaly* names a number of treaties before the Dawes Act that provided for allotment. The earliest he names is the Creek removal treaty of 1832 (171–74).

27. Patricia Nelson Limerick, *The Legacy of Conquest*, 198–99.

28. Hoxie argues, and my own research has shown, that around 1900 reformers begin to question the ability of individual land ownership to effect immediate assimilation (*A Final Promise*, 117). For a breakdown of the number of acres allotted during the periods in question, see Janet McDonnell, *The Dispossession of the American Indian, 1887–1934*, 6–18.

29. Morgan, *Ancient Society*, 511–12.

30. Alice C. Fletcher, "Land, Law, Education—The Three Things Needed by the Indian," 33.

31. Susan L. Mizruchi, *The Science of Sacrifice: American Literature and Modern Social Theory*, 31–32. Mizruchi is not speaking specifically about Native Americans, but about the prevalence of sacrifice across the spectrum of late nineteenth-century social theory.

32. See Homi Bhabha, "DissemiNation: Time, Narrative, and the Margins of the Modern Nation," in *Nation and Narration*, ed. Bhabha, 291–322.

33. Unsurprisingly, this period was marked by a new nostalgia for the frontier past. As Hoxie writes, "The [Native American] race would become more important for what it represented than for what it might become." His chapter, "The Transformation of the Indian Question" (*A Final Promise*, 83–113), contains an excellent discussion of the portrayal of Indians at the 1893 Columbian Exposition and other exhibitions of the period.

34. *Proceedings of the Fifth Annual Meeting of the Lake Mohonk Conference of the Friends of the Indian, 1887*, 64.

35. Fletcher was the only ethnographer truly active—attending conferences, delivering speeches, writing articles—in the Indian reform groups, and her burgeoning career in the late nineteenth century tells something of the social milieu in which both Indian reform and ethnography operated. See Joan Mark's biography, *A Stranger in Her Native Land: Alice Fletcher and the American Indians*. Hoxie writes that Powell "remained a firm advocate of Indian assimilation," and Frank Hamilton Cushing often lent his support (*A Final Promise*, 24, 262n).

36. R. H. Pratt, in *Proceedings of the Twentieth Annual Meeting of the Lake Mohonk Conference of the Indian*, ed. Isabel C. Barrows, 136.

37. Philip C. Garrett, "Indian Citizenship," *Proceedings of the Fourth Annual Lake Mohonk Conference, 1886*, 8.

38. Pratt, in *Proceedings of the Twentieth Annual Meeting of the Lake Mohonk Conference of the Indian*, 136.

39. For general biographical information on John Wesley Powell, see John Upton Terrell, *The Man Who Rediscovered America: A Biography of John Wesley Powell*, and William Culp Darrah, *Powell of the Colorado*. On Powell's transition from geology to anthropology, see Terrell, 125, and Hinsley, *The Smithsonian and the American Indian*, 138–39.

40. John Wesley Powell, "Report of the Director," *First Annual Report of the Bureau of Ethnology to the Secretary of the Smithsonian Institution, 1879–'80*, xiv.

41. Frank Hamilton Cushing, "The Need of Studying the Indian in Order to Teach Him," in *The Twenty-Eighth Annual Report of the Board of Indian Commissioners, 1896*, 109–14.

42. Quoted in Darnell, *And Along Came Boas*, 37.

43. John Wesley Powell, "Indian Linguistic Families of America North of Mexico," *Seventh Annual Report of the Bureau of Ethnology to the Secretary of the Smithsonian Institution, 1885–'86*: 35–36.

44. Darnell argues that Powell, in fact, coined the term acculturation (*And Along Came Boas*, 40). I have taken the phrase from the first "Report of the Director," *First Annual Report of the Bureau of Ethnology*, xxviii.

45. Darnell, *And Along Came Boas*, 47.

46. Darnell argues: "Language held the place of honour in the American paradigm which persisted from the BAE to Boasian anthropology on at least two grounds: (1) Language was understood to be the symbolic form par excellence, the characteristic which distinguished humans from all other species . . . ; (2) Language provided the most plausible method to classify the otherwise nearly overwhelming cultural diversity of aboriginal North America" (*And Along Came Boas*, xii–xiii). Hinsley points out that one major influence upon Powell's attitude toward language and, consequently, on the Bureau's work in linguistics, was William Dwight Whitney, an American linguist whose European admirers would later include Ferdinand de Saussure (*The Smithsonian and the American Indian*, 158–59). On Boas's philological orientation, see Briggs and Bauman, "'The Foundation of All Future Researches,'" 498–99 and 526 n68.

47. John Wesley Powell, "Report of the Director," *Second Annual Report of the Bureau of Ethnology to the Secretary of the Smithsonian Institution, 1880–'81*, xvii.

48. I have followed McGee's own practice of not placing periods after his initials.

49. John Wesley Powell, "Report of the Director," *Twenty-Second Annual Report of the Bureau of Ethnology to the Secretary of the Smithsonian Institution, 1900–'01*, x. McGee was actually writing under Powell's name. Hinsley points out that during the final years of Powell's life, McGee wrote all of the official reports and letters related to Bureau business on Powell's behalf (*The Smithsonian and the American Indian*, 246).

50. Hinsley, *The Smithsonian and the American Indian*, 110, 156–64.

51. David Murray, *Forked Tongues: Speech, Writing, and Representation in American Indian Texts*, 15–19.

52. Hinsley, *The Smithsonian and the American Indian*, 154.

53. L. G. Moses, *The Indian Man: A Biography of James Mooney*, 11–12. I have relied on Moses's well-documented work for biographical information regarding Mooney. Also useful is William M. Colby, "Routes to Rainy Mountain: A Biography of James Mooney, Ethnologist."

54. Darnell, *And Along Came Boas*, 70–72, 75, and 80–81. The sole ethnologist with a university degree was Albert Samuel Gatschet.

55. Moses, *The Indian Man*, 18–20.

56. For a thorough account of popular representations of the Ghost Dance prior to and following the Wounded Knee massacre, see Christina Klein, "'Everything of Interest in the Late Pine Ridge War Are Held by Us for Sale': Popular Culture and Wounded Knee," 45–68.

57. Just as I have alternated the use of "Indian" and "Native American," I will alternate the use of "Sioux" and "Lakota." "Sioux," like many such terms, is a name by which this people did not originally refer to themselves. "Lakota," often a preferred term today, is the name of one of the three dialects spoken by members of the Sioux nation.

58. As Raymond J. DeMallie put it: "For the whites . . . Indian dancing symbolized impending war. . . . [I]t suggested that the Indians were expecting to die, caught up in a frenzy of reckless fatalism" ("The Lakota Ghost Dance: An Ethnohistorical Account," 392).

59. James P. Boyd, *Recent Indian Wars, Under the Lead of Sitting Bull, and Other Chiefs; with A Full Account of the Messiah Craze, and Ghost Dances,* 189; quoted in DeMallie, "The Lakota Ghost Dance," 393.

60. A much more complete account of the historical details of the events leading up to the Wounded Knee massacre can be found in Robert M. Utley's *The Last Days of the Sioux Nation.*

61. "The Last of Sitting Bull," 1.

62. James Mooney, *The Ghost-Dance Religion and the Sioux Outbreak of 1890,* 871. The *Ghost-Dance Religion* originally appeared as part two of the *Fourteenth Annual Report of the Bureau of Ethnology to the Secretary of the Smithsonian Institution, 1892–'93.* This Nebraska edition maintains the original Bureau pagination. Further references to this edition appear parenthetically within the text.

Mooney's estimate of "very nearly 300" Lakotas "killed on the field, or who later died from wounds and exposure," was higher than any official estimate.

63. "The Indian Massacre," 4.

64. Sidney W. Mintz, "Sows' Ears and Silver Linings: A Backward Look at Ethnography," 171. For recent discussions of the Ghost Dance itself, see DeMallie, "The Lakota Ghost Dance" and Alice Kehoe, *The Ghost Dance: Ethnohistory and Revitalization.*

65. White defines emplotment as "the way by which a sequence of events fashioned into a story is gradually revealed to be a story of a particular kind" (*Metahistory: The Historical Imagination in Nineteenth-Century Europe,* 7). White does not, however, describe a circular structure of emplotment, as I do. Further, my discussion of "tragic realism" modifies White's division of narrative into four categories: tragedy, comedy, romance, and satire.

66. White, *Metahistory,* 9.

67. This emphasis on suffering as something to be managed and limited rather than eliminated comports with the widespread interest in establishing an "economy of pain," as described by Wai Chee Dimock in "The Economy of Pain: The Case of Howells."

68. Merrill E. Gates, "Address of President Gates," *Proceedings of the Ninth Annual Lake Mohonk Conference,* 8.

69. John Wesley Powell, "Report of the Director," *Fourteenth Annual Report of the Bureau of Ethnology,* lx.

70. Michael Hittman, *Wovoka and the Ghost Dance,* ed. Don Lynch, expanded ed., 63–105. Hittman's book was first published in 1990 under the auspices of the Yerrington Paiute Tribe, which holds the copyright.

71. Hittman points out that the political nature of Wovoka's teachings "has been altogether ignored" (*Wovoka and the Ghost Dance,* 153).

72. Hittman writes that there is no historical evidence that Wovoka actually attended or "performed" at the Midwinter Fair in San Francisco (Ibid., 127).

73. William James, "The Dilemma of Determinism," in *"The Will to Believe" and "Human Immortality,"* 145–83. James declares soft determinism, which he eschews, to be "the determinism which allows considerations of good and bad to mingle with those of cause and effect in deciding what sort of a universe this may rationally be held to be" (166).

74. Manganaro, "Textual Play, Power, and Cultural Critique," 33.

75. Clifford Geertz, "Thick Description: Toward an Interpretive Theory of Culture," in *The Interpretation of Cultures,* 3–30.

76. According to Julian Rice, the Lakota word "oya'te" is customarily translated as either "people" or "nation." One may speak of the "Lakota oya'te"—but one may also use the word when referring to, say, a representative of the buffalo nation whom one meets in a vision. The word can refer to any group of like-minded people or spirits seeking to cooperate in an effort

for a common survival. Rice points out, however, that the word does not connote the kind of governmental apparatus—a regimented hierarchy, a police force, a military force, etc.—that English speakers usually associate with the English word "nation" (personal communication). In the dictionary published by the Smithsonian in 1890, to which Mooney presumably had access, the word is defined as "a people, nation, tribe, band" (Stephen Return Riggs, *A Dakota-English Dictionary*, ed. James Owen Dorsey, 397).

77. See DeMallie, "The Lakota Ghost Dance," 390.

78. The possibilities that I *do* mention regarding the significance of this song illustrate, I hope, what Arnold Krupat has referred to as a criticism of the "subjunctive," the "domain of *if-I-were-you*, or *should-it-turn-out that*" (*Ethnocriticism*, 28). For the foundation of a less tentative and more complete approach than mine, see DeMallie, "The Lakota Ghost Dance."

79. Cushing, "The Need of Studying the Indian in Order to Teach Him," 111, 109.

80. Eliza McFeely, "Palimpsest of American Identity: Zuni, Anthropology and American Identity at the Turn of the Century," 202–6. McFeely describes how the reviews of the Brooklyn exhibition focused upon the role of Cushing in making Zuni culture accessible.

5. Culture and the Making of Native American Literature

1. Quoted in Joan Mark, *A Stranger in Her Native Land*, 273.

2. Nancy J. Parezo, "The Formation of Ethnographic Collections: The Smithsonian Institution in the American Southwest," 19.

3. Consider, for instance, Craig S. Womack's critique of the Creek narratives that Boasian John Swanton published in *Myths and Tales of the Southeastern Indians* (1929), an annual report of the Bureau of American Ethnology. Swanton's texts, according to Womack, "do not connect to a living human community. The tellings occur in a vacuum. They are artifacts; they have no bearing on contemporary concerns. They are self-fulfilling evidence amassed by the BAE to prove the popular 'vanishing American' theory so widespread during Swanton's time" (*Red on Red: Native American Literary Separatism*, 98).

4. D. G. Brinton, *Aboriginal American Authors and Their Productions*, 59. This pamphlet ends with an advertisement for Brinton's own "Library of Aboriginal American Literature."

5. Steven Conn, *Museums and American Intellectual Life, 1876–1926*, 75–113.

6. Svetlana Alpers, "The Museum as a Way of Seeing," in *Exhibiting Cultures: The Poetics and Politics of Museum Display*, ed. Ivan Karp and Steven D. Levine, 27, 31.

7. The following sources have been especially helpful to my understanding the history of folklore studies in the United States: Rosemary Lévy Zumwalt, *American Folklore Scholarship: A Dialogue of Dissent*; William K. McNeil, "A History of American Folklore Scholarship Before 1908;" and Susan A. Dwer-Shick, "The American Folklore Society and Folklore Research in America, 1888–1940."

8. Zumwalt, *American Folklore Scholarship*, 10.

9. Ibid., 9–10.

10. Ibid., 48.

11. Kate Chopin, *Bayou Folk and A Night in Acadie*, 157.

12. Gavin Jones briefly discusses Leland's work on dialects of English spoken by immigrants in *Strange Talk*, 52–53.

13. For a more thorough account of Leland's work, particularly his manipulation of stories to fit his scholarly goals, see Thomas C. Parkhill, *Weaving Ourselves into the Land: Charles Godfrey Leland, Indians, and the Study of Native American Religions*.

14. Charles Godfrey Leland, "Legends of the Passamaquoddy; With Drawings on Birch Bark by a Quadi Indian," 668–77; Leland, "The Edda among the Algonquin Indians," 222–34.

15. Charles G. Leland, *Algonquin Legends*, 2.

16. Ibid., 13.

17. Leland further advanced this idea years later when, with a linguist, he reprinted

the same texts in the form of epic poetry, organized into verse lines and cantos, in Charles Godfrey Leland and John Dyneley Prince, *Kulóskap the Master and Other Algonkin Poems*.

18. George B. Grinnell's *Pawnee Hero Stories and Folk-Tales* is an example of his own collection. In *The Punishment of the Stingy and Other Stories*, Grinnell acknowledges his debt to Boas (x), whose *Chinook Texts* (1894) Grinnell used as a source.

19. Charles L. Briggs, "Metadiscursive Practices and Scholarly Authority in Folkloristics," 404.

20. Michael Castro, *Interpreting the Indian: Twentieth-Century Poets and the Native American*, 3–45; Helen Carr, *Inventing the American Indian*, 206–29; and Kenneth Lincoln, *Singing with the Heart of a Bear: Fusions of Native and American Poetry, 1890–1999*, 28–59. For a wider perspective on Anglo-American primitivism, see the articles collected in Elazar Barkan and Ronald Bush, eds., *Prehistories of the Future: The Primitivist Project and the Culture of Modernism*.

21. Briggs, "Metadiscursive Practices and Scholarly Authority in Folkloristics," 397–400.

22. The reinscription of Native disappearance as the basis of American exceptionalism would reach its fullest expression in Mary Austin's *The American Rhythm*, in which Austin explains how she "awoke to the relationships that must necessarily exist between aboriginal and later American forms" (19).

23. Natalie Burlin Curtis, *The Indians Book*, xxvii.

24. Joel Chandler Harris, *Uncle Remus*, 39.

25. Such formulations were frequently found in social thought that built upon the evolutionary thought of Herbert Spencer (Lears, *No Place of Grace*), 144–49.

26. See, for example, Brian Swann, ed., *On the Translation of Native American Literature*.

27. Arnold Krupat, *The Turn to the Native*, 32–36. Krupat argues here for a strategy of reading Native American literature as engaged in acts of "anti-imperial translation." While I find this argument persuasive, I am not attempting to make the same claim for the texts I discuss here. However, like Krupat, I am interested in the ways in which translation creates certain possibilities for making complex statements about the place of Native peoples within the English-speaking world.

28. At this point in his life, Powell was not in good health, and consequently much that appeared under his name was actually composed by his aide WJ McGee, who shared Powell's general principles vis-à-vis culture and anthropology. I have not been able to determine, however, whether or not McGee is the author of the introduction to Cushing's collection.

29. John Wesley Powell, introduction to Frank Hamilton Cushing, *Zuñi Folk Tales*, vii.

30. Thomas Frederick Crane, *Italian Popular Tales*, 252–53.

31. Cushing, *Zuñi Folk Tales*, 411.

32. James A. Boon, "Accenting Hybridity: Postcolonial Cultural Studies, a Boasian Anthropologist, and I," in John Carlos Rowe, ed., *"Culture" and the Problem of the Disciplines*, 161.

33. A. LaVonne Brown Ruoff, editor's introduction to S. Alice Callahan, *Wynema: A Child of the Forest*, xvii. For an account of Callahan's failure to address issues of tribal nationalism or culture, see Womack, *Red on Red*, 107–29.

34. Elisabeth Luther Cary, "Recent Writings by American Indians," 21.

35. For biographical information on Eastman and Zitkala-Ša, see Raymond Wilson, *Charles Eastman, Santee Sioux*, and Dexter Fisher's foreword to Zitkala-Ša's autobiographical *American Indian Stories*, v–xx. I discuss La Flesche's biography at greater length below.

36. Cary, "Recent Writings by American Indians," 21.

37. Eastman, Zitkala-Ša, and La Flesche were also all members of the assimilationist Society of American Indians (SAI); Hazel Hertzberg describes the SAI in detail in *The Search for an American Indian Identity: Modern Pan-Indians*. Robert Allen Warrior describes the SAI as playing a key role in the development of twentieth-century American Indian history in *Tribal Secrets: Recovering American Indian Intellectual History*, 5–14.

More specifically, for Eastman's involvement with Garland's naming project, see Wilson, *Ohiyesa*, 120–30; Zitkala-Ša discusses her own teaching at Carlisle in *American Indian Stories*, 81–92; and I explain La Flesche's role in the Omaha allotment in the text that follows.

38. Elaine Goodale Eastman, in fact, served as an editor to all of Eastman's writing, a fact Eastman mentions in his second autobiography, *From Deep Woods to Civilization*, 185–86. The extent of her editorial intervention, however, is not precisely known and has been the subject of some debate. See, for example, William Oandasan, "A Cross-Disciplinary Note on Charles Eastman (Santee Sioux)," 75–78; and Carol Lea Clark, "Charles A. Eastman (Ohiyesa) and Elaine Goodale Eastman: A Cross-Cultural Collaboration," 271–80. For Charles Eastman's experience at the Pine Ridge agency during the Wounded Knee massacre of 1890, see *From Deep Woods to Civilization*, 92–115.

The collections in which the two appear as co-authors are *Wigwam Evenings: Sioux Folk Tales Retold* and *Smoky Day's Wigwam Evenings: Indian Stories Retold*.

39. Eastman and Eastman, *Wigwam Evenings*, 30, 87, 37.

40. Michaelsen, *The Limits of Multiculturalism*, 76–83.

41. Charles A. Eastman (Ohiyesa), *Red Hunters and the Animal People*, vii. Further references to this edition are parenthetically within the body of the text.

42. Frederick Douglass, *Narrative of the Life of Frederick Douglass, an American Slave*, xii. Wendell Phillips uses this common figure of speech in his prefatory letter.

43. Susan Bernadin, "The Lessons of a Sentimental Education: Zitkala-Ša's Autobiographical Narratives," 221.

44. Cary, "Recent Writings by American Indians," 24.

45. Quoted in Dexter Fisher, foreword to *American Indian Stories*, vi.

46. Zitkala-Ša, *Old Indian Legends*, vi. Further references to this edition are made parenthetically within the body of the text.

47. Eastman and Eastman, *Wigwam Evenings*, 64–69. See also Stephen Return Riggs, *Dakota Grammar, Texts, and Ethnography*, ed. James Owen Dorsey, Contributions to North American Ethnology, vol. 9, 95–104.

48. The controversy surrounding the ancestry of Joseph La Flesche revolves around the question of whether his mother belonged to the Omaha or the Ponca tribe. For a brief account of the dispute, see R. H. Barnes, *Two Crows Denies It: A History of Controversy in Omaha Sociology*, 37–49. In *Iron Eye's Family*, Norma Jean Kidd provides biographical information on the La Flesche family based on archival resources, including the family papers.

49. Kidd, *Iron Eye's Family*, 60–62.

50. Mark, *A Stranger in Her Native Land*, 183 (on the Queen Victoria resemblance); 207 (on the adoption); 132 and 309 (on the gossip). Mark explains that Fletcher and La Flesche decided not to make the adoption fully legal, for fear that Francis would have to forego using La Flesche as his last name.

51. Mark, *A Stranger in Her Native Land*, 88–101.

52. Quoted in Robin Ridington and Dennis Hastings (In'aska), *Blessing for a Long Time: The Sacred Pole of the Omaha Tribe*, 97. Ridington and Hastings's book more completely discusses the importance of the Sacred Pole, La Flesche's role in removing it from the Omahas, and the recent return of the Pole to the tribe.

53. Ridington and Hastings, *Blessing for a Long Time*, 236–37.

54. La Flesche's denunciation of the tribal sacred becomes even more baffling in light of the fact that when, independent of Fletcher, he began to write about the Osages, he almost exclusively focused upon sacred ceremonies and rituals.

55. Fletcher to Putnam, October 1907, quoted in Mark, *A Stranger in Her Native Land*, 318–19.

56. Alice Fletcher and Francis La Flesche, *The Omaha Tribe*, 2 vols., 245–51.

57. Herbert, *Culture and Anomie*, 8–19.

58. Fletcher and La Flesche, *The Omaha Tribe*, 134, 217, 113.

59. Ibid., 614–15.

60. Ibid., 641.

61. See Fletcher, "Flotsam and Jetsam from Aboriginal America," 12–14; La Flesche, "An Indian Allotment," 2686–88; and Mark, *A Stranger in Her Native Land*, 266–68.

62. That same year, Small, Maynard also published Fletcher's *Indian Story and Song*, her first book aimed at a general audience.

63. Francis La Flesche, *The Middle Five*, xv. Further references to this edition are made parenthetically within the body of the text.

64. The "boy book" tradition is most frequently discussed in the context of Twain's works. See, for example, Albert E. Stone, Jr., *The Innocent Eye: Childhood in Mark Twain's Imagination*, 62–72; Jim Hunter, "Mark Twain and the Boy-Book in Nineteenth-Century America," 430–38; Judith Fetterly, "The Sanctioned Rebel," 293–94; and Alan Gribben, "'I Did Wish Tom Sawyer Was There': Boy-Book Elements in *Tom Sawyer* and *Huckleberry Finn*," in *One Hundred Years of Huckleberry Finn: The Boy, His Book, and American Culture*, eds. Robert Sattelmeyer and J. Donald Crowley, 149–70. For a more recent discussion of this tradition in a different critical context, see Stephen Mailloux, *Reception Histories: Rhetoric, Pragmatism, and American Cultural Politics*, 138–40.

65. Thomas Bailey Aldrich, *The Story of a Bad Boy*, 1.

66. See Bederman, *Manliness and Civilization*, generally, for one account of this anxiety. Philip J. Deloria has documented how these same worries about gender roles led some Euro-Americans in the early decades of the twentieth century to encourage their children to "play Indian" through summer camps and the scouting movement (*Playing Indian*, 95–127).

67. "Book Reviews," 581.

68. Fletcher and La Flesche, *The Omaha Tribe*, 34–35.

69. I should like to be especially clear about my method of interpretation here. I am basing my judgments of the episodes in *The Middle Five* on what La Flesche would (with Fletcher) write later to be true of Omaha life and its standards of conduct. The matter of La Flesche's accuracy in his memoir or in his ethnography is beyond the scope of my book.

70. During the period when La Flesche published his book, Native American boarding schools were, in fact, promoting athletics as means of shaping the masculine identity of their students. In the 1930s, several schools would even develop boxing teams, which became a source of both pan-Indian and tribal pride. See John Bloom, *To Show What an Indian Can Do*, 61–72.

71. Fletcher and La Flesche, *The Omaha Tribe*, 432.

72. For example, Franz Boas gave *A Study of Omaha Music* a highly favorable review in the *Journal of American Folk-Lore* 7 (1894): 169–71.

73. Mark, *Stranger in a Native Land*, 216. The letter from Fletcher, written in 1893, was directed to her mentor, Frederic Ward Putnam.

74. Fletcher and La Flesche, *The Omaha Tribe*, 364–65.

75. Renato Rosaldo, *Culture and Truth: The Remaking of Social Analysis*, 216. I am indebted to David E. Johnson and Scott Michaelsen for their discussion of this passage and of cultural "borders" in "Border Secrets: An Introduction," in *Border Theory: The Limits of Cultural Politics*, eds. Michaelsen and Johnson, 1–39, esp. 3.

76. Michel de Certeau, *The Practice of Everyday Life*, trans. Steven F. Rendell, 30. De Certeau, too, emphasizes the agency of actors placed in circumstances like those of the boys of *The Middle Five*, more than is appropriate for La Flesche's text, but his nuanced attempt to balance the imposition of systems of action and knowledge (culture) with the "creativity" of those on whom they are imposed has been useful to me.

77. Craig S. Womack has recently made a similar argument on how literature allows for the "creative change" that "the anthropological definition of culture denies" (*Red on Red*, 42). I agree with this assessment, but I also think La Flesche shows that this definition of culture has also been crucial to the development of Native American literature.

78. The name Big Elk was held by two other men before Joseph La Flesche's father, but it seems *The Middle Five* refers to the final Big Elk, a man Fletcher and La Flesche praise in the Omaha tribe for trying "to face his people toward civilization" (84).

79. Frank La Flèche [Francis La Flesche], "My First Buffalo Hunt," in James Owen Dorsey, *The Ȼegiha Language*, Contributions to North American Ethnology, vol. 6, 466–67. According to Dorsey, La Flesche's first hunt occurred when he about twelve, which would have been about two to four years after he entered the mission school. Dorsey, however, is surely incorrect when he estimates the year of La Flesche's first hunt as 1856, since La Flesche's birthdate was usually given as 1857.

80. Hartley B. Alexander, "Francis La Flesche," 328.

81. James Parins and Daniel F. Littlefield Jr., introduction to Francis La Flesche, *Ke-ma-ha: The Omaha Stories of Francis La Flesche*, ed. Parins and Littlefield, xii, xxi–xxxi. This volume includes several of these stories, including a fragment of the novel, "Ne-ma-ha" (112–29). My own sense is that La Flesche's assimilationist novel may have been at least partly inspired by the life of his father, who learned to speak French as a child, worked at a trading post, and later decided to begin earning and distributing the gifts that would enable him to become a chief.

82. Hertzberg, *The Search for an American Indian Identity*, 259–84. Hertzberg states that Richard Henry Pratt, speaking in favor of a prohibition upon peyote use, called La Flesche a "victim" of the Bureau of American Ethnology and attacked him for "not lifting up his race" (262).

83. On Native sovereignty and self-determination, see Vine Deloria, Jr., and Clifford Lytle, *The Nations Within: The Past and Future of American Indian Sovereignty*. Womack's *Red on Red*, meanwhile, provides the best example of how this concept might be applied to a body of Native American literature.

84. I quote from Omaha tribal chair Doran Morris's speech upon the presentation of sacred objects to the tribe in 1991 (quoted in Ridington and Hastings, *Blessing for a Long Time*, 230). I am deeply indebted to Ridington and Hastings for their account of the repatriation of sacred objects to the Omaha tribe.

6. Beyond Boas

1. Henry Louis Gates Jr., preface to *Zora Neale Hurston: Critical Perspectives Past and Present*, eds. Gates and K. A. Appiah, xi.

2. Krupat addresses this topic in his chapter, "Ethnography and Literature: A History of Their Convergence," which engages more recent developments within anthropology more rigorously than I do. Krupat provides a brief discussion of Hurston as part of his broader history (*Ethnocriticism*, 49–80, esp. 73–74).

3. Castro, *Interpreting the Indian*, 4–45, and Lincoln, *Sing With the Heart of a Bear*, 28–59.

4. Houston Baker Jr., *The Workings of the Spirit: The Poetics of Afro-American Women's Writing*, 95–97. For another example of this reading of Hurston's relationship to Boas and Boasian anthropology, see Susan Edwards Meisenhelder, *Hitting a Straight Lick with a Crooked Stick: Race and Gender in the Work of Zora Neale Hurston*, 15–18.

5. Hazel V. Carby, "The Politics of Fiction, Anthropology, and the Folk: Zora Neale Hurston," in *New Essays on* Their Eyes Were Watching God, ed. Michael Awkward, 71–93.

6. Zora Neale Hurston, *Mules and Men*, in *Folklore, Memoirs, and Other Writings*, ed. Cheryl A. Wall, 9. Further references to this work are made parenthetically within the text.

For biographical information about Hurston, I have relied upon Robert E. Hemenway, *Zora Neale Hurston*. In addition, Cheryl A. Wall's chapter, "Zora Neale Hurston's Traveling Blues" in *Women of the Harlem Renaissance*, (139–99) offers some biographical details that have come to light since Hemenway's biography was published. Of the many other sources available on the context of the Harlem Renaissance, the most valuable to me have been:

Nathan I. Huggins, *Harlem Renaissance*; David Levering Lewis, *When Harlem Was in Vogue*; and George Hutchinson, *The Harlem Renaissance in Black and White*.

7. Karen Jacobs, "From 'Spy-Glass' to 'Horizon': Tracking the Anthropological Gaze in Zora Neale Hurston," 329–31.

8. Ella Cara Deloria, a Dakota linguist and ethnographer who worked with Boas, offers another example of someone undertaking this endeavor during the period Hurston was writing. Deloria not only published accomplished works of social science, such as *Dakota Texts* (1932) and *Dakota Grammar* (1941), but she also wrote a novel, *Waterlily*, that was published posthumously.

9. Margaret Mead, *Coming of Age in Samoa*, 12–13. For a useful comparison of Mead and Hurston, see Deborah Gordon, "The Politics of Ethnographic Authority: Race and Writing in the Ethnography of Margaret Mead and Zora Neale Hurston," in *Modernist Anthropology*, ed. Manganaro, 146–62.

10. Jacobs, "From 'Spy-Glass' to 'Horizon,'" 330.

11. Berthold Laufer, review of *Culture and Ethnology* by Robert H. Lowie, 90.

12. Alfred L. Kroeber, "The Superorganic," in *The Nature of Culture*, 40.

13. Ibid., 51. Kroeber later disavowed both phrases. In his 1952 introduction to the essay, he wrote that he wanted to "retract, as unwarranted reification, the references . . . to organic and superorganic 'substances,' entities, or fabrics" in the essay (23).

14. Edward Sapir, "Culture, Genuine and Spurious," in *Culture, Language and Personality*, ed. David G. Mandelbaum, 93. Richard Handler provides a more complete discussion of Sapir's thought about the relationship between the individual and culture in "Anti-Romantic Romanticism: Edward Sapir and the Critique of American Individualism," 1–13.

15. Richard Handler, "Ruth Benedict and the Modernist Sensibility," in *Modernist Anthropology*, ed. Marc Manganaro, 172. Handler compares these earlier versions of the chapters of *Patterns of Culture* with the finished volume.

16. Mark Helbling, "'My Soul Was With the Gods and My Body in the Village': Zora Neale Hurston, Franz Boas, Melville Herskovits, and Ruth Benedict," 290–92; Hurston to Boas, 20 Aug. 1934, Franz Boas Papers, American Philosophical Society, Philadelphia.

17. Handler's discussion of Benedict in "Ruth Benedict and Modernist Sensibility" offers a more complete account of Benedict's work (163–80, esp. 172, 178–80). Handler argues that Benedict puts forward an "individualizing vision" in *Patterns of Culture*, one that sees cultures acting as holistic individuals. Susan Hegeman also offers a persuasive interpretation of Benedict's *Patterns of Culture* as a meditation on the relationship between the individual and culture, in her *Patterns for America*, 94–116.

18. Ruth Benedict, *Patterns of Culture*, 46.

19. Ibid., 47.

20. Ibid., 2–3.

21. Zora Neale Hurston, "Characteristics of Negro Expression," in *Folklore, Memoirs, and Other Writings*, 830. Further references to this edition of the article are made parenthetically within the text.

22. Lynda Marion Hill's *Social Rituals and the Verbal Art of Zora Neale Hurston* uses Hurston's interest in drama and performance as an interpretive lens through which to read her entire career, a project useful to my discussion here.

23. In his reading of the same article, Walter Benn Michaels argues that Hurston's piece actually suggests the opposite—that racial identity binds the African American intellectual to the folk and therefore affirms the primacy of racial essentialism (*Our America*, 87–94). While I have found Michaels's critique of Hurston instructive, I am contending here that she is describing a process of cultural identification not determined by biological race.

24. Lukács, "Narrate or Describe?" 110–48.

25. Hurston, *Dust Tracks on a Road*, in *Folklore, Memoirs, and Other Writings*, 683; see also Hemenway, *Zora Neale Hurston*, 20–21.

26. Zora Neale Hurston, *The Complete Stories*, 202.

27. Zora Neale Hurston, "Hoodoo in America," *The Journal of American Folk-Lore* 44 (1931): 317–418.

28. On Herskovits's role in the Boasian anthropology of the 1920s, see Walter Jackson, "Melville Herskovits and the Search for Afro-American Culture," in *Malinowski, Rivers, Benedict and Others: Essays on Culture and Personality*, ed. George W. Stocking Jr., 95–126.

29. Langston Hughes, *The Big Sea*, 239.

30. Quoted in Jackson, "Melville Herskovits and the Search for Afro-American Culture," 107.

31. Hemenway, *Zora Neale Hurston*, 91–92. A letter from Hurston to Boas about the difficulty she was having on this trip is telling. Hurston writes, "You see, the negro is not living his lore to the extent of the Indian. He is not on a reservation, being kept pure. His negroness is being rubbed off by a close contact with white culture" (Hurston to Boas, undated [1927], Boas Papers). This comment points to the rhetoric of authenticity that was part of cultural anthropology, as well as to the degree to which Boasian cultural anthropology was developed through the study of American indigenous populations.

32. Hurston, *Dust Tracks on a Road*, 687.

33. Zora Neale Hurston, "Cudjo's Own Story of the Last American Slaver," 648–63. The book that appears to have been Hurston's source is Emma Langdon Roche, *Historic Sketches of the South*, esp. 73–122. Notably, Hurston returned to interview Cudjo Lewis again and then produced a fictionalized account of Lewis's life, "Barracoon." See Lynda Marion Hill, *Social Rituals and the Verbal Art of Zora Neale Hurston*, 61–72, for a description of this manuscript.

34. Mason not only disapproved of Hurston's involvement with academic institutions, but she legally controlled the results of Hurston's fieldwork from this trip. On Hurston's relationship to Mason, see Hemenway, *Zora Neale Hurston*, 104–14.

35. Hurston to Mason, 10 March 1931; quoted in Wall, "Zora Neale Hurston's Traveling Blues," 156.

36. Michael E. Staub makes this point, but goes farther by arguing that Hurston turns "the text as a whole into a *mock(ing)* ritual reenactment of standard fieldwork methods" (emphasis added) (*Voices of Persuasion: Politics of Representation in 1930s America*, 81). I agree that the prose offers a staged reenactment, but I hope my discussion of *Mules and Men* shows that Hurston's engagement with the conventions of ethnography, even with its elements of parody, is a complex effort to theorize the nature of culture rather than a send-up of disciplinary practices.

37. As Marc Manganaro points out, this type of self-reflexive writing has become more common in cultural anthropology because of what he calls the "textual turn" within the field ("Textual Play, Power and Cultural Critique," 16).

38. Hurston to Boas, 20 Aug. 1934, Boas Papers.

39. This argument is more fully elaborated in D. A. Boxwell, "'Sis Cat' as Ethnographer: Self-Presentation and Self-Inscription in Zora Neale Hurston's *Mules and Men*," 605–17.

40. *Mules and Men* also includes a much shorter "Hoodoo" section, an edited version of Hurston's "Hoodoo in America" from the *Journal of American Folk-Lore*. I do not give extensive attention to this section, which was possibly added at the request of an editor to lengthen the volume, nor do I discuss the arguments that have been made about the unity of the volume. While I disagree with his discussion of Hurston's relationship to Boas, I do find Houston Baker Jr.'s, argument in this respect persuasive. Baker explains that, in "Hoodoo," Hurston finds the folk rituals and customs necessary to heal the fractured gender relations that drive her from central Florida. See Baker, *Workings of the Spirit*, 88–97.

41. Hurston may be poking fun at her own inexperience during her first, unsuccessful field trip to Eatonville. During that trip, she wrote that "a great many people say, 'I used to know some of that old stuff, but I done forgot it all'" (Hurston to Boas, undated [1927], Boas Papers).

42. Boas to Hurston, 3 May 1927, Boas Papers.

43. Michael E. Staub persuasively argues that *Mules and Men* textualizes the oral dynamics of "signifying"—a term that, following Henry Louis Gates, Jr., he defines as "an indirect way of speaking in which that which is spoken encodes one message or meaning as it more explicitly states something else entirely" (*Voices of Persuasion*, 86).

44. I have in mind, in particular, the turn toward the crafting of "life stories" by figures such as Paul Radin and Ruth Underhill. I am grateful to Joel Pfister for pointing out these similarities.

45. Zora Neale Hurston, *Their Eyes Were Watching God*, in *Novels and Stories*, ed. Cheryl A. Wall, 186.

46. Deborah Plant writes, "Hurston's presentation and analysis of folktales highlight an ethos of pragmatism, emphasizing self-preservation and individualistic action" (*Every Tub Must Sit On Its Own Bottom: The Philosophy and Politics of Zora Neale Hurston*, 48). Plant sees such textual moments as examples of Hurston's individualistic philosophy. While I largely agree with her assessment, I would argue that what *Mules and Men* reflects is a conflict between this individualistic impulse and the group-centered concepts inherent to ethnography.

47. Mead, *Coming of Age in Samoa*, 13. Handler discusses this trend in Boasian anthropology in "Ruth Benedict and the Modernist Sensibility," 163–80.

48. Cheryl A. Wall, for example, has pointed out that the gender relations in the town of Eatonville take place on notably different terms than those in the work camps of Polk County ("Zora Neale Hurston's Traveling Blues," 161–71). For other critical arguments on this topic, see: Meisenhelder, *Hitting a Straight Lick with a Crooked Stick*, 25–35; Mary Katherine Wainwright, "Subversive Female Folk Tellers in *Mules and Men*," in *Zora in Florida*, eds. Steve Glassman and Kathryn Lee Seidel, 62–75; and Benigno Sánchez-Eppler, "Telling Anthropology: Zora Neale Hurston and Gilberto Freyre Disciplined in Their Field Home Work," 464–88.

49. According to Hemenway's biography, the drafting of *Mules and Men* was "largely completed" between March 1930 and September 1932; Hurston wrote *Jonah's Gourd Vine* between July and October of 1932 (*Zora Neale Hurston*, 160, 188–89).

50. Zora Neale Hurston, *Jonah's Gourd Vine*, in *Novels and Stories*, 58. Further citations to this edition are made parenthetically within the text.

51. In an article that remained unpublished in her lifetime, Hurston wrote that John de Conquer "is the success story that all weak people create to compensate for their weakness" ("Folklore and Music," in *Folklore, Memoirs, and Other Writings*, 884).

52. Hurston also published a transcription of the same sermon—which she originally heard from the Reverend C. C. Lovelace in Eau Gallie, Florida, in 1929—in Nancy Cunard's *Negro* anthology, released the same year as *Jonah's Gourd Vine*. See Hurston's "A Sermon," in *Negro: Anthology Made By Nancy Cunard*, 50–54.

53. Consider the opening sentence of chapter 14: "To Janie's strange eyes, everything in the Everglades was big and new" (*Their Eyes Were Watching God*, 280).

54. Hurston, "Dance Songs and Tales from the Bahamas," 294–312.

55. I share Hazel V. Carby's sense that "*Their Eyes Were Watching God* is a text concerned with the tensions arising from Hurston's position as writer in relation to the folk as community that she produces in her writing" ("The Politics of Fiction, Anthropology, and the Folk: Zora Neale Hurston," 82).

56. Hurston, *Their Eyes Were Watching God*, 200.

57. Ibid., 232.

58. Carby, "The Politics of Fiction, Anthropology, and the Folk," 82–87.

59. Richard Wright, review of *Their Eyes Were Watching God* in *Zora Neale Hurston: Critical Perspectives Past and Present*, eds. Gates and Appiah, 17. William J. Maxwell has recently provided a provocative re-reading of the Hurston-Wright debate by arguing that the two authors shared more common ground than has been previously acknowledged. Both Hurston

and Wright, Maxwell shows, were interested in the impact of the migration of black laborers to the north upon rural African American communities. See Maxwell's chapter, "Black Belt/Black Folk: The End(s) of the Richard Wright–Zora Neale Hurston Debate," in his *New Negro, Old Left: African-American Writing and Communism Between the Wars*, 153–78.

60. Hurston, *Their Eyes Were Watching God*, 332.

61. Henry Louis Gates Jr., *The Signifying Monkey: A Theory of Afro-American Literary Criticism*, 214.

62. Kingston's most prominent critic has been Frank Chin; see Chin's "Come All Ye Asian American Writers of the Real and the Fake," in *The Big Aiiieeeee!: An Anthology of Chinese American and Japanese American Literature*, ed. Jeffery Paul Chan et al., 4–8. Patricia P. Chu provides a highly useful account of the Kingston-Chin controversy in "*Tripmaster Monkey*, Frank Chin, and the Chinese Heroic Tradition," 117–39.

Gloria Bird criticizes Sherman Alexie's representation of the Spokane/Coeur d'Alene reservation in "The Exaggeration of Despair in Sherman Alexie's *Reservation Blues*," 47–52. Louis Owens extends her critique in *Mixedblood Messages: Literature, Film, Family, Place*, 47–52.

Works Cited

Aldrich, Thomas Bailey. *The Story of a Bad Boy.* 1895. Reprint, Hanover, N.H.: University Press of New England, 1990.

———. "Unguarded Gates." *Atlantic* 70 (1892): 57–58.

Alexander, Hartley B. "Francis La Flesche." *American Anthropologist* 35 (1933): 328–31.

Allen, James Lane. "Realism and Romance." *Documents of American Realism and Naturalism.* Edited by Donald Pizer. Carbondale: Southern Illinois University Press, 1998. 99–103.

Alpers, Svetlana. "The Museum as a Way of Seeing." *Exhibiting Cultures: The Poetics and Politics of Museum Display.* Edited by Ivan Karp and Steven D. Levine. Washington: Smithsonian Institution Press, 1991. 25–32.

"The American Type." *New York Globe and Commercial Advertiser,* 17 Dec. 1909, 3.

Andrews, H. A., et al. "Bibliography of Franz Boas." *Memoirs of the American Anthropological Association* 61 (1943): 67–109.

Arnold, Matthew. *Culture and Anarchy.* Edited by Samuel Lipman. New Haven, Conn.: Yale University Press, 1994.

Austin, Mary. *The American Rhythm.* New York: Harcourt, Brace and Company, 1923.

Baker, Houston, Jr. *Modernism and the Harlem Renaissance.* Chicago: University of Chicago Press, 1987.

———. *The Workings of the Spirit: The Poetics of Afro-American Women's Writing.* Chicago: University of Chicago Press, 1991.

Baker, Lee D. *From Savage to Negro: Anthropology and the Construction of Race, 1896–1954.* Berkeley and Los Angeles: University of California Press.

Bannister, Robert C. *Social Darwinism.* Philadelphia: Temple University Press, 1979.

Barkan, Elazar, and Ronald Bush, eds. *Prehistories of the Future: The Primitivist Project and the Culture of Modernism.* Stanford: Stanford University Press, 1995.

Barnes, R. H. *Two Crows Denies It: A History of Controversy in Omaha Sociology*. Lincoln: University of Nebraska Press, 1984.

Bay, Mia. *The White Image in the Black Mind: African-American Ideas about White People, 1830–1925*. New York: Oxford University Press, 2000.

Bederman, Gail. *Manliness and Civilization: A Cultural History of Gender and Race in the United States, 1880–1917*. Chicago: University of Chicago Press, 1995.

Bell, Michael Davitt. *The Problem of American Realism: Studies in the Cultural History of a Literary Idea*. Chicago: University of Chicago Press, 1993.

Bendix, Regina. *In Search of Authenticity: The Formation of Folklore Studies*. Madison: University of Wisconsin Press, 1997.

Benedict, Ruth. *Patterns of Culture*. Boston: Houghton Mifflin, 1934.

Bentley, Nancy. *The Ethnography of Manners: Hawthorne, James, Wharton*. Cambridge: Cambridge University Press, 1995.

Bernadin, Susan. "The Lessons of a Sentimental Education: Zitkala-Ša's Autobiographical Narratives." *Western American Literature* 32 (1997): 212–38.

Best, Felton O. *Crossing the Color Line: A Biography of Paul Laurence Dunbar, 1872–1906*. Dubuque, Iowa: Kendall/Hunt Publishing Company, 1996.

Bhabha, Homi. "DissemiNation: Time, Narrative, and the Margins of the Modern Nation." *Nation and Narration*. Edited by Bhabha. New York: Routledge, 1990. 291–322.

Bieder, Robert E. *Science Encounters the Indian, 1820–1880*. Norman: University of Oklahoma Press, 1986.

Bird, Gloria. "The Exaggeration of Despair in Sherman Alexie's *Reservation Blues*." *Wicazo Sa Review* 11 (1995): 47–52.

Bixler, Phyllis. *Frances Hodgson Burnett*. Boston: Twayne Publishers, 1984.

Bloom, John. *To Show What an Indian Can Do*. Minneapolis: University of Minnesota Press, 2000.

Blount, Marcellus. "The Preacherly Text: African American Poetry and Vernacular Performance." *PMLA* 107 (1992): 582–93.

Boas, Franz. "An Anthropologist's Credo." *The Nation* 147 (1938): 201–4.

———. *Anthropology and Modern Life* 1928. Reprint, New York: W. W. Norton & Company, 1962.

———. *Changes in Bodily Form of Descendants of Immigrants*. U.S. Senate Document no. 208. Washington, D.C.: GPO, 1911.

———. *Chinook Texts*. Smithsonian Institution, Bureau of American Ethnology Bulletin 20. Washington, D.C.: GPO, 1894.

———. "Eskimo Tales and Songs." *The Journal of American Folk-Lore* 7 (1894): 45–50.

———. *Franz Boas among the Inuit of Baffin Island, 1883–1884: Journals and Letters*. Edited by Ludger Müller-Wille. Translated by William Barr. Toronto: University of Toronto Press, 1998.

———. *The Mind of Primitive Man*. New York: Macmillan, 1911.

———. "Museums of Ethnology and Their Classification," *Science* 9 (1887): 587–89, 614.

———. "The Occurrence of Similar Inventions in Areas Widely Apart." *Science* 9 (1887): 485–86.

———. Papers. American Philosophical Society, Philadelphia.

———. "The Problem of the American Negro." *Yale Quarterly Review* 10 (1921): 284–95.

———. *Race, Language, and Culture*. 1940. Reprint, Chicago: University of Chicago Press, 1982.

———. Review of *A Study of Omaha Music*, by Alice C. Fletcher, aided by Francis La Flesche. *Journal of American Folk-Lore* 7 (1894): 169–71.

———. Review of *The Passing of the Great Race*, by Madison Grant. *The New Republic* 9 (1917): 305–7.

———. Review of *The Rising Tide of Color against White World-Supremacy*, by Lathrop Stoddard. *The Nation* 111 (1920): 656.

———. "Some Principles of Museum Administration." *Science* 25 (1907): 921–33.

———. "What is Race?" *The Nation* 120 (1925): 89–91.

"Book Reviews." Review of *The Middle Five*, by Francis La Flesche. *Southern Workman* 29 (Oct. 1900): 581.

Boon, James A. "Accenting Hybridity: Postcolonial Cultural Studies, a Boasian Anthropologist, and I." *"Culture" and the Problem of the Disciplines.* Edited by John Carlos Rowe. New York: Columbia University Press, 1998. 141–70.

Bourdieu, Pierre. *Distinction.* Translated by Richard Nice. Cambridge: Harvard University Press, 1984.

Boxwell, D. A. "'Sis Cat' as Ethnographer: Self-Presentation and Self-Inscription in Zora Neale Hurston's *Mules and Men.*" *African-American Review* 26 (1992): 605–17.

Boyd, James P. *Recent Indian Wars, Under the Lead of Sitting Bull, and Other Chiefs; with A Full Account of the Messiah Craze, and Ghost Dances.* Philadelphia: Publishers Union, 1891.

Boyesen, Hjalmar Hjorth. *Literary and Social Silhouettes.* New York: Harper and Brothers, 1894.

Briden, Earl F. "Kemble's 'Specialty' and the Pictoral Countertext of *Huckleberry Finn.*" In Mark Twain, *Adventures of Huckleberry Finn.* Edited by Gerald Graff and James Phelan. New York: Bedford Books, 1995. 383–406.

Briggs, Charles L. "Metadiscursive Practices and Scholarly Authority in Folkloristics." *Journal of American Folklore* 106 (1993): 387–434.

Briggs, Charles L., and Richard Bauman. "'The Foundation of All Future Researches': Franz Boas, George Hunt, Native American Texts, and the Construction of Modernity." *American Quarterly* 51 (1999): 479–528.

Brinton, Daniel Garrison. *Aboriginal American Authors and Their Productions.* Philadelphia, 1883.

———. "The Aims of Anthropology." *Popular Science Monthly* 48, no. 1 (1896): 59–72.

———. *Races and Peoples: Lectures on the Science of Ethnography.* New York: N. D. C. Hodges, 1890.

Brodhead, Richard H. *Cultures of Letters: Scenes of Reading and Writing in Nineteenth-Century America.* Chicago: University of Chicago Press, 1993.

Brooks, Peter. *Reading for the Plot.* New York: Alfred A. Knopf, 1990.

Burnett, Frances Hodgson. *Louisiana.* 1880. Reprint, New York: Charles Scribner's Sons, 1886.

Cable, George Washington. "Creole Slave Songs." *Century* 31 (1886): 807–28.

———. *The Negro Question: A Selection of Writings on Civil Rights in the South.* Edited by Arlin Turner. Garden City, N.Y.: Doubleday, 1958.

———. "A Protest Against Dialect." *Critic* n.s. 4 (1884): 52–53.

Callahan, S. Alice. *Wynema: A Child of the Forest.* Edited and with an introduction by A. LaVonne Brown Ruoff. 1891. Reprint, Lincoln: University of Nebraska Press, 1997.

Carby, Hazel V. "The Politics of Fiction, Anthropology, and the Folk: Zora Neale Hurston." *New Essays on* Their Eyes Were Watching God. Edited by Michael Awkward. New York: Cambridge University Press, 1990. 71–93.

Carr, Helen. *Inventing the American Indian.* New York: New York University Press, 1996.

Cary, Elisabeth Luther. "Recent Writings by American Indians." *The Book Buyer* 24 (1902): 20–25.

Castro, Michael. *Interpreting the Indian: Twentieth-Century Poets and the Native American.* 1983. Reprint, Norman: University of Oklahoma Press, 1991.

Chatman, Seymour. *Coming to Terms: The Rhetoric of Narrative in Fiction and Film.* Ithaca, N.Y.: Cornell University Press, 1990.

Chesnutt, Charles W. *The Conjure Woman and Other Tales.* Edited and with an introduction by Richard H. Brodhead. Durham, N.C.: Duke University Press, 1993.

———. *Essays and Speeches.* Edited by Joseph R. McElrath Jr., Robert C. Leitz III, and Jesse S. Crisler. Stanford, Calif.: Stanford University Press, 1999.

————. *The Journals of Charles W. Chesnutt.* Edited Richard H. Brodhead. Durham, N.C.: Duke University Press, 1993.

————. *The Marrow of Tradition* 1901. Reprint, New York: Penguin, 1993.

————. *"To Be an Author": Letters of Charles W. Chesnutt, 1889-1905.* Edited by Joseph R. McElrath Jr., and Robert C. Leitz III. Princeton: Princeton University Press, 1997.

Chin, Frank. "Come All Ye Asian American Writers of the Real and the Fake." *The Big Aiiieeeee!: An Anthology of Chinese American and Japanese American Literature.* Edited by Jeffery Paul Chan et al. New York: Meridian, 1991. 1–92.

Chopin, Kate. *Bayou Folk and A Night in Acadie.* 1894 and 1897. Reprint, New York: Penguin, 1999.

Chu, Patricia P. *"Tripmaster Monkey,* Frank Chin, and the Chinese Heroic Tradition." *Arizona Quarterly* 53 (1997): 117–39.

Clark, Carol Lea. "Charles A. Eastman (Ohiyesa) and Elaine Goodale Eastman: A Cross-Cultural Collaboration." *Tulsa Studies in Women's Literature* 13 (1994): 271–80.

Clifford, James. "On Ethnographic Allegory." *Writing Culture: The Poetics and Politics of Ethnography.* Edited by Clifford and George E. Marcus. Berkeley and Los Angeles: University of California Press, 1986. 98–121.

————. *The Predicament of Culture: Twentieth-Century Ethnography, Literature, and Art.* Cambridge: Harvard University Press, 1988.

Colbron, Grace Isabel. "Across the Colour Line." Review of *The Uncalled* by Paul Laurence Dunbar. *Bookman* 8 (1898): 338–41.

Colby, William M. "Routes to Rainy Mountain: A Biography of James Mooney, Ethnologist." Ph.D. diss., University of Wisconsin–Madison, 1977.

Cole, Douglas. *Franz Boas: The Early Years, 1858–1906.* Seattle: University of Washington Press, 1999.

————. "'The Value of a Person Lies in His *Herzensbildung*': Franz Boas' Baffin Island Letter-Diary, 1883–1884." *Observers Observed: Essays on Ethnographic Fieldwork.* Edited by George W. Stocking Jr. Madison: University of Wisconsin Press, 1983. 13–52.

Conn, Steven. *Museums and American Intellectual Life, 1876–1926.* Chicago: University of Chicago Press, 1998.

Craddock, Charles Egbert. [Mary Noailles Murfree.] "The Dancin' Party at Harrison's Cove." *Atlantic* 41 (1878): 576–86.

Crane, Thomas Frederick. *Italian Popular Tales.* Boston: Houghton, Mifflin and Company, 1885.

Crawford, Nelson Antrim. "The Indian As He Is." Review of *American Indian Life,* ed. by Elsie Clews Parsons. *Bookman* 55 (1922): 636–37.

[Cultee, Charles.] "Coyote Establishes Fishing Taboos." In Nina Baym, gen. ed. *The Norton Anthology of American Literature.* 2 vols. 5th ed. New York: W. W. Norton & Co., 1996. 1: 140–46.

Cunningham, Virginia C. *Paul Laurence Dunbar and His Song.* New York: Dodd, Mead & Company, 1947.

Curtis, Natalie Burlin. *The Indians Book.* 1907. Reprint, New York: Harper and Brothers, 1923.

Cushing, Frank Hamilton. "My Adventures in Zuñi." *Zuñi: Selected Writings of Frank Hamilton Cushing.* Edited by Jesse Green. Lincoln: University of Nebraska Press, 1979. 46–134.

————. "The Need of Studying the Indian in Order to Teach Him." *The Twenty-Eighth Annual Report of the Board of Indian Commissioners, 1896.* Washington, D.C.: GPO, 1897. 109–14.

————. *Zuñi Breadstuff.* New York: Museum of the American Indian, 1920.

————. *Zuñi Folk Tales.* Introduction by John Wesley Powell. New York: G. P. Putnam's and Sons, 1901.

Darnell, Regna. *And Along Came Boas: Continuity and Revolution in Americanist Anthropology.* Amsterdam and Philadelphia: John Benjamins Publishing Company, 1998.

————. *Daniel Garrison Brinton: The "Fearless Critic" of Philadelphia.* Philadelphia: Department of Anthropology, University of Pennsylvania, 1988.

Darrah, William Culp. *Powell of the Colorado*. Princeton: Princeton University Press, 1951.

Darrow, Clarence. "Realism in Literature and Art." *Documents of American Realism and Naturalism*. Edited by Donald Pizer. Carbondale: Southern Illinois University Press, 1998.

de Certeau, Michel. *The Practice of Everyday Life*. Translated by Steven F. Rendell. Berkeley and Los Angeles: University of California Press, 1984.

Deacon, Desley. *Elsie Clews Parsons: Inventing Modern Life*. Chicago: University of Chicago Press, 1997.

Degler, Carl N. *In Search of Human Nature: Biology and Culture in American Social Science*. New York: Oxford University Press, 1991.

Deloria, Philip J. *Playing Indian*. New Haven, Conn.: Yale University Press, 1998.

Deloria, Vine, Jr., and Clifford Lytle, *The Nations Within: The Past and Future of American Indian Sovereignty*. 1984. Reprint, Austin: University of Texas Press, 1998.

DeMallie, Raymond J. "The Lakota Ghost Dance: An Ethnohistorical Account." *Pacific Historical Review* 51 (1982): 385–405.

Dilworth, Leah. *Imagining Indians in the Southwest: Persistent Visions of a Primitive Past*. Washington, D.C.: Smithsonian Institution Press, 1996.

Dimock, Wai Chee. "The Economy of Pain: The Case of Howells." *Raritan* 9, no. 4 (1990): 99–119.

Douglass, Frederick. *Narrative of the Life of Frederick Douglass, an American Slave*. 1845. Reprint, Garden City, N.Y.: Doubleday & Company, 1963.

Du Bois, W. E. B. "The Conservation of Races." *Writings*. Edited by Nathan Huggins. New York: Library of America, 1986. 815–26.

———. *Dusk of Dawn*. In *Writings*. Edited by Nathan Huggins. New York: Library of America, 1986. 549–802.

Duden, Barbara. "Rereading Boas: A Woman Historian's Response to Carl N. Degler." *Culture Versus Biology in the Thought of Franz Boas and Alfred L. Kroeber*, by Carl N. Degler. New York: Berg Publishers, 1989. 24–28.

Dunbar, Paul Laurence. *The Collected Poetry of Paul Laurence Dunbar*. Edited by Joanne Braxton. Charlottesville: University Press of Virginia, 1993.

———. *Folks from Dixie*. New York: Dodd, Mead & Company, 1898.

———. *In Old Plantation Days*. New York: Dodd, Mead & Company, 1903.

———. *Majors and Minors*. 1896. Reprint, Miami: Mnemosyne Publishing Company, 1969.

———. "Unpublished Letters of Paul Laurence Dunbar to a Friend." *Crisis* 20 (June 1920): 73–76.

Dwer-Shick, Susan A. "The American Folklore Society and Folklore Research in America, 1888–1940." Ph.D. diss., University of Pennsylvania, 1979.

Eastman, Charles A. (Ohiyesa). *From Deep Woods to Civilization*. 1916. Reprint, Lincoln: University of Nebraska Press, 1977.

———. *Red Hunters and the Animal People*. New York: Harper and Brothers, 1904.

Eastman, Charles A. (Ohiyesa), and Elaine Goodale Eastman. *Smoky Day's Wigwam Evenings: Indian Stories Retold*. Boston: Little, Brown, 1910.

———. *Wigwam Evenings: Sioux Folk Tales Retold*. Boston: Little, Brown, 1909.

"Environmentalist." *Time*, 11 May 1936, 37–42.

Evans, Brad. "Cushing's Zuni Sketchbooks: Literature, Anthropology, and American Notions of Culture." *American Quarterly* 49 (1997): 717–45.

Fabian, Johannes. *Time and the Other: How Anthropology Makes Its Object*. New York: Columbia University Press, 1983.

Fetterly, Judith. "The Sanctioned Rebel." *Studies in the Novel* 3 (1971): 293–304.

Fletcher, Alice C. "Flotsam and Jetsam from Aboriginal America." *Southern Workman* 28.1 (1899): 12–14.

———. "Indian Songs." *Century* 47 (1894): 421–32.

———. "Land and Education for the Indian." *Southern Workman* 14 (1885): 6.

―――. "Land, Law, Education—The Three Things Needed by the Indian." *Southern Workman* 14.3 (1885): 33–34.

―――. "On Indian Education and Self-Support." *Century* 26 (1883): 312–15.

Fletcher, Alice, and Francis La Flesche. *The Omaha Tribe*. 2 vols. 1911. Reprint, Lincoln: University of Nebraska Press, 1992.

"The Free Parliament." *Critic* n.s. 12 (1889): 158.

Frank, Gelya. "Jews, Multiculturalism, and Boasian Anthropology." *American Anthropologist* 99 (1997): 731–45.

Fredrickson, George. *The Black Image in the White Mind*. Middletown, Conn.: Wesleyan University Press, 1971.

Garland, Hamlin. *Crumbling Idols: Twelve Essays on Art Dealing Chiefly with Literature, Painting, and the Drama*. Edited by Jane Johnson. 1894. Reprint, Cambridge: Harvard University Press, 1960.

―――. "Boy Life on the Prairie." *The American Magazine*. n.s. 2 (1888): 299–303, 571–77, 684–90.

―――. *Prairie Folks*. Chicago: F. J. Schulte & Company, 1892.

―――. *A Son of the Middle Border*. 1917. Reprint, New York: Penguin, 1971.

Garrett, Philip C. "Indian Citizenship." *Proceedings of the Fourth Annual Lake Mohonk Conference, 1886*. Philadelphia: Indian Rights Association, 1887. 8–11.

Gates, Henry Louis, Jr. "Dis and Dat: Dialect and the Descent." *Afro-American Literature: The Reconstruction of Instruction*. Edited by Dexter Fisher and Robert B. Stepto. New York: The Modern Language Association of America, 1979. 88–119.

―――. Preface to *Zora Neale Hurston: Critical Perspectives Past and Present*. Edited by Gates and K. A. Appiah. New York: Amistad Press, 1993. xi–xv.

―――. *The Signifying Monkey: A Theory of Afro-American Literary Criticism*. New York: Oxford University Press, 1988.

Gates, Merrill E. "Address of President Gates." *Proceedings of the Ninth Annual Meeting of the Lake Mohonk Conference of the Friends of the Indian, 1891*. The Lake Mohonk Conference, 1891. 3–12.

―――. "Address of President Merrill E. Gates." *Proceedings of the Fourteenth Annual Meeting of the Lake Mohonk Conference of Friends of the Indian, 1896*. Edited by Isabel C. Barrows. The Lake Mohonk Conference, 1897. 7–13.

Gayle, Addison, Jr. "Literature as Catharsis: The Novels of Paul Laurence Dunbar." *A Singer in the Dawn: Reinterpretations of Paul Laurence Dunbar*. Edited by Jay Martin. New York: Dodd, Mead & Company, 1975. 139–51.

Geertz, Clifford. *The Interpretation of Cultures*. New York: Basic Books, 1973.

Genette, Gérard. *The Aesthetic Relation*. Translated by G. M. Goshgarian. Ithaca, N.Y.: Cornell University Press, 1999.

Gilder, Richard Watson. "Certain Tendencies in Current Literature" *Documents of American Realism and Naturalism*. Edited by Donald Pizer. Carbondale: Southern Illinois University Press, 1998. 104–14.

Gilmore, Paul. "The Indian in the Museum: Henry David Thoreau, Okah Tubbee, and Authentic Manhood." *Arizona Quarterly* 54, no. 2 (1998): 25–63.

Glazener, Nancy. *Reading for Realism: The History of a U.S. Literary Institution*. Durham, N.C.: Duke University Press, 1997.

Glick, Leonard B. "Types Distinct from Our Own: Franz Boas on Jewish Identity and Assimilation." *American Anthropologist* 84 (1982): 545–65.

Gordon, Deborah. "The Politics of Ethnographic Authority: Race and Writing in the Ethnography of Margaret Mead and Zora Neale Hurston." *Modernist Anthropology: From Fieldwork to Text*. Edited by Marc Manganaro. Princeton, N.J.: Princeton University Press, 1990. 146–62.

Gribben, Alan. "'I Did Wish Tom Sawyer Was There': Boy-Book Elements in *Tom Sawyer* and *Huckleberry Finn*." *One Hundred Years of Huckleberry Finn: The Boy, His Book, and*

American Culture. Edited by Robert Sattelmeyer and J. Donald Crowley. Columbia: University of Missouri Press, 1985. 149–70.

Grinnell, George Bird. *Pawnee Hero Stories and Folk-Tales.* 1889. Reprint, Lincoln: University of Nebraska Press, 1961.

———. *The Punishment of the Stingy and Other Stories.* 1901. Reprint, Lincoln: University of Nebraska Press, 1982.

Handler, Richard. "Anti-Romantic Romanticism: Edward Sapir and the Critique of American Individualism." *Anthropological Quarterly* 62 (1989): 1–13.

———. "Boasian Anthropology and the Critique of American Culture." *American Quarterly* 42 (1990): 252–73.

———. "Ruth Benedict and the Modernist Sensibility." *Modernist Anthropology: From Fieldwork to Text.* Edited by Marc Manganaro. Princeton, N.J.: Princeton University Press, 1990. 163–80.

Harper, Kenn. *Give Me My Father's Body: The Life of Minik, the New York Eskimo.* 1986. Reprint, South Royalton, Vt.: Steerforth Press, 2000.

Harris, Joel Chandler. *Uncle Remus: His Songs and Sayings.* 1880. Reprint, with an introduction by Robert Hemenway, New York: Penguin, 1982.

Harris, Marvin. *The Rise of Anthropological Theory.* New York: Thomas Y. Crowell, 1968.

Hegeman, Susan. *Patterns for America: Modernism and the Concept of Culture.* Princeton, N.J.: Princeton University Press, 1999.

Helbling, Mark. "'My Soul Was With the Gods and My Body in the Village': Zora Neale Hurston, Franz Boas, Melville Herskovits, and Ruth Benedict." *Prospects* 22 (1997): 285–322.

Hemenway, Robert. "The Functions of Folklore in Charles Chesnutt's *The Conjure Woman.*" *Journal of the Folklore Institute* 13 (1976): 283–309.

———. *Zora Neale Hurston.* Urbana: University of Illinois Press, 1977.

Hendrick, Burton J. "The Skulls of Our Immigrants." *McClure's Magazine* 35 (1910): 36–50.

Herbert, Christopher. *Culture and Anomie: Ethnographic Imagination in the Nineteenth Century.* Chicago: University of Chicago Press, 1991.

Herskovits, Melville J. *Franz Boas: The Science of Man in the Making.* New York: Charles Scribner's Sons, 1953.

Hertzberg, Hazel. *The Search for an American Indian Identity: Modern Pan-Indians.* Syracuse, N.Y.: Syracuse University Press, 1971.

Higham, John. *Strangers in the Land: Patterns of American Nativism 1860–1925.* 2nd ed. 1955. Reprint, New Brunswick, N.J.: Rutgers University Press, 1988.

Hill, Lynda Marion. *Social Rituals and the Verbal Art of Zora Neale Hurston.* Washington, D.C.: Howard University Press, 1996.

Hinsley, Curtis M. *The Smithsonian and the American Indian: Making a Moral Anthropology in Victorian America.* 1981. Reprint, Washington, D.C.: Smithsonian Institution Press, 1994.

———. "Zunis and Brahmins: Cultural Ambivalence in the Gilded Age." *Romantic Motives: Essays on Anthropological Sensibility.* Edited by George W. Stocking Jr. Madison: University of Wisconsin Press, 1989. 169–205.

Hittman, Michael. *Wovoka and the Ghost Dance.* Edited by Don Lynch. Expanded ed. Lincoln: University of Nebraska Press, 1997.

Hofstadter, Richard. *Social Darwinism in American Thought, 1860–1915.* Philadelphia: University of Pennsylvania Press, 1945.

Howard, June. "Unraveling Regions, Unsettling Periods: Sarah Orne Jewett and American Literary History." *American Literature* 68 (1996): 365–84.

Howells, William Dean. "Editor's Study," *Harper's Monthly* 74 (1887): 983–87.

———. *A Hazard of New Fortunes.* 1890. Reprint, New York: Meridian, 1994.

———. Introduction to *Lyrics of Lowly Life* by Paul Laurence Dunbar. 1896. Reprint, Secaucus, N.J.: Citadel Press, 1984. xiii–xx.

———. "Life and Letters." *Harper's Weekly* 40 (27 June 1896): 630.

————. "The Man of Letters as a Man of Business." *Literature and Life: Studies.* New York: Harper and Brothers, 1902. 1–35.

————. "Mr. Charles W. Chesnutt's Stories." *Atlantic* 85 (1900): 699–701.

————. *The Rise of Silas Lapham.* Edited Walter J. Meserve. Vol. 12 of *A Selected Edition of William Dean Howells.* Bloomington: Indiana University Press, 1971.

————. *Selected Literary Criticism.* 3 vols. Edited by Ulrich Halfmann, Donald Pizer, and Ronald Gottesman. Vols. 13, 21, 30 of *A Selected Edition of William Dean Howells.* Bloomington: Indiana University Press, 1993.

Hoxie, Frederick. *A Final Promise: The Campaign to Assimilate the Indians, 1880–1920.* Lincoln: University of Nebraska Press, 1984.

Huggins, Nathan I. *Harlem Renaissance.* New York: Oxford University Press, 1971.

Hughes, Langston. *The Big Sea.* 1940. Reprint, New York: Hill and Wang, 1993.

Huhndorf, Shari M. *Going Native: Indians in the American Cultural Imagination.* Ithaca, N.Y.: Cornell University Press, 2001.

Hunter, Jim. "Mark Twain and the Boy-Book in Nineteenth-Century America." *College English* 24 (1963): 430–38.

Hurston, Zora Neale. "Characteristics of Negro Expression." *Folklore, Memoirs, and Other Writings.* Edited by Cheryl A. Wall. New York: Library of America, 1995. 830–46.

————. *The Complete Stories.* New York: HarperCollins, 1995.

————. "Cudjo's Own Story of the Last American Slaver." *Journal of Negro History* 12 (1927): 648–63.

————. "Dance Songs and Tales from the Bahamas." *Journal of American Folk-Lore* 43 (1930): 294–312.

————. "Folklore and Music." *Folklore, Memoirs, and Other Writings.* Edited by Cheryl A. Wall. New York: Library of America, 1995. 875–94.

————. "Hoodoo in America." *The Journal of American Folk-Lore* 44 (1931): 317–418.

————. *Jonah's Gourd Vine.* In *Novels and Stories.* Edited by Cheryl A. Wall. New York: Library of America, 1995. 1–171.

————. *Mules and Men.* In *Folklore, Memoirs, and Other Writings.* Edited by Cheryl A. Wall. New York: Library of America, 1995. 1–267.

————. "A Sermon." *Negro: Anthology Made By Nancy Cunard.* London: Wishart & Co., 1934. 50–54.

————. *Their Eyes Were Watching God.* In *Novels and Stories.* Edited by Cheryl A. Wall. New York: Library of America, 1995. 173–333.

Hutchinson, George. *The Harlem Renaissance in Black and White.* Cambridge: Harvard University Press, 1995.

Hyatt, Marshall. *Franz Boas: The Dynamics of Ethnicity.* Westport, Conn.: Greenwood Press, 1990.

Hyman, Stanley Edgar. "Freud and Boas: Secular Rabbis?" *Commentary* 17 (1954): 264–67.

"The Indian Massacre." *New York Times,* 31 Dec. 1890, 4.

Jacknis, Ira. "The Ethnographic Object and the Object of Ethnography in the Early Career of Franz Boas." *Volksgeist as Method and Ethic.* Edited by George W. Stocking Jr. Madison: University of Wisconsin Press, 1996. 185–214.

————. "Franz Boas and Exhibits: On the Limitations of the Museum Method of Anthropology." *Objects and Others: Essays on Museums and Material Culture.* Edited by George W. Stocking Jr. Madison: University of Wisconsin Press, 1985. 75–111.

Jackson, Walter. "Melville Herskovits and the Search for Afro-American Culture." *Malinowski, Rivers, Benedict and Others: Essays on Culture and Personality.* Edited by George W. Stocking Jr. Madison: University of Wisconsin Press, 1986. 95–126.

Jacobs, Karen. "From 'Spy-Glass' to 'Horizon': Tracking the Anthropological Gaze in Zora Neale Hurston." *Novel: A Forum on Fiction* 30 (1997): 329–60.

Jacobson, Matthew Frye. *Barbarian Virtues: The United States Encounters Foreign Peoples at Home and Abroad.* New York: Hill and Wang, 2000.

James, Henry. "William Dean Howells." *Harper's Weekly* 30 (19 June 1886): 394–95.

James, William. "The Dilemma of Determinism." *"The Will to Believe" and "Human Immortality."* New York: Dover, 1956. 145–83.

Jefferson, Thomas. *Notes on the State of Virginia.* In *Writings.* Edited by Merrill D. Peterson. New York: Library of America, 1984. 123–325.

Johnson, David E., and Scott Michaelsen. "Border Secrets: An Introduction," *Border Theory: The Limits of Cultural Politics.* Edited by Michaelsen and Johnson. Minneapolis: University of Minnesota Press, 1997. 1–39.

Johnson, James Weldon. *Along This Way.* 1933. Reprint, New York: Viking, 1968.

Jones, Gavin. *Strange Talk: The Politics of Dialect Literature in Gilded Age America.* Berkeley and Los Angeles: University of California Press, 1999.

Kallen, Horace M. "Democracy versus the Melting-Pot: A Study of American Nationality." *Theories of Ethnicity: A Classical Reader.* Edited by Werner Sollors. New York: New York University Press, 1996. 67–92.

Kaplan, Amy. *The Social Construction of American Realism.* Chicago: University of Chicago Press, 1988.

Keeling, John. "Paul Dunbar and the Mask of Dialect." *Southern Literary Journal* 25 (1993): 24–38.

Kehoe, Alice. *The Ghost Dance: Ethnohistory and Revitalization.* Fort Worth, Tex.: Holt, Rinehart and Winston, 1989.

Kidd, Norma Jean. *Iron Eye's Family.* Lincoln, Nebr.: Johnsen Publishing, 1969.

Klein, Christina. "'Everything of Interest in the Late Pine Ridge War Are Held by Us for Sale': Popular Culture and Wounded Knee." *The Western Historical Quarterly.* 25 (1994): 45–68.

Kroeber, Alfred L. *The Nature of Culture.* Chicago: University of Chicago Press.

Kroeber, Alfred L. and Clyde Kluckhohn. *Culture: A Critical Review of Concepts and Definitions.* Cambridge: Harvard University Press, 1952.

Krupat, Arnold. *Ethnocriticism: Ethnography, History, Literature.* Berkeley and Los Angeles: University of California Press, 1992.

———. *The Turn to the Native: Studies in Criticism and Culture.* Lincoln: University of Nebraska Press, 1996.

Kuper, Adam. *Culture: The Anthropologists' Account.* Cambridge: Harvard University Press, 1999.

———. *The Invention of Primitive Society: Transformations of an Illusion.* New York: Routledge, 1988.

La Flèche, Frank [Francis La Flesche]. "My First Buffalo Hunt." *The Ȼegiha Language.* By James Owen Dorsey. Contributions to North American Ethnology, vol. 6. Washington, D.C.: GPO, 1890. 466–67.

La Flesche, Francis. "An Indian Allotment." *Independent* 52 (1900): 2686–88.

———. *Ke-ma-ha: The Omaha Stories of Francis La Flesche.* Edited and introduction by James Parins and Daniel F. Littlefield Jr. Lincoln: University of Nebraska Press, 1995.

———. *The Middle Five.* 1900. Reprint, Lincoln: University of Nebraska Press, 1978.

"The Last of Sitting Bull." *New York Times,* 16 Dec. 1890, 1.

Laufer, Berthold. Review of *Culture and Ethnology* by Robert H. Lowie. *American Anthropologist* 20 (1918): 87–91.

Lears, T. Jackson. *No Place of Grace: Antimodernism and the Transformation of American Culture, 1880–1920.* 1981. Reprint, Chicago: University of Chicago Press, 1994.

Leland, Charles Godfrey. *Algonquin Legends.* 1884. Reprint, New York: Dover, 1992.

———. "The Edda among the Algonquin Indians." *Atlantic* 54 (1884): 222–34.

———. "Legends of the Passamaquoddy; With Drawings on Birch Bark by a Quadi Indian." *Century* 6 (1884): 668–77.

Leland, Charles Godfrey, and John Dyneley Prince. *Kulóskap the Master and Other Algonkin Poems.* New York: Funk & Wagnalls Company, 1902.

Lewis, David Levering. *When Harlem Was in Vogue.* New York: Oxford University Press, 1981.

Limerick, Patricia Nelson. *The Legacy of Conquest.* New York: W. W. Norton & Company, 1987.

Lincoln, Kenneth. *Singing with the Heart of a Bear: Fusions of Native and American Poetry, 1890–1999.* Berkeley and Los Angeles: University of California Press, 2000.

Liss, Julia E. "German Culture and German Science in the *Bildung* of Franz Boas." *Volksgeist as Method and Ethic.* Edited by George W. Stocking Jr. Madison: University of Wisconsin Press, 1996. 155–84.

Livingstone, David N. *Nathaniel Southgate Shaler and the Culture of American Science.* Tuscaloosa: University of Alabama Press, 1987.

Lukács, Georg. "Narrate or Describe?" In *Writer and Critic and Other Essays.* Edited and translated by Arthur Kahn. London: Merlin Press, 1970. 110–48.

Mabie, Hamilton Wright. "Two New Novelists." *Outlook* 64 (1900): 440–41.

———. "A Typical Novel." Edited by Donald Pizer. Carbondale: Southern Illinois University Press, 1998. 60–69.

Mackethan, Lucinda H. "Plantation Fiction, 1865–1900." *The History of Southern Literature.* Gen. ed. Louis D. Rubin Jr. Baton Rouge: Louisiana State University Press, 1985. 209–18.

Mailloux, Stephen. *Reception Histories: Rhetoric, Pragmatism, and American Cultural Politics.* Ithaca, N.Y.: Cornell University Press, 1998.

Manganaro, Marc. "Textual Play, Power, and Cultural Critique: An Orientation to Modernist Anthropology." Introduction to *Modernist Anthropology: From Fieldwork to Text.* Edited by Marc Manganaro. Princeton, N.J.: Princeton University Press, 1990. 3–47.

Mark, Joan. *Four Anthropologists.* New York: Science History Publications, 1980.

———. *A Stranger in Her Native Land: Alice Fletcher and the American Indians.* Lincoln: University of Nebraska Press, 1988.

Martin, Jay, and Gossie H. Hudson, eds. *The Paul Laurence Dunbar Reader.* New York: Dodd, Mead & Company, 1975.

Mason, Otis T. "The Natural History of Folk-Lore." *Journal of American Folk-Lore* 4 (1891): 97–105.

Maxwell, William J. *New Negro, Old Left: African-American Writing and Communism Between the Wars.* New York: Columbia University Press, 1999.

McDonnell, Janet. *The Dispossession of the American Indian, 1887–1934.* Bloomington: Indiana University Press, 1991.

McFeely, Eliza. "Palimpsest of American Identity: Zuni, Anthropology and American Identity at the Turn of the Century." Ph.D. diss., New York University, 1996.

McNeil, William K. "A History of American Folklore Scholarship Before 1908." Ph.D. diss., Indiana University, 1980.

Mead, Margaret, ed. *An Anthropologist at Work: Writings of Ruth Benedict.* 1959. Reprint, Westport, Conn.: Greenwood Press, 1977.

———. *Coming of Age in Samoa.* New York: William Morrow and Company, 1928.

Meisenhelder, Susan Edwards. *Hitting a Straight Lick with a Crooked Stick: Race and Gender in the Work of Zora Neale Hurston.* Tuscaloosa: University of Alabama Press, 1999.

Metcalf, Eugene Wesley, Jr. "The Letters of Paul and Alice Dunbar: A Private History." Ph.D. diss., University of California, Irvine, 1973.

Michaels, Walter Benn. *The Gold Standard and the Logic of Naturalism.* Berkeley and Los Angeles: University of California Press, 1987.

———. *Our America: Nativism, Modernism, and Pluralism.* Durham, N.C.: Duke University Press, 1995.

———. "Political Science Fictions." *New Literary History* 31 (2000): 649–64.

Michaelsen, Scott. *The Limits of Multiculturalism: Interrogating the Origins of American Anthropology.* Minneapolis: University of Minnesota Press, 1999.

Mintz, Sidney W. "Sows' Ears and Silver Linings: A Backward Look at Ethnography." *Current Anthropology* 41 (2000): 169–89.

Mizruchi, Susan L. *The Science of Sacrifice: American Literature and Modern Social Theory.* Princeton, N.J.: Princeton University Press, 1998.

Mooney, James. *The Ghost-Dance Religion and the Sioux Outbreak of 1890.* 1896. Reprint, Lincoln: University of Nebraska Press, 1991.

Morgan, Lewis Henry. *Ancient Society.* 1877. Reprint, Gloucester, Mass.: Peter Smith, 1974.

Morse, James Herbert. "The Native Element in Fiction," *Century* 26 (1883): 362–75.

Moses, L. G. *The Indian Man: A Biography of James Mooney.* Urbana: University of Illinois Press, 1984.

———. *Wild West Shows and the Images of American Indians, 1883–1933.* Albuquerque: University of New Mexico Press, 1996.

Murray, David. *Forked Tongues: Speech, Writing, and Representation in American Indian Texts.* Bloomington: Indiana University Press, 1991.

Nagel, James, ed. *Critical Essays on Hamlin Garland.* Boston: G. K. Hall & Company, 1981.

Norris, Frank. "Zola as a Romantic Writer." *Documents of American Realism and Naturalism.* Edited by Donald Pizer. Carbondale: Southern Illinois University Press, 1998. 168–69.

"A Note Not Heard Before." *Arena* 19 (Feb. 1898): 286.

Nott, Josiah, and George R. Gliddon. *Types of Mankind.* Philadelphia: Lippincott, Grambo & Co., 1854.

Oandasan, William. "A Cross-Disciplinary Note on Charles Eastman (Santee Sioux)." *American Indian Culture and Research Journal* 7, no. 2 (1983): 75–78.

Otis, D. S. *The Dawes Act and the Allotment of Indian Lands.* 1934. Reprint, Norman: University of Oklahoma Press, 1973.

Owens, Louis. *Mixedblood Messages: Literature, Film, Family, Place.* Norman: University of Oklahoma Press, 1998.

Page, Thomas Nelson. *In Ole Virginia, or Marse Chan and Other Stories.* 1887. Reprint, New York: Charles Scribner's Sons, 1890.

Parezo, Nancy J. "The Formation of Ethnographic Collections: The Smithsonian Institution in the American Southwest." *Advances in Archaeological Method and Theory* 10 (1987): 1–47.

Parkhill, Thomas C. *Weaving Ourselves into the Land: Charles Godfrey Leland, Indians, and the Study of Native American Religions.* Albany, N.Y.: State University of New York Press, 1997.

Parsons, Elsie Clews, ed. *American Indian Life.* 1922. Reprint, Lincoln: University of Nebraska Press, 1991.

———. Papers. American Philosophical Society, Philadelphia.

Peck, H. T. "An Afro-American Poet." *Bookman* 4 (1897): 568.

Pellew, George. "The New Battle of the Books." *Documents of American Realism and Naturalism.* Edited by Donald Pizer. Carbondale: Southern Illinois University Press, 1998. 115–21.

———. "Ten Years of American Literature." *Critic* n.s. 15 (17 Jan. 1891): 29–31.

Plant, Deborah. *Every Tub Must Sit on Its Own Bottom: The Philosophy and Politics of Zora Neale Hurston.* Urbana: University of Illinois Press, 1995.

Powell, John Wesley. "Indian Linguistic Families of America North of Mexico." *Seventh Annual Report of the Bureau of Ethnology to the Secretary of the Smithsonian Institution, 1885–'86.* Washington, D.C.: GPO, 1891. 7–142.

———. "Report of the Director." *First Annual Report of the Bureau of Ethnology to the Secretary of the Smithsonian Institution, 1879–'80.* Washington, D.C.: GPO, 1881. xi–xxxiii.

———. "Report of the Director." *Second Annual Report of the Bureau of Ethnology to the Secretary of the Smithsonian Institution 1880–'81.* Washington, D.C.: GPO, 1883. xv–xxxvii.

———. "Report of the Director." *Fourteenth Annual Report of the Bureau of Ethnology to the Secretary of the Smithsonian Institution, 1892–'93.* Washington, D.C.: GPO, 1896. xv–lxi.

———. "Report of the Director." *Twenty-Second Annual Report of the Bureau of Ethnology to the Secretary of the Smithsonian Institution 1900–'01.* Washington, D.C.: GPO, 1904. ix–xliv.

———. *Report on the Methods of Surveying the Public Domain to the Secretary of the Interior at the Request of the National Academy of Sciences.* Washington, D.C.: GPO, 1878.

Preston, George. "Folks from Dixie." Review of *Folks from Dixie*, by Paul Laurence Dunbar. *Bookman* 7 (1898): 348–49.

Price, Kenneth M. "Charles Chesnutt, the *Atlantic Monthly*, and the Intersection of African-American Fiction and Elite Culture." *Periodical Literature in Nineteenth-Century America*. Edited by Price and Susan Belasco Smith. Charlottesville: University Press of Virginia, 1995. 257–74.

Prucha, Francis Paul. *American Indian Treaties: The History of a Political Anomaly*. Berkeley and Los Angeles: University of California Press, 1994.

———, ed. *Americanizing the American Indians: Writings by the "Friends of the Indian" 1880–1900*. Cambridge: Harvard University Press, 1973.

———. *The Great Father: The U.S. Government and the Indians*. 2 vols. Lincoln: University of Nebraska Press, 1984.

Ricoeur, Paul. *Time and Narrative*. 3 vols. Translated by Kathleen McLaughlin and David Pellauer. Chicago: University of Chicago Press, 1984.

Ridington, Robin, and Dennis Hastings (In'aska). *Blessing for a Long Time: The Sacred Pole of the Omaha Tribe*. Lincoln: University of Nebraska Press, 1997.

Riggs, Stephen Return. *A Dakota-English Dictionary*. Edited by James Owen Dorsey. 1890. Reprint, Minneapolis: Minnesota Historical Society, 1992.

———. *Dakota Grammar, Texts, and Ethnography*. Edited by James Owen Dorsey. Contributions to North American Ethnology, vol. 9. Washington, D.C.: GPO, 1893.

Roche, Emma Langdon. *Historic Sketches of the South*. New York: Knickerbocker Press, 1914.

Rohner, Ronald P., comp. and ed. *The Ethnography of Franz Boas*. Translated by Hedy Parker. Chicago: University of Chicago Press, 1969.

Rosaldo, Renato. *Culture and Truth: The Remaking of Social Analysis*. Boston: Beacon Press, 1993.

Ross, Dorothy. *The Origins of American Social Science*. New York: Cambridge University Press, 1991.

Sapir, Edward. *Culture, Language and Personality*. Edited by David G. Mandelbaum. Berkeley and Los Angeles: University of California Press, 1960.

Samuels, Shirley, ed. *The Culture of Sentiment: Race, Gender, and Sentimentality in Nineteenth-Century America*. New York: Oxford University Press, 1992.

Sánchez-Eppler, Benigno. "Telling Anthropology: Zora Neale Hurston and Gilberto Freyre Disciplined in Their Field Home Work." *American Literary History* 4 (1992): 464–88.

"Say Aliens Soon Get American Physique." *New York Times*, 17 Dec. 1909, 18.

Sewall, William H., Jr. "Geertz, Cultural Systems, and History: From Synchrony to Transformation." *Representations* 59 (1997): 35–55.

Simon, Myron. *A Singer in the Dawn: Reinterpretations of Paul Laurence Dunbar*. Edited by Jay Martin. New York: Dodd, Mead & Company, 1975. 114–33.

Skaggs, Merrill Macguire. "Varieties of Local Color." *The History of Southern Literature*. Gen. ed. Louis D. Rubin Jr. Baton Rouge: Louisiana State University Press, 1985. 219–27.

Slote, Ben. "Listening to 'The Goophered Grapevine' and Hearing Raisins Sing." *American Literary History* 6 (1994): 684–94.

Smedley, Audrey. *Race in North America: Origin and Evolution of a Worldview*. Boulder, Colo.: Westview Press, 1993.

Sollors, Werner. "A Critique of Pure Pluralism." *Reconstructing American Literary History*. Edited by Sacvan Bercovitch. Cambridge: Harvard University Press, 1986. 250–79.

———. "The Goopher in Charles Chesnutt's Conjure Tales: Superstition, Ethnicity, and Modern Metamorphoses." *Letteratura d'America* 6, no. 27 (Spring 1985): 107–29.

———. *Neither Black nor White Yet Both*. New York: Oxford University Press, 1996.

Southern Matron. "'Marse Chan' Again." *Critic* n.s. 4 (1884): 114

Staub, Michael E. *Voices of Persuasion: Politics of Representation in 1930s America*. New York: Cambridge University Press, 1981.

Stepan, Nancy. *The Idea of Race in Science.* London: Archon Books, 1982.

Stepto, Robert. "'The Simple But Intensely Human Inner Life of Slavery': Storytelling, Fiction and the Revision of History in Charles W. Chesnutt's 'Uncle Julius Stories.'" *History and Tradition in Afro-American Culture.* Edited by Günter H. Lenz. Frankfurt: Campus Verlag, 1984. 29–55.

Stocking, George W., Jr. *The Ethnographer's Magic and Other Essays in the History of Anthropology.* Madison: University of Wisconsin Press, 1992.

————. *Race, Culture, and Evolution: Essays in the History of Anthropology.* New York: The Free Press, 1968.

————. "The Turn-of-the-Century Concept of Race." *Modernism/Modernity* 1, no. 1 (1994): 4–16.

————, ed. Volksgeist *as Method and Ethic: Essays on Boasian Ethnography and the German Anthropological Tradition.* Madison: University of Wisconsin Press, 1996.

Stone, Albert E., Jr. *The Innocent Eye: Childhood in Mark Twain's Imagination.* New Haven, Conn.: Yale University Press, 1961.

Stowe, Harriet Beecher. *Oldtown Folks.* Edited by Dorothy Berkson. New Brunswick, N.J.: Rutgers University Press, 1987.

————. *Uncle Tom's Cabin.* Edited by Elizabeth Ammons. New York: W. W. Norton and Company, 1994.

Stronks, James B. "Paul Laurence Dunbar and William Dean Howells." *The Ohio Historical Quarterly* 67 (1958): 95–108.

Sundquist, Eric J. *To Wake the Nations: Race in the Making of American Literature.* Cambridge: Harvard University Press, 1994.

Swann, Brian, ed. *On the Translation of Native American Literature.* Washington, D.C.: Smithsonian Institution Press, 1992.

Terrell, John Upton. *The Man Who Rediscovered America: A Biography of John Wesley Powell.* New York: Weybright and Talley, 1969.

Thayer, William Roscoe. "The New Story-Tellers and the Doom of Realism." *Documents of American Realism and Naturalism.* Edited by Donald Pizer. Carbondale: Southern Illinois University Press, 1998. 159–66.

Thompson, Maurice. "The Analysts Analyzed," *Critic.* n.s. 6 (1886): 19–22.

Twain, Mark. "What Paul Bourget Thinks of Us." *Collected Tales, Sketches, Speeches, and Essays.* 2 vols. Edited by Louis Budd. New York: Library of America, 1992. 2: 164–79.

Tylor, E. B. *Primitive Culture.* 2 vols. 1871. Reprint, New York: Henry Holt and Company, 1883.

U.S. Board of Indian Commissioners. *The Fifteenth Annual Report of the Board of Indian Commissioners.* Washington, D.C.: GPO, 1883.

U.S. Bureau of the Census. *Negro Population in the United States, 1790–1915.* 1918. Reprint, New York: Arno Press, 1968.

————. *Statistical Abstract of the United States: 1991.* 111th edition. Washington, D.C.: GPO, 1991.

Utley, Robert M. *The Last Days of the Sioux Nation.* New Haven, Conn.: Yale University Press, 1963.

Vizenor, Gerald. *Manifest Manners: Postindian Warriors of Survivance.* Hanover, N.H.: Wesleyan University Press/University Press of New England, 1994.

Wainwright, Mary Katherine. "Subversive Female Folk Tellers in *Mules and Men*." *Zora in Florida.* Edited by Steve Glassman and Kathryn Lee Seidel. Orlando: University of Central Florida Press, 1991. 62–75.

Wald, Priscilla. *Constituting Americans: Cultural Anxiety and Narrative Form.* Durham, N.C.: Duke University Press, 1995.

Walker, Francis A. "Immigration and Degradation." *Forum* 11 (1891): 634–44.

Wall, Cheryl A. *Women of the Harlem Renaissance.* Bloomington: Indiana University Press, 1995.

Warner, Charles Dudley. *A Little Journey in the World.* 1889. Reprint, Ridgewood, N.J.: The Gregg Press, 1967.

Warren, Kenneth W. *Black and White Strangers: Race and American Literary Realism*. Chicago: University of Chicago Press, 1993.

Warrior, Robert Allen. *Tribal Secrets: Recovering American Indian Intellectual History*. Minneapolis: University of Minnesota Press, 1995.

Welsh, Herbert. *The Helplessness of the Indians Before the Law with an Outline of Proposed Legislation*. Philadelphia: Indian Rights Association, 1886.

Werner, Craig. "The Framing of Charles W. Chesnutt: Practical Deconstruction in the Afro-American Tradition." *Southern Literature and Literary Theory*. Edited by Jefferson Humphries. Athens: University of Georgia Press, 1990. 339–65.

Wexler, Laura. *Tender Violence: Domestic Visions in an Age of U.S. Imperialism*. Chapel Hill: University of North Carolina Press, 2000.

"What America Is Doing for the Children of Immigrants: Prof. Boas Gives Startling Results of Inquiry." *New York Times*, 26 Dec. 1909, 5: 3.

White, Hayden. *Metahistory: The Historical Imagination in Nineteenth-Century Europe*. Baltimore: Johns Hopkins University Press, 1973.

Williams, Raymond. *The Country and the City*. New York: Oxford University Press, 1973.

———. *Culture and Society, 1870–1950*. London: Chatto & Windus Ltd., 1958.

———. *Keywords: A Vocabulary of Culture and Society*. 1976. Reprint, London: Flamingo, 1981.

Williams, Vernon, J. *Rethinking Race: Franz Boas and His Contemporaries*. Lexington: The University Press of Kentucky, 1996.

Wilson, Raymond. *Charles Eastman, Santee Sioux*. Urbana: University of Illinois Press, 1983.

Womack, Craig S. *Red on Red: Native American Literary Separatism*. Minneapolis: University of Minnesota Press, 1999.

Wonham, Henry B. "'An Art to Be Cultivated': Ethnic Caricature and American Literary Realism." *American Literary Realism* 32 (2000): 185–219.

Wright, Richard. Review of *Their Eyes Were Watching God*, by Zora Neale Hurston. *Zora Neale Hurston: Critical Perspectives Past and Present*. Edited by Henry Louis Gates Jr., and K. A. Appiah. New York: Amistad Press, 1993. 16–17.

Young, J. C. *Colonial Desire: Hybridity in Theory, Culture and Race*. New York: Routledge, 1995.

Zagarell, Sandra A. "*Country's* Portrayal of Community and the Exclusion of Difference." *New Essays on* The Country of the Pointed Firs. Edited by June Howard. New York: Cambridge University Press, 1994.

Zitkala-Ša. *American Indian Stories*. Foreword by Dexter Fisher. 1921. Reprint, Lincoln: University of Nebraska Press, 1985.

———. *Old Indian Legends*. 1901. Reprint, Lincoln: University of Nebraska Press, 1985.

Zumwalt, Rosemary Lévy. *American Folklore Scholarship: A Dialogue of Dissent*. Bloomington, Indiana University Press, 1988.

Index

aesthetic value, xxi, 12, 36–37, 47–48, 64–65, 72, 83, 118, 126, 133–34, 192n. 35

African Americans: animals in the stories of, 137–38; authorship, xvi, xxvii; and cakewalks, 85, 87; caricatures of, 37, 64–65; culture heroes of, 180–81; in dialect poetry, 72–73; discrimination against, xv, 15–16, 36, 62, 68, 72, 17; in ethnography, 167–69, 172–77; in fiction, 64–68, 73–74, 78–79, 83–87, 178–85; folklore of, 80–83, 131, 174–76; and labor, 175; and literary "material," 61, 71; and "Negro Problem," 63, 95; in plantation tradition, 66–68; portrayed in American literary realism, 61–63; and publication of folklore, 80–83, 131; racial theories of, 13–16; reactions of, to Boasian culture concept, 16, 192n. 48; religious practices of, 170; in Sioux story, 141; songs of, 35–36, 73, 77–78, 179

Agassiz, Louis, 14–15

Aldrich, Thomas Bailey, 42, 150

Alexie, Sherman, 186, 215n. 62

Algonquin-language narratives, 129

Allen, James Lane, 53

allotment, 96–97, 144–45

American Anthropological Association, 28, 32

American Anthropologist, 4, 9

American Folk-Lore Society, xix, 127

American Indian Life, 29, 31–34

American Indians. *See* Native Americans

Americanization. *See* assimilation

American literary realism. *See* realism, American literary

American Museum of Natural History, 6, 125, 191n. 24, 196n. 103

American school of ethnology, 14

animals: depictions of, 136–39

anthropology: "armchair," 100–101; and assimilation, 122; Boas's organization of, 9; connection to Indian reform, 97; criticism against, 89–90; and distance, 164–65; as ironic science, 11, 191n. 34; professionalization of, xvi, 4, 90–91, 190–91n. 10; recent critique of culture by, xxii; shift from deduction to induction, 100–101; and textual production, 9–11; as textual production, 89–90, 115

Anzaldúa, Gloria, 156

231

Michael A. Elliott is assistant professor of English at Emory University, where he teaches courses in nineteenth-century American and Native American literature. He held fellowships from the Charles Warren Center at Harvard University and the American Philosophical Society in Philadelphia while completing the research for this book.